DOMINANCE & DECLINE

DOMINANCE & DECLINE

MAKING SENSE
OF RECENT
CANADIAN ELECTIONS

ELISABETH GIDENGIL
NEIL NEVITTE
ANDRÉ BLAIS
JOANNA EVERITT
PATRICK FOURNIER

UNIVERSITY OF TORONTO PRESS

Library and Archives Canada Cataloguing in Publication

Dominance and decline : making sense of recent Canadian elections / Elisabeth Gidengil ... [et al.].

Includes bibliographical references and index.
Also issued in electronic format.
ISBN 978-1-4426-0389-9

1. Canada. Parliament—Elections—History—21st century. 2. Canada—Politics and government—1993–2006. 3. Canada—Politics and government—2006–. 4. Elections—Canada—History—21st century. 5. Voting—Canada—History—21st century.
I. Gidengil, Elisabeth, 1947–

JL193.D64 2012   324.971'07   C2011-908549-6

We welcome comments and suggestions regarding any aspect of our publications—please feel free to contact us at news@utphighereducation.com or visit our Internet site at www.utppublishing.com.

North America
5201 Dufferin Street
North York, Ontario, Canada, M3H 5T8

2250 Military Road
Tonawanda, New York, USA, 14150

ORDERS PHONE: 1–800–565–9523
ORDERS FAX: 1–800–221–9985
ORDERS E-MAIL: utpbooks@utpress.utoronto.ca

UK, Ireland, and continental Europe
NBN International
Estover Road, Plymouth, PL6 7PY, UK
ORDERS PHONE: 44 (0) 1752 202301
ORDERS FAX: 44 (0) 1752 202333
ORDERS E-MAIL: enquiries@nbninternational.com

RECYCLED
Paper made from recycled material
FSC® C103567

This book is printed on paper containing 100% post-consumer fibre.

The University of Toronto Press acknowledges the financial support for its publishing activities of the Government of Canada through the Canada Book Fund.

Printed in Canada

Designed by Daiva Villa, Chris Rowat Design

CONTENTS

FIGURES AND TABLES

FIGURES

TABLES

ACKNOWLEDGEMENTS

The first decade of the twenty-first century was an extraordinary one in Canada's electoral history. At the turn of the century, the Liberal Party of Canada appeared to be unbeatable. A mere eight years later, the party suffered a crushing defeat. This book sets out to explain how a political party can go from dominance to decline in the space of just a few years.

Such an in-depth investigation would have been impossible had it not been for the generous support that the Canadian Election Study (CES) has received. The scientific communities in every major advanced industrial state conduct comprehensive studies of their national elections. These studies provide an essential record of the democratic experience of a country. They furnish a reference point, enabling those experiences to be compared with past elections and with experiences in other democracies, and they provide unique opportunities for different national scientific communities to contribute to the advancement of knowledge about the dynamics of political behaviour and the functioning of democracy. We have been fortunate that both the Social Sciences and Humanities Research Council of Canada and Elections Canada have understood the importance of conducting such studies in Canada. We would particularly like to thank Alain Pelletier at Elections Canada for working with us on developing questions that relate to the agency's strategic objectives. We would also like to express our thanks to the Institute for Research on Public Policy (IRPP) for its financial contribution to the 2000 Canadian Election Study, and we are grateful to our universities for both financial support and release time. The

Québec members of the team also benefited from funding from the Fonds de recherche du Québec–Société et culture.

Special thanks are also due to the Institute for Social Research (ISR) at York University and Jolicoeur & Associés who conducted all or part of the surveys on which this book is based. We would particularly like to thank ISR's director, David Northrup. Uncertainty over the timing of the elections complicated the task of getting the CES into the field, but David was always there for us. We are extremely grateful for his patience, grace under pressure, and, above all, his commitment to high-quality survey research.

One of the most enjoyable aspects of working on this project was the opportunity to work closely with a number of talented graduate students and postdoctoral fellows. We would especially like to express our thanks to Benjamin Ferland, Andrea Lawlor, Jason Roy, and Melanee Thomas at McGill University; Delia Dumitrescu, Mike Medeiros, Alexandre Morin Chassé, and Silvina Danesi at Université de Montréal; Yannick Dufresne and Nick Ruderman at the University of Toronto; and Kurt Goddard at the University of New Brunswick.

Finally, we have been very fortunate to work with an editor who believed in the project. We very much appreciate the strong commitment that Michael Harrison has shown. We are also grateful to Karen Taylor for making the copyediting process so painless and to the anonymous reviewers who provided us with valuable feedback.

INTRODUCTION

Coming out of the 2000 federal election, Liberal dominance seemed assured. No party since the 1950s had won three successive majority governments. Yet, less than a dozen years later, the party suffered its most devastating defeat ever. For the first time in its history, the party long considered Canada's "natural governing party" was reduced to being the third party in Parliament. The seeds of that historic defeat are to be found in the series of elections held between 2004 and 2008. The 2004 election marked the end of Liberal dominance: the party lost its majority and barely managed to hold on to power. In the 2006 election, the Liberals could not even muster a minority victory, and, in 2008, they suffered a crushing defeat, recording their second lowest ever share of the vote. The Liberals' fall from grace was accompanied by the rapid rise to power of the Conservative Party. The party had only come into existence in 2003 when the Canadian Alliance and the Progressive Conservatives merged. In the space of just two elections, the new party was able to displace the Liberals and form the government. Meanwhile, the New Democratic Party (NDP) rescued itself from the threat of electoral oblivion by doubling its share of the vote between the 2000 and 2004 elections. But the NDP seemed to be unable to capitalize on the Liberals' decline, and its support remained stalled in the next two elections. And while the Bloc Québécois (BQ) continued to dominate in Québec, its share of the vote fluctuated. Finally, the Green Party appeared to be emerging from the electoral margins, capturing

Figure 0.1 *Party Vote Shares, 2000–2011*

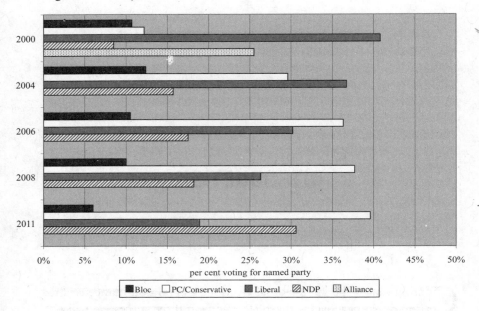

nearly seven per cent of the vote in 2008, only to see its support drop below 4 per cent in 2011.

The contours of Canadian elections were clearly shifting in the first decade of the new millennium (see Figure 0.1). For only the third time in Canada's history, voters delivered three successive minority parliaments.[1] This book explores the major fault lines that appeared in Canada's electoral landscape in the elections leading up to the 2011 electoral earthquake. It addresses a series of critical questions. What led to the Liberals' dramatic decline? Why did it take four elections for the Conservative Party to achieve a majority? Why was the NDP unable to capitalize sooner on the Liberals' electoral woes? How much did the Greens' success in 2008 owe to the unique electoral circumstances? And what accounts for the volatility of the Bloc vote?

The Chrétien Majority: 2000–2004

Prior to the 2004 election, the Liberal Party had enjoyed the reputation of being one of the most successful political parties in any contemporary democracy. It had been out of office for only 21 of the previous 100 years. Such was its success that it had acquired the label of "the Government Party" (Whitaker 1977). The Liberals' most recent period of electoral dominance had begun with the 1993 election. That election saw the Progressive Conservative government suffer the worst defeat of any government in a postindustrial democracy. It also saw the near demise of the NDP and the rise of the Reform Party in the West and the Bloc Québécois in Québec. With their third successive majority in the 2000 election, the Liberals appeared to be secure in their government supremacy. But after 2000, the underpinnings of their historical electoral support gradually eroded.

The key event during Jean Chrétien's final term as prime minister was the sponsorship scandal. The Liberals had once dominated federal elections in Québec, but they never recovered from the repatriation of the Canadian Constitution in 1982, which Pierre Trudeau's Liberal government undertook without the support of that province's government. Two failed attempts under the Progressive Conservatives to bring Québec into the Constitution—the 1987 Meech Lake Accord and the 1992 Charlottetown Accord—reinvigorated the sovereignty movement, culminating in the 1995 Québec sovereignty referendum. The referendum proved to be extremely divisive: 49.4 per cent of Quebecers supported an option that could have led to the province's eventual separation from the rest of the country.

One of the Chrétien government's responses to the surge in support for sovereignty was to create a $250 million sponsorship program to increase Quebecers' awareness of Canada's contributions to Québec. But criticisms of the program and allegations of corruption and mismanagement of money began to surface around 2000. The sponsorship program was temporarily suspended, and then reinstated, amid questions about suspicious contracts and bogus reports. Eventually, Auditor General Shelia Fraser conducted an audit. In December 2003, shortly before Fraser's initial report was produced, Chrétien resigned and was replaced by Paul Martin, the former finance minister. The very first decision Martin made as prime minister, announced the day his new cabinet was sworn in, was to cancel the sponsorship program. Over the next few months, Martin took several steps to deal with the brewing scandal. When the report revealed that embezzlement of funds had occurred, Martin moved quickly to establish the Commission of Inquiry into the Sponsorship Program and Advertising Activities, led by Justice John H. Gomery. Prime Minister Martin claimed that he was unaware of any financial irregularities, but he was forced nonetheless to go into the 2004 federal election with the spectre of the sponsorship scandal and accusations of Liberal Party corruption hanging over his head.

The Liberals went into that election facing a newly united Conservative Party. The merger of the Canadian Alliance and the Progressive Conservatives had put an end to the so-called fight for the right that began when the populist, right-wing Reform Party achieved its electoral breakthrough in 1993 by winning 52 seats, all in western Canada. In the 1997 election, Reform attempted to break out of its western heartland and win seats in vote-rich Ontario, but it failed to achieve this goal (Nevitte et al. 2000). Recognizing that the failure to win seats in Ontario hampered its prospects of forming the government, Reform transformed itself into the Canadian Alliance in 2000 in the hopes of attracting the support of Progressive Conservatives. However, the Alliance had limited success in improving on Reform's performance. Although its share of the vote increased, the Alliance only managed to win two seats east of Manitoba. With Stephen Harper's assumption of the role of leader of the Canadian Alliance in 2002 and Peter MacKay's election as Progressive Conservative leader in early 2003, discussions between the two parties about a possible merger to stop the vote splitting on the right reached a successful conclusion. The new party's leadership convention, held in March of 2004, selected Stephen Harper as the party's leader on the first ballot.

The 2004 Election: The Liberals Lose their Majority

In the hopes of avoiding more revelations about the sponsorship scandal and in an effort to give the new party as little time to prepare as possible, Martin called an election for June 28, 2004. Martin and Harper were not the only new players in federal politics in 2004. In 2003, the NDP, Canada's traditional party of the left, selected Jack Layton, a Toronto politician, as its new leader, replacing Alexa McDonough. Gilles Duceppe, leader of the Bloc Québécois, was the only party leader with previous political experience at the helm of a federal party going into the 2004 election campaign.

The Liberals went into that campaign believing that they would do better under Paul Martin than they had under Jean Chrétien. But the party floundered during the campaign. Within the party, there was infighting between the Martin and Chrétien supporters. That, coupled with the ever-present cloud from the sponsorship scandal, undoubtedly goes some distance toward accounting for the party's poor performance. Support for the new Conservative Party grew during the first half of the campaign, prompting speculations about a possible Conservative majority. But the Liberals hung on to the core of their party's support and eked out a minority government with 135 seats, a decline of 37 seats from the 2000 election.

The Liberals were the only party to lose seats in the 2004 federal election. The new Conservative Party took 99 seats, up from the 72 that it held at the dissolution of Parliament. The NDP increased the number of seats that it won from 14 to 19. The BQ increased its seat count from 33 to 54. The

Greens, who, under the leadership of Jim Harris, had run candidates in all 308 ridings for the first time, won no seats, but the party doubled its electoral support to 4.3 per cent of the popular vote.

The Martin Minority and the 2006 Election

The Liberal minority government limped along for 18 months before it was forced to call another election. The party faced threats of defeat over its 2005 spring budget, which eventually passed with the support of independent members of the House of Commons and the support of Conservative member Belinda Stronach who crossed the floor to join the Liberal caucus.

Same-sex marriage posed another challenge to the Liberals. Starting in 2003, a series of provincial Supreme Court rulings had made same-sex marriage legal in eight provinces and one territory. As the Canadian Constitution makes it clear that the definition of marriage is the sole responsibility of the federal government, these rulings challenged Ottawa to step into the same-sex marriage debate. Because this was a politically contentious issue, the government asked the Supreme Court of Canada in the summer of 2003 to rule on whether limiting marriage to heterosexual couples was legally possible given the Canadian Charter of Rights and Freedoms. This request had effectively removed the issue from debate in the 2004 election. However, the Supreme Court's ruling in December 2004 that same-sex marriage was constitutional forced the Martin minority government to address it in the first months of 2005. Bill C-38 was introduced in February 2005 amid much controversy, particularly in the Liberal caucus. As a result, Martin required all of his cabinet ministers to support the legislation, but allowed back-bench Liberal MPs a free vote. A final vote was held in the House of Commons on June 28, 2005, and the legislation passed with the support of most members of the Liberal, NDP, and Bloc caucuses. The majority of the Conservative members voted against the bill. It quickly passed in the Senate and received royal assent in July 2005.

Perhaps the most contentious issue during the life of this government was the sponsorship scandal. The Gomery Commission had begun its public hearings in the fall of 2004, and they lasted nine months. They were intensely covered by the media, and they produced startling testimonies that left no doubt that there had been corruption. Advertising agencies had received lavish amounts of money for very little actual work, and some of that money had been funnelled back into Liberal Party coffers. Judge Gomery's first report, released in the fall of 2005, confirmed that there had been serious wrongdoing, but it cleared all politicians of guilt except for the former minister of public works. Most relevant here, it explicitly stated that "Mr. Martin . . . is entitled, like other Ministers in the Québec caucus, to be exonerated from any blame for carelessness or misconduct" (Canada. Commission of Inquiry into the Sponsorship Program and Advertising Activities 2005, 77).

Despite this conclusion, support for the Liberals dropped. The opposition seized the political opportunity, and the Conservatives introduced a non-confidence motion. The motion passed on November 28, 2005, and the following day Paul Martin asked Governor General Michaëlle Jean to dissolve Parliament and call an election. Election day was set for January 23, 2006, resulting in an eight-week campaign.

The Conservative campaign in 2005–06 was a disciplined one. Individual MPs were prohibited from speaking to the media without the central campaign's permission, and there were far fewer political gaffes than there had been 18 months earlier. The party dominated the news coverage during the first half of the campaign with a series of policy-per-day announcements on issues such as the Goods and Services Tax and a child-care allowance. The Liberals, by contrast, delayed their major policy announcements until after the Christmas and New Year holidays believing that voters would not be paying close attention to the campaign until early January. The NDP directed its campaign attacks at the Liberals in an effort to counter Liberal arguments that only they could keep the Conservatives from office.

On December 27, 2005, the Royal Canadian Mounted Police announced that it was investigating the office of Liberal Finance Minister Ralph Goodale for possible insider trading, which allegedly occurred before the government announced in late November that it would not impose a tax on income trusts. News of a criminal investigation both deflected attention from the Liberal Party's key policy announcements released at the same time and played into the opposition parties' hands; they resumed their attacks about corruption within the Liberal ranks.

By early January, the Conservatives were clearly leading in the polls and had begun to make a breakthrough in Québec, displacing the Liberals as the most preferred party after the Bloc. As in the 2004 election, the Liberals countered with an advertising campaign implying that the Conservatives had a "hidden agenda"—but to little avail. On election day, the Conservatives eked out a minority government with 124 seats. The Liberals fell to 103 seats in Parliament; they lost seats to the Conservatives in what had once been the Liberal heartland—in Ontario and Québec. The Bloc dropped to 51 seats, and the NDP rose to 29, with gains in Ontario, British Columbia, and the North West Territories.

The Harper Minority: 2006–2008

Following the Liberal election defeat, Paul Martin stepped down as party leader. In March of 2006, he was replaced by interim party leader Bill Graham, and the Liberal Party set a leadership convention date for early December of 2006. Several leadership contenders stepped forward. Michael Ignatieff, a newly elected MP who had only recently returned to Canada after several years living in the United States, was one of the frontrunners, as was Bob Rae, the former NDP premier of Ontario in the early 1990s. But it was Stéphane Dion, a cabinet minister from Québec under Jean Chrétien, who somewhat unexpectedly ended up as the new party leader. Dion was best known as the author of the Clarity Act, which had established the conditions under which the federal government would enter into negotiations with a province following a vote to secede. He began the leadership campaign as a dark horse but emerged from the leadership fray with 55 per cent of the delegates' support in the fourth round of voting.

In the months after the leadership convention, the Conservative Party launched a series of attack ads portraying Dion as an indecisive and ineffectual leader and criticizing his record as environment minister. Internal tensions quickly began to appear within the Liberal Party as supporters of Ignatieff's leadership bid became increasingly critical of Dion's leadership. The party's failure to win three critical by-elections in September 2007 (particularly its loss in the riding of Outremont, which had been a Liberal stronghold since the 1930s) heightened internal party discontent.

With the Liberals in disarray, the Conservative government moved legislation to put into effect several of the party's campaign promises. It lowered the federal Goods and Services Tax from 7 per cent to 6 per cent. Income tax cuts for middle-income earners were introduced, as was a $1,200 per child childcare payment labelled the "Universal Child Care Benefit." The Liberals criticized the Conservatives' agenda but then put themselves in the awkward position of voting for these legislative proposals to avoid precipitating an election for which they were not prepared. The NDP voted regularly against the Conservative budgets and its proposal to extend the Canadian mission in Afghanistan. The Bloc varied in its support or opposition to various pieces of legislation. No party was in a position to enter into a third election campaign in less than four years.

The Liberals were not the only party to get a new leader in the aftermath of the 2006 election. Jim Harris announced his intention to step down in April 2006 after almost three years as leader of the Green Party. A leadership vote was held at the party's annual convention in August 2006, and Elizabeth May, a former executive director of the Sierra Club of Canada, won on the first ballot with 65 per cent of the vote. In November 2006, May ran in a federal by-election in London North Centre, finishing second with 26 per cent of the vote. In March 2007, May announced that she would run against Cabinet Minister Peter MacKay in his Central Nova riding. Liberal Leader Stéphane Dion took the position that his party would not run a candidate against May in return for her agreement not to run a Green candidate against him in his riding of Saint-Laurent-Cartierville. That announcement was roundly criticized by the other parties and sharpened internal disagreements among the Liberals.

The 2008 Election

Despite the new law establishing fixed-date elections, it became clear over the summer of 2008 that the government was preparing for an election. The economy had started to slow down, and economic forecasts were weaker than expected. As well, there was a sense that the US election in the fall of 2008, which likely would result in a victory for the Democratic Party, might influence Canadian voters and reduce the Conservatives' chances of making electoral gains if the Canadian election were held after the American election.

At the end of August, Stephen Harper met the three leaders of the parliamentary opposition parties with the stated goal of searching for common ground between their parties and his fall legislative agenda. The search failed. Conservative Leader Harper claimed that Parliament had become increasingly "dysfunctional," and, on September 7, 2008, he called on Governor General Michaëlle Jean to request that she dissolve Parliament and call an election for October 14.

The Conservatives argued that the election was about leadership, and they framed the election as a choice between a thoughtful, approachable, yet decisive Harper and a weak and ineffectual Dion. The Liberals focused on their "green shift" proposals that included an eco-tax on carbon emissions and the reduction of personal and corporate income taxes. Both the Conservatives and the NDP criticized this proposal, arguing that it would stifle the economy by driving up prices and not encourage the reduction of emissions in the most cost-effective areas. In an approach that was exactly opposite of that employed in 2006, the NDP focused its attacks on the Conservatives, attempting to sideline the Liberals and present the NDP as the only viable alternative to the current government. Similarly, Gilles Duceppe, the Bloc leader, argued that the only way to prevent the Conservatives from winning a majority was to vote for his party. The Green Party took on a more significant role in this campaign than it had in the past. For the first time in Canada's history, it was allowed to participate in the televised leaders' debates. However, this concession only occurred after much negotiating and pressure to reverse the initial opposition of all parties but the Liberals, and the reported refusal of Jack Layton and Stephen Harper to participate in the debate if Elizabeth May was involved.

At the start of the election campaign, the Conservatives claimed that the Canadian economy was strong. But the global financial crisis that began in the United States in early October became a critical issue over the course of the election. The fall of major American financial and securities companies and the spiralling subprime mortgage crisis set off a ripple effect in economies across the world. This was particularly the case in Ontario and Québec, whose economies were closely tied to that of the United States.

As the campaign progressed, it became clear that this economic crisis had the potential to rival the depression of the 1930s. The opposition parties claimed that the Conservatives' economic policies were contributing to the economic downturn, while the Conservatives argued that the situation would have been worse under the Liberals. The leadership debates focused increasingly on the state of the country's economy. The Conservatives' goal was to present their party as offering a calm and measured response to this crisis. To others, it seemed that the Harper-led Conservatives were unresponsive and unsympathetic to the economic concerns of Canadian voters. Conservative support, which had been hovering in the high 30s during the last few weeks of September, slipped to the low 30s after the debates, and those ratings did not rebound until the last few days of the campaign.

When all of the ballots had been counted on October 14, the Conservatives won a plurality, but they took only 143 seats, insufficient for a legislative majority. The Liberals experienced their worst election results in over 20 years; they took only 77 seats and 26 per cent of the popular vote. The NDP increased its seat count from 29 to 37 seats. The Bloc dropped by two seats. The Green Party won no seats in the election but increased its vote share yet again to almost 7 per cent.

The 2011 election produced a very different outcome. The Conservatives won the majority that had eluded them in the previous three elections. For the first time ever, the Liberals came in third, and the NDP formed the official opposition for the first time in the party's history. The Bloc vote was swamped by the unprecedented "orange surge" of NDP support in Québec. And, despite winning a seat, the Greens received their lowest share of the vote in a decade.

The parties' electoral fortunes changed dramatically in that election, but the fault lines that produced these shifts were already becoming apparent in the previous decade. This book explores those fault lines. It begins with the 2000 election. Coming out of that election, the Liberals appeared to be unbeatable, yet, a mere eight years later, the party suffered a humiliating defeat from which it could not recover. The analyses that follow explore the roots of Liberal dominance in 2000 and show how the party went from dominance to decline in the next three elections.

The Canadian Election Studies

To explore the electoral dynamics of the decade, we draw on data from the 2000, 2004, 2006, and 2008 Canadian Election Study (CES) surveys.[2] These data come from random digit dialling telephone surveys and self-administered mail-back questionnaires; they provide a rich source of information about Canadians' vote choices, attitudes, and behaviours in these four elections. In each election, between 3,257 and 4,323 respondents were surveyed during the campaign period. After the election, as many of these respondents as possible were re-interviewed. Thus, data from each election can be analyzed as a cross-section or as a panel.[3]

In addition, since the 2004, 2006, and 2008 elections occurred so closely together, the CES has a panel component that spans all three elections. In both 2006 and 2008, efforts were made to re-contact participants who had answered all of the previous waves of the study. Although there was a degree of attrition in the panel that occurred during each election, a total of 1,138 individuals from the 2004 campaign study participated in some or all of the subsequent waves of the 2006 and 2008 CES. These data provide an uncommon opportunity to track the same respondents over all three elections and learn more about the stability or change in their attitudes and behaviours.[4]

Outline of the Book

These unique data enable us to compare the impact of various common explanations for the parties' changing electoral fortunes[5] in the four elections and to explore the implications that electoral volatility and a succession of minority governments had for Canadians' satisfaction with Canadian democracy. It should be stressed at the outset that we are interested in how the parties fared as opposed to the specific campaign strategies, events, or media commentary that characterized each campaign. For this reason, we do not focus on the media coverage, advertisements, or events such as leaders' debates that make each election unique. Instead, we look at those long- and short-term forces that are present in every election. Some of these factors (social background characteristics, values, and even party identification) are more enduring, while others (the state of the economy, key issues, or evaluations of a party's leader) may change from one election to another. Throughout the book, we ask these questions: What are the relationships between these long- and short-term forces, and how might the linkages between them have an effect on voting behaviour?

It should also be noted that our primary focus in this book is on English-speaking Canada. The reason for this is that, since 1993, federal elections have unfolded very differently in Québec due to the role played by the Bloc Québécois. Until the 2011 election at least, the Bloc was a significant electoral force in Québec that was not present elsewhere in the country. Because it would be extremely difficult within the confines of a book of this nature to reproduce all of our analyses in each chapter for Québec, a separate chapter is devoted specifically to that province. However, in examining electoral behaviour in Québec, we are driven by the question as to whether Quebecers are really that different from other Canadians and, if they are different, on what dimensions they differ.

Chapter 1 provides the theoretical framework that guides the analysis throughout the book. It begins with a review of the major approaches that have been used to explain voting behaviour (the sociological, social-psychological, and rational choice models), and it assesses their strengths and limitations. We then describe the analytical model and explain how simulations can help to identify the role that different factors play in explaining individual vote choice.

Chapters 2 to 8 probe the specific long- and short-term factors that form the basis of our approach. Chapter 2 considers social cleavages in Canada and then examines the social bases of party support in Canada across the four elections. Because social background characteristics are enduring at the individual level and slow to change at the aggregate level, their role in accounting for electoral outcomes has often been underestimated, if not dismissed or ignored. However, this chapter argues that, although people's social background characteristics may not change, their *effects* can, depending on the circumstances of the particular election. In presenting this argument, Chapter 2 answers questions such as these: How successful was the Conservative Party in broadening its electoral base? Did the Liberals lose their core supporters? Did the NDP rebuild its traditional support base, or did it appeal to a new type of voter?

Chapter 3 considers whether, and how, fundamental values and beliefs shape vote choices. These factors typically receive little attention in the literature on voting and elections in Canada. Certainly, some Canadians may have difficulty understanding abstract terms like left and right. But this does not mean that their vote choices are devoid of these kinds of considerations. This chapter explores some basic values and beliefs (for instance beliefs about the role of the state and traditional morality) and examines the impact of these values on vote choice and party vote shares across the four elections. This exploration enables us to answer several questions about the role of values and beliefs in explaining electoral dynamics. For example, to what extent did the Conservatives' success reflect their growing ability to attract voters beyond their traditional right-wing constituency? Were the Liberals and the NDP increasingly competing for voters who share the same value space? Was the typical Conservative voter an economic conservative, a social conservative, or both?

The extent to which Canadians develop psychological attachments to their political parties is a matter of considerable debate. One of the earliest election studies concluded that the concept of party identification was "almost inapplicable" in Canada. Subsequent studies have offered a more tempered assessment, and the conventional view now is that Canadians' ties to political parties are highly flexible. The 2004–2006–2008 CES panel provides a unique opportunity to examine whether Canadians do indeed have meaningful attachments to political parties. Chapter 4 tracks the size of each party's partisan core across the four elections and uses the 2004–2006–2008 panel to examine just how many people remained loyal to their party and how many defected. This analysis concludes with the acid test of party identification, namely partisans' willingness to vote for a party other than the one they commonly identify with. If their party attachment is meaningful, they should still consider themselves partisans, even though short-term forces (like the sponsorship scandal or an unpopular leader) have induced them to vote against their party. The chapter ends with a consideration of the role of party identification in explaining the parties' changing electoral fortunes. Notably, it asks, were the Liberals simply losing votes, or were they losing partisans as well?

Chapters 5 to 8 turn to the short-term influences on vote choice. Chapter 5 begins with an investigation of voters' perceptions of the economy. According to the simple reward-and-punish model, voters reward the incumbent party for good economic times and punish it for bad times. In practice, however, economic voting is a less straightforward matter. The chapter compares the impact of economic perceptions on vote choice and party vote shares across the four elections and addresses a series of critical questions about economic voting. Which matters more: perceptions of how the economy is doing or voters' evaluations of their own financial circumstances? Are voters even-handed: are they as ready to reward as they are to punish? Did the onset of the economic crisis limit the Liberals' losses in 2008 and deny the Conservatives a majority?

Issues typically matter more than economic perceptions, but some issues matter more than others. Even a high-profile issue may matter little to the election outcome if opinion is evenly divided. Under those conditions, the votes of those on opposing sides will cancel out one another. Chapter 6 assesses the impact of a variety of issues that figured in the four elections. Did opposition to same-sex marriage help to boost the Conservative vote? How big a price did the Liberals pay for the sponsorship scandal? Was focusing so much attention on the green shift in 2008 a strategic blunder for the Liberals?

Chapter 7 tracks voters' evaluations of the party leaders and assesses the impact of these evaluations on both vote choice and vote shares. Leaders may have a powerful effect on individual vote choice, but the leaders' popularity does not always translate into a substantial impact on party vote shares. Leader evaluations are likely to have the most impact on an election outcome when one leader is markedly more—or less—popular than the others. Did evaluations of Stephen Harper contribute to the growing success of the Conservative Party? Did positive evaluations of Jack Layton help revive the NDP's electoral fortunes? How much of the Liberals' loss of support can be attributed to increasingly unpopular leaders?

Chapter 8 puts the spotlight on strategic considerations. Some voters will opt for their second-choice party if their preferred party has no chance of winning in their local riding. As the Liberals' electoral fortunes declined, they became more vulnerable to strategic defections. Voters who wanted to see the Conservative candidate defeated might have voted NDP if they thought its candidate had a better chance than the Liberal candidate of winning the local race. How much of the drop in the Liberals' vote share was attributable to this sort of strategic voting? This chapter also examines a novel set of strategic calculations. How did Canadians feel about minority governments? Did those feelings change in the light of experience? Did some voters factor views about minority government into their vote calculus, and, if they did, which parties paid the price?

Chapter 9 considers the Greens' performance in the 2008 election, the election where the party made great—albeit temporary—gains. There were simply too few Green voters in the earlier elections to permit a reliable analysis, and, even in 2008, the small number of Green voters means that the decision to vote for the party cannot be modelled in the same way as the decision to vote for one of the larger parties. Small parties in single-member, winner-take-all elections face challenges. But Green voting is not an entirely novel phenomenon. There are successful Green parties in Europe and New Zealand. The chapter investigates what role social background characteristics, fundamental values and beliefs, partisanship, economic perceptions, issues, and leader evaluations played in Green voting. Where did Green Party voters come from? Were they new voters? Did Green success come at the expense of the Liberals? What role did strategic voting play

INTRODUCTION

in the choice among the Greens, the Liberals, and the NDP? Did positive evaluations of Elizabeth May help the party? Are the Greens a single-issue party, or do they have broader appeal?

Chapter 10 examines the determinants of individual vote choice and the parties' vote shares in Québec. The focus is on the linguistic cleavage, views about Québec sovereignty, economic perceptions, issues, and leadership. The chapter addresses several questions. What was the relative weight of these different factors? Did they matter more—or less—than they did in the rest of Canada? Was sovereignty still the overriding determinant of Québec voters' choices? How much did the sponsorship scandal or leader unpopularity hurt the Liberals? Why were the Conservatives able to break through and win seats in 2006? Did the ebb and flow of support for sovereignty affect the Bloc?

In the concluding chapter, we step back to assess the strategic challenges facing each party and to consider the implications of our findings for the future of the Canadian party system and the durability of the partisan configuration that emerged in the wake of the 2011 election. The discussion highlights what we learned about voting behaviour in a period of unprecedented electoral volatility and minority government.

Notes

1 The first time Canada had three successive minority parliaments was in the 1920s. Strictly speaking, there were four minority governments between 1921 and 1926 because Governor General Byng invited the Conservatives to form a minority government when Mackenzie King's Liberals lost the support of the Progressives. However, the minority government formed by Mackenzie King following the 1926 election was able to function as if it were a majority government thanks to the support of Liberal-Progressive, Progressive, Labour, and Independent MPs (Russell 2008, 24). The second time Canada had three minority parliaments in a row was in the 1960s. Diefenbaker's Progressive Conservative minority was replaced by two successive Liberal minority governments led by Lester Pearson.

2 The studies were funded by the Social Sciences and Humanities Research Council of Canada and by Elections Canada. The fieldwork was conducted by the Institute for Social Research at York University.

3 In 2000, the campaign survey lasted from October 24 to November 26, 2000, while the post-election survey ran from November 28, 2000 until February 12, 2000. In 2004, respondents were surveyed during the campaign period (May 23–June 27, 2004), the post-election period (July 5–September 19, 2004), and, for those who responded to the post-election survey, in a mail-back survey that was distributed from one week after they had been re-interviewed to the

end of November 2004. In 2006, the campaign wave of the survey extended from November 30, 2005 to January 22, 2006. No interviews were conducted between December 22 and December 27, 2005 or between December 30, 2005 and January 1, 2006. The post-election survey ran from January 24, 2006 to March 27, 2006. There was no mail-back survey for this election. The campaign survey in 2008 was only conducted in the final two and a half weeks of the election (September 26–October 13, 2008). The post-campaign survey began on October 15 and ran until December 23, 2008. As in 2004, the 2008 mail-back survey began shortly after respondents were contacted for the post-campaign survey.

4 To ensure that each election was useful for regional comparisons or multivariate analyses, the panel responses in the 2006 and 2008 were augmented with a new randomly selected sample.

5 By changing electoral fortunes, we mean changing vote shares as opposed to changing electoral outcomes. Electoral outcomes depend not just on the parties' vote shares but on how votes get translated into seats.

CHAPTER ONE

EXPLAINING VOTE CHOICE

A multitude of factors might potentially influence an individual's choice of party: social identities, normative beliefs, party attachments, economic conditions, the issues of the day, and perceptions of the party leaders, to name the most obvious. How much weight these factors carry in the decision calculus varies from one individual to another and from one election to the next. To add to the explanatory challenge, the factors that explain individual vote choice do not necessarily have the same importance when it comes to explaining the parties' vote shares. The challenge is to find a model of voting behaviour that is comprehensive and yet sufficiently theoretically motivated that it amounts to more than simply a "laundry list" of all the factors that might explain why people vote the way they do.

The very first survey-based academic voting studies offered a sociological explanation that emphasized voters' social background characteristics and social interactions. There has been a revival of interest in the sociological approach, but that approach was for many years eclipsed by a social-psychological model that emphasized attitudinal influences. However, the two approaches are actually quite compatible. This compatibility has been recognized in the development of composite models ("bloc recursive models") that seek to incorporate all of the major explanatory factors. As such, they contrast with rational choice models that put a premium on parsimony.

Evaluating both the strengths and limitations of the various approaches helps to clarify our choice of model to explain the dynamics of electoral change between 2000 and 2008.

The Sociological Model

The sociological model, developed by Paul Lazarsfeld and colleagues (1944) at Columbia University, was based on their 1940 study of voting in Erie County, Ohio. The Columbia team actually began with a view of voting behaviour that mimicked the marketplace: voters choose between political parties in much the same way that they choose which brand of a product to buy. Election campaigns were likened to advertising campaigns; and voters were expected to weigh the merits of the competing parties, just as they might weigh the merits of competing brands in the marketplace, hesitating between one party and another until they made their final choice on election day. This consumer preference model failed, however, to capture the realities of voting behaviour not least of all because voters exhibited an unexpected degree of "brand loyalty" (Miller 1983, 100). Indeed, most voters knew how they were going to vote even before the campaign began. In retrospect, the disappointing performance of the consumer preference model might well have reflected the particular electoral context. President Franklin D. Roosevelt was running for a third term of office, and, by 1940, most voters knew enough about him to have formed clear preferences about him. In any case, the Columbia researchers were sufficiently dissatisfied with the performance of that particular approach that they abandoned the consumer preference model altogether and turned instead to an approach that emphasized voters' social background characteristics.

At the core of the sociological approach is the premise that "a person thinks, politically, as he [sic] is socially" (Lazarsfeld, Berelson, and Gaudet 1968, 27). The Columbia researchers found that the strongest predictors of vote choice were socio-economic status, religion, and type of community. Taken together, these three social background characteristics went a long way toward explaining people's vote choice: 70 per cent of respondents voted in ways that were consistent with the vote tendencies of those who shared similar characteristics. Accordingly, Lazarsfeld and his colleagues combined the three characteristics into an index of political predisposition (IPP) that classified voters on a scale ranging from those with strong Democratic predispositions (Catholic, urban, low socio-economic status) at one extreme to those with strong Republican predispositions (Protestant, rural, high socio-economic status) at the other extreme.

Undue focus on that index led many to equate their model with a crude sociological approach. Niemi and Weisberg (1993) in *Classics in Voting*

Behaviour summarize the point succinctly: "The Columbia explained the 1940 election with a sociological model, rela.. socioeconomic status (education, income, and social class), religion, anu place of residence (urban or rural) to their vote" (p. 8). Understood that way, a sociological approach would simply involve finding the best combination of social background characteristics for predicting vote choice and, as such, would be theoretically uninteresting.

The early version of the sociological approach faced several criticisms. One was that the approach left little room for "politics." Neither issues nor candidates figured very prominently in the sociological models, and thus the approach seemed inappropriately "apolitical" for such a political event as an election. Others criticized the approach for being too descriptive. Relating social background characteristics to vote choice reveals little about the underlying motivations of voters. Yet others pointed out that the approach suffered from weak predictive accuracy. When researchers at the University of Michigan replicated IPP on a nationwide sample, they found that it did not do very well in predicting how people voted: only 61 per cent of their respondents voted in line with the IPP prediction (Janowitz and Miller 1952, 717). Simply using coin flips to predict whether people voted Republican or Democrat would have achieved 50 per cent accuracy. Finally, the sociological model was also criticized for being too static. Social background characteristics remain more or less stable from one election to the next, but parties' vote shares fluctuate. The clear implication is that a sociological model is unlikely to be of much help when it comes to explaining electoral dynamics. In a nutshell, the sociological model necessarily "failed because it tried to use things that did not change to explain things that did" (Clarke, Kornberg, and Scotto 2009, 274).

The Columbia researchers probably left themselves open to some of these criticisms by claiming too much. They wrote, for example, that "social characteristics determine political preference" (Lazarsfeld, Berelson, and Gaudet 1968, 27) and suggested that "a large part of the study of voting deals not with why votes change but rather with why they do not" (Berelson, Lazarsfeld, and McPhee 1954, 315). But, in retrospect, there may be much more to this approach than the critics suggest.

First, it is not entirely fair to dismiss the sociological approach as "simply descriptive." On the contrary, Lazarsfeld and his colleagues (1968) were keenly interested in the "psychological mediators which connect the social situation and the individual decision" (p. xxiv). Nor did they neglect the influence of the candidates and the issues of the day. They also recognized that an index of political predisposition was going to be less valid when applied to a nationwide as opposed to a community-wide sample

(p. xxviii). In any case, how well IPP predicts vote choice is too crude a criterion for evaluating the model's performance. The index was a scale whose extremes corresponded to the most loyal partisans of the two competing parties. But what about people located in the middle range of the scale? Their choices would be much harder to predict because they are more likely to divide their votes more or less equally between the parties. The predictive accuracy of the scale was thus very much a function of how voters were distributed between the extremes. Finally and most important, a sociological model is not necessarily static. Most social background characteristics certainly are either fixed or relatively stable, but this does not mean that they cannot have dynamic effects. People's "values" on these variables are typically determined long before the election, but the political effects of these variables can vary, depending on the electoral context.

The key insight of the Columbia school's sociological model was that "voting is essentially a group experience. People who work or live or play together are likely to vote for the same candidates" (Lazarsfeld, Berelson, and Gaudet 1968, 137). From this perspective, knowing voters' socio-economic status, religious affiliation, and place of residence does matter because it provides important clues about their social networks. Social categories indicate people's contacts with friends and family and neighbours and workmates, and, in that sense, they represent live social dynamics not just static categories.

The Columbia researchers saw voting as a social process. Social interactions helped to explain changing voting patterns because group members react to changing political landscapes through the lens of shared values and interests. Opinion leaders play a key role in getting group members to vote in ways that correspond to the group's overall interests. These opinion leaders are group members who exhibit more interest in campaigns and pay more attention to the media. In short, regarding vote choice as a kind of group decision does not mean that group voting is static.

A second dynamic element in the Columbia model can potentially come from cross-pressures. The vote decision is construed as "the net effect of a variety of pressures" (Berelson, Lazarsfeld, and McPhee 1954, 56). If different pressures work in different directions, then these pressures can also have dynamic effects. People take on a variety of social identities, and these may not be mutually reinforcing when it comes to vote choice. Religious affiliation, for example, may push voters in one direction, but their regional identity might push them in the opposite direction. In Canada, for example, Catholics have traditionally been more likely than Protestants to vote Liberal. Western Canadians, meanwhile, have been much less likely than residents of other regions to vote Liberal. As a result, Catholics living in western Canada could well feel cross-pressured. One possibility, of course, is that some cross-pressured voters might simply lose interest and not vote at all. But those who do vote may well switch parties from one election to the next. And their vote choice in any one particular election could well depend on their particular personal contacts at the time, or on which social identity gets cued in that particular election.

The Columbia researchers advanced the concept of cross-pressures by developing the notion of a "breakage effect" in their study of the 1948 election. When a citizen's primary groups are not homogeneous politically, the dominant partisan climate of opinion in the community will break through (Berelson, Lazarsfeld, and McPhee 1954). Berelson and colleagues (1954) also theorized that "contact breeds consensus": the more people interact with a group, the more likely they are to share the dominant partisanship of that group. A Catholic who is a regular churchgoer, for example, would be more likely to vote Liberal than one who rarely or never worships. These notions go well beyond a crude social analysis that simply shows different voting patterns in different social categories.

The Social-Psychological Model

The main theoretical rival to the sociological approach, the social-psychological model, was developed by researchers at the University of Michigan. Pioneered by Campbell and colleagues (Campbell et al. 1960) and tested in their study of the 1952 US presidential election, the social-psychological model was motivated by the perceived shortcomings of the Columbia model. The Michigan researchers challenged the Columbia model on both empirical and theoretical grounds. Empirically, IPP performed poorly when applied to the entire country. And theoretically, according to the Michigan school, the Columbia model could not explain why social groups differed in their voting patterns. More important, the sociological approach could not explain electoral dynamics because the distribution of social background characteristics changes too slowly between elections to account for short-term fluctuations in the vote. Electoral dynamics, they argued, could only be explained by incorporating factors that vary in the short term.

Where the Columbia model views voting as a social process, the Michigan model sees voting as a response to psychological forces. The key to understanding the dynamics of electoral behaviour, according to the Michigan school, had to do with voters' reactions to changes in the political landscape: "The individual's attitudes toward the elements of national politics comprise a field of forces that determines his [sic] action in an immediate sense" (Campbell et al. 1960, 120). Two forces were of paramount importance:

voters' evaluations of the candidates and voters' issue attitudes. Moreover, both of these forces were linked to a key antecedent psychological factor: voters' emotional attachment to a political party. This focus on the political parties, the candidates, and the issues plainly responded to one major perceived shortcoming of the sociological model, namely, that it was apolitical.

Campbell and his colleagues adopted a metaphor, the "funnel of causality," to describe their approach. The funnel metaphor highlighted a series of causal chains that resulted in a particular vote choice. The axis of the funnel was time, and the links in the chain were prioritized according to their proximity to the actual vote. Social background characteristics such as ethnicity, race, region, and religion, along with social status characteristics such as education, occupation, and class as well as parental characteristics such as partisanship were at the mouth of the causal funnel. The Michigan researchers conceptualized these factors as influencing a person's party identification. They defined party identification as a feeling of closeness or psychological attachment to a political party that is formed early in the life cycle and is strongly influenced by parental partisanship. Accordingly, partisanship followed social background characteristics in the causal chain and was viewed as the key long-term—or distal—influence on the vote. Party identification could have a direct effect on vote choice, but its influence could also be mediated via issue attitudes and candidate evaluations. These were viewed as the most important short-term—or proximate—influences, and they formed the next link in the causal chain. Other short-term factors such as campaign events reported by the media and conversations about the election with family and friends came toward the end of the causal funnel, closer to vote choice itself. But the main focus was on party identification, candidate evaluations, and issue attitudes rather than on the campaign communications near the tip of the funnel or on the social characteristics at its mouth.

Campbell and his colleagues (1960) were primarily interested in the psychological forces that influence vote choice. In their view, exploring "the infinite regress of antecedent factors" (p. 33) was unnecessary because party identification represented "a perfect distillation" (p. 34) of all the factors in people's life histories that could influence their predisposition to support a particular party. Concentrating on attitudes that were highly proximate to voters' actual decisions, they argued, was the key to maximizing explanatory power.

The Michigan approach explains vote choice by the intensity and partisan direction of attitudes. A voter who identifies with the Republican Party, shares the Republicans' positions on the issues, and likes the Republican candidate is very likely to vote Republican. People who identify with a political party will tend to perceive the issues and the candidates through the filter of their party attachment. But party identification does not necessarily predetermine their vote. How people vote in a given election depends on the interaction between their inclination to support a particular party and the short-term attitudinal forces that are specific to that particular election. If the short-term forces are sufficiently strong, some partisans may defect and vote for another political party.

Not surprisingly, the Michigan approach also attracted some criticism. First, some questioned the utility of relying on explanatory variables that were conceptually very close to vote choice itself. Variables that are proximate to the vote will certainly do a better job of explaining it in the statistical sense, but how much is really learned by arguing that people tend to vote for the party with which they identify or for the presidential candidate they like the best? Campbell and his colleagues (1960) concede that focusing on attitudinal variables risks "prediction without understanding" (p. 35). But prediction is not the primary goal of voting behaviour research. Our distant ancestors could predict the lunar cycle, but they could not account for it. Relying too heavily on factors close to the vote threatens to introduce a similar dilemma. What we need to know is why people identify with one party rather than another, why they like one candidate more than the others, and why they stand where they do on the issues of the day. And this means that we have to delve further back in the funnel of causality.

Questions can also be raised abut the causal paths. Do the causal arrows run in the direction that the funnel of causality assumes? First, as Campbell and his colleagues (1960) acknowledged, "Measurement close to the behaviour runs the risk of including values that are determined by the event we are trying to predict—that is, the vote decision" (p. 35). For example, some voters may decide to vote for the incumbent party based on its perceived handling of the economy and then simply assume that the party shares their positions on other issues. Second, there is the causal status of party identification to consider. It is certainly plausible that party identification influences evaluations of the candidates and issue attitudes. But it is also reasonable to expect that party identification may be affected by those very same factors. Indeed, the Michigan researchers themselves recognized that party allegiance can come under pressure when people develop attitudes that are inconsistent with their party identification, and "if this pressure is intense enough, a stable partisan identification may actually be changed" (Campbell et al. 1960, 135). But, at the end of the day, they contended that the influence of party identification on these attitudes was much more important than any reverse effect.

The Michigan approach has also been criticized for paying insufficient attention to the social element. Social psychology is supposed to explain human behaviour in terms of its social context, yet the social-psychological model treats voting very much as an individual behaviour. This difference in emphasis is perhaps understandable. After all, the social-psychological approach adopted by the Michigan school was grounded in a rejection of the assumptions of the sociological approach. Indeed, its developers stressed the differences "to the point of exaggeration: so that the differences received more attention than the similarities" (Miller 1983, 107).[1] Yet there is clearly some common ground. Both the Columbia and Michigan models assume that voters have a predisposition toward a particular party and that the likelihood of defections from that party is inversely related to the strength of that partisan predisposition. They differ, though, when it comes to identifying what lies behind the predisposition. In the Michigan model, it is rooted in a psychological attachment to a political party. In the Columbia model, its basis is mutually reinforcing social group memberships. Arguably, the differences between the two models may be a matter of emphasis. The Columbia school paid much more attention to the social background characteristics at the mouth of the funnel of causality and to the communications networks near its tip, whereas the Michigan researchers focused on the psychological mediators. Given the benefit of a longer historical perspective, it is not difficult to see why Lewis-Beck and his colleagues (2008) arrived at the judgment that "a combination of the two is more powerful than the two taken separately" (p. 19).

Multistage Models

Combining the sociological and the social-psychological approaches is very much the motivation behind the multistage bloc-recursive approach that was developed by Miller and Shanks (1996) in *The New American Voter*. The authors point to an important limitation of the analyses reported in *The American Voter*. The metaphor of a funnel of causality was supposed to represent the ways in which causally prior variables have an indirect impact on the vote by influencing more proximate psychological "forces." Yet party identification was the only variable whose indirect as well as direct effects on the vote were actually examined in any detail by Campbell and his colleagues. The Miller and Shanks "multi-stage model is based on a more differentiated set of assumptions concerning the sequence in which voters acquired their 'positions' on different types of explanatory variables" (p. 210). And it explicitly represents the linkages between causal factors that are closer to the mouth of the funnel.

According to Miller and Shanks, all of the potentially relevant explanatory factors can be conceptualized as a series of blocs. The blocs are then ordered according to their presumed proximity to the vote. Variables are located in the same bloc if they can be assumed to occupy a similar position in the temporal sequence. In other words, it is assumed that they are all caused by factors that are further back in the causal sequence and that they all exert a causal influence on blocs of variables that are further along in the sequence. The analysis proceeds in stages. At the first stage, the vote model includes only social background characteristics. Variables included in this bloc are necessarily exogenous: they may be influenced by other variables in the same bloc, but they are clearly causally prior to political preferences. At the second stage, the next bloc of variables is added and the model is re-estimated. This process of adding blocs and re-estimating the model is repeated until all of the blocs have been incorporated.

Entering blocs of variables in stages makes it possible to estimate the total impact of each explanatory factor, as opposed to only that portion that is not mediated via more proximate factors. Estimating a single model containing all of the explanatory factors would necessarily underestimate the effects of those factors that are more distant from the actual vote choice. The multistage bloc-recursive approach introduces another significant advance; it also guards against projection effects. Projection occurs when more proximate variables are strongly affected by more distant ones. Perceptions of how well the incumbent has handled the economy, for example, may well be shaped by partisan loyalties. A voter who identifies with the incumbent's party is apt to judge the performance more favourably simply by virtue of being a partisan. In the bloc-recursive approach, more proximate variables are only credited with that part of their effect that cannot be explained by causally prior variables.

There are two potential problems with this approach. The first concerns the assumed causal ordering. The assumptions concerning the temporal sequence are crucial. If they are wrong, the method will either seriously overestimate or seriously underestimate the effect of a given explanatory factor, depending on whether it is entered too soon or too late. This means that it is important to provide a careful rationale for the chosen ordering. There is also the risk of persuasion effects with this approach. The model assumes that the causal arrows all run in one direction. For example, Miller and Shanks assume that voters' own policy preferences are causally prior to their candidate evaluations. It is possible, though, that some voters like a candidate for other reasons, and, because they like the candidate, they are "persuaded" to adopt the candidate's policy preferences as their own.

Miller and Shanks acknowledge this potential problem, but counter that such persuasion effects are likely to be only moderate and certainly less serious than the potential impact of projection effects.

Anderson and Stephenson (2010a) conclude that the bloc-recursive approach results in "a very powerful model of vote choice and knowledge of how the various factors interact with each other" (p. 14). They are critical, though, of the lack of attention to the relative importance of the different blocs of variables. This oversight is easily remedied by looking, for example, at the improvement in fit or the increase in the percentage of variance explained when blocs are added. The more serious criticism is the absence of a powerful theoretical rationale for grounding predictions about the relative importance of each of the blocs. This is a challenge, not least because the relative importance of different blocs of explanatory factors might well vary from one election to another, both across time and across contexts.

Finally, Miller and Shanks (1996) themselves recognize that the model assumes that all voters' decision paths go through each of the stages in exactly the same order. Clearly, though, many voters will not engage in such lengthy reasoning chains. Indeed, the evidence suggests that voters often make use of short cuts. Some voters may even rely on simple sociodemographic cues such as the degree of social similarity between themselves and the party leaders when it comes to figuring out how to vote (Cutler 2002). Lewis-Beck and his colleagues (2008) suggest that the assumption of homogeneity in causal ordering is "heroic" (p. 410). The failure to account for heterogeneity in the decision calculus is not unique to the bloc-recursive approach, however. It applies to all of the models reviewed here. The problem is that by "having the same expectations for all voters, and treating them equally in our analyses, we run the risk of distorting the true effects of particular variables by averaging them out over the population" (Anderson and Stephenson 2010b, 281). As a result, the effects of some variables will be significantly overestimated for some voters and significantly underestimated for others. The extent to which this inaccuracy qualifies as "a problem" depends on the purpose at hand. If the objective is to understand what factors influence electoral outcomes, as it is here, then it is the average effects that are of interest.

Rational Choice Models
Rational choice offers a theoretical alternative that seeks to provide a much more parsimonious explanation of vote choice. Anthony Downs's *An Economic Theory of Democracy* (1957) was a pioneering effort that explicitly attempted to apply economic reasoning to the behaviour of political par-

ties and voters. Unlike other pioneers in the field, Downs eschewed psychological considerations almost completely. His core assumption was that "conscious rationality prevails" (p. 4). In the context of voting behaviour, this idea implies that people will vote for the party they believe will provide them with the most benefits. Downs defines benefits as "streams of utility derived from government activity" (p. 36). The rational voter will always choose the course of action that yields the highest utility. Thus, the vote decision calculus entails a comparison of the benefits that would accrue to the voter if each party were in office. For the incumbent party, the best basis for estimating future performance is what that party has done in its current term of office. And because "it would be irrational to compare the current performance of one party with the expected future performance of another" (p. 40), the rational voter compares the incumbent's performance with the performance that the opposition party would have produced had it been in power. The latter, of course, is purely hypothetical, but Downs maintains that it is better to compare an actual with a hypothetical than to compare two hypotheticals. A similar decision process applies to a multiparty system, but with allowance for strategic calculations: if the preferred party's chances of winning are perceived to be very low, the rational alternative is to vote for the next preferred party in the hopes of defeating the least preferred party. This utility-maximizing model has not only informed subsequent work on strategic voting but also sparked a vast literature on economic voting. Economic voting models postulate that voters engage in a reward-and-punish calculus whereby their decision to vote for the incumbent party (or not) hinges on their assessments of its economic performance.

Downs's theorizing has also underpinned spatial models of party competition. Here, the assumption is that voters will choose the party that is closest to them on a left-right ideological scale. This Downsian issue proximity model of vote choice has been generalized to predict that voters will vote for the party that is closest to them in the issue space. The primary challenge to this spatial model has come from the directional model developed by Rabinowitz and his colleagues (Macdonald, Listhaug, and Rabinowitz 1991; Rabinowitz and Macdonald 1989). The directional model postulates that there are two sides or directions in a given policy domain and that voters systematically prefer the parties that are on their side of the issue over those that are on the other side. According to this approach, a voter never prefers a party on the opposite side of the issue to one on the same side, even if the former is "closer" than the latter. Moreover, among the parties on their side, voters prefer the party that is perceived to take the strongest stand in favour of that side unless that party is perceived to lie beyond the region of acceptability. Thus, the expectation is that voters will penalize parties that are deemed to be extreme or irresponsible. Whether the directional model works better than the spatial model remains an unsettled matter, but, in Canada at least, the evidence has clearly favoured the proximity model (Johnston, Fournier, and Jenkins 2000; see also Blais, Nadeau et al. 2001a).

Both models work from parsimonious and powerful assumptions but each is vulnerable to perceptual biases. Voters may be apt to attribute their own position to the party they prefer or to assume that the party they prefer takes the same side. Both models are also vulnerable to the criticism that they assume that the issues defining party competition are primarily positional in nature (Stokes 1963). The issue proximity model presumes that voters choose among an ordered set of alternatives, while the directional model maintains that voters face a choice of sides. Stokes's objection was that "many of the issues that agitate our politics do not involve even a shrivelled set of two alternatives of government action" (p. 372). According to Stokes, election campaigns often revolve around what he terms "valence issues." Valence issues have no sides. Instead, they are characterized by a general consensus about a particular goal, such as a healthy economy or a clean environment. No party will campaign in favour of higher unemployment or more pollution. Instead, the parties campaign on claims that they will be the best party for dealing with the issue. In Canada, health care qualifies as a valence issue; each party claims that it would be best when it comes to improving health care. The Liberal Party's green shift, on the other hand, was clearly a positional issue; the major parties took different sides.

The valence politics model occupies a central place in the approach developed by Clarke and his colleagues (Clarke et al. 2004; Clarke, Kornberg, and Scotto 2009). They aimed to avoid the shortcomings of models based on the "narrow concept of rationality" that underpinned Downs's work (Downs 1957, 6). They question the analogy between the political arena and the market place and suggest that Downs greatly underestimated the importance of non-rational considerations in people's evaluations and perceptions of the political realm. They also point out that models that rely on a narrow concept of rationality tend not to perform well empirically. This failing is most obvious when it comes to "the paradox that ate rational choice theory" (Grofman 1993, 93). From a strict rationality perspective, it is irrational to vote.

The perspective adopted by Clarke and his colleagues also builds on Fiorina's (1981) reconception of party identification and on more recent work on low-information rationality (see, for example, Lupia and McCubbins

1998; Sniderman, Brody, and Tetlock 1991). Fiorina views party identification as "a running tally of retrospective evaluations" of party promises and performance (p. 251). Socialization influences may dominate in young adulthood, but party identification is subject to modification in the light of experience. That perspective is entirely consistent with a rational choice conception that sees party identification as being driven by cognitive rather than affective considerations. The implication is that party ties are flexible.[2] According to Clarke and his colleagues (2009), "flexible partisan attachments that encapsulate a storehouse of information about past party and party leader performance provide easily accessible cues that enable voters to make their decisions quickly and at relatively low cost" (p. 279). That perspective fits with low-information rationality arguments that suggest that people can rely on a variety of information short cuts, or heuristics, to help them arrive at the choices they would make if they were fully informed. The other critical cues in the valence politics model are party leader images. Voters' impressions of the leaders' characters and competence can serve as short cuts to help people judge which party is going to do the best job of providing sound management of the country's affairs.

In sum, the valence politics model focuses on "how judgments about parties' likely performance in office affect electoral choice . . . [and] how such judgments are conditioned by cognitive shortcuts, such as leadership images and party identification" (Clarke et al. 2004, 10). These factors can certainly provide important insights into parties' changing electoral fortunes. But it is fair to ask, how much explanatory leverage is gained if we settle for an explanation that people vote for the party they think will do the best job? Important questions are left unanswered. Why do people choose to identify with one party rather than another? And why do some people view the same leader's character and competence very differently? There is also the question of empirical fit. The economy is the quintessential valence issue: a healthy economy is universally appealing; no party is going to campaign in favour of higher unemployment or lower incomes. Yet (as we will see in Chapter 5) economic voting is weak in Canada. Finally, there may be a risk of circularity: party identification and leader images shape evaluations of parties' likely performance in office, but performance evaluations influence party identification and leader images.

The Analytic Strategy[3]
The analyses that follow adopt the multistage, bloc-recursive approach. For our purposes, it represents a useful simplification of what is undoubtedly a complex and heterogeneous decision process. We do not assume that

Figure 1.1 *The Multistage Explanatory Model*

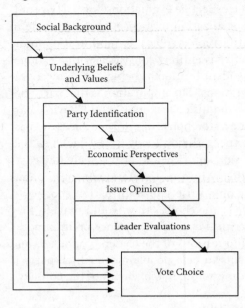

voters necessarily reason in stages, or that they all factor the same considerations into their decision calculus. Those would, indeed, be "heroic" assumptions (Lewis-Beck et al. 2008, 410), and they would not hold up under most circumstances (see Johnston et al. 1996; Roy 2009). Rather, the driving assumption is that this explanatory schema (see Figure 1.1) captures a sequence in which many voters do participate, if only incompletely. Moreover, this approach has two other virtues: it is comprehensive in the sense that it captures a wide range of considerations that plausibly motivate vote choice, and it minimizes possible projection effects that can arise when more proximate variables are strongly affected by more distant ones (see above).

Recall that the basic insight underlying the multistage model is that explanatory factors differ in their proximity to the vote. Where people stand on the issues of the day and how they feel about the party leaders, for example, are closer in time to the actual vote than such longer-term predispositions as party identification and basic values and beliefs. These longer-term predispositions can have a direct effect on vote choice: some voters are such strong partisans that their vote is decided long before the election is called. Importantly, though, predispositions can also affect vote choice indirectly by influencing more proximate factors. For example, a social conservative is likely to oppose same-sex marriage.

The first bloc of variables comprises social background characteristics. Critics of the sociological model would find this an odd starting point for any attempt to explain electoral dynamics in the four elections held between 2000 and 2008. After all, any change in the sociodemographic composition of the electorate during that period would be modest at best, far too small to explain the changes in party fortunes. However, it is difficult to make sense of voting behaviour in Canada unless the effects of certain key social background characteristics are taken into account (Blais et al. 2002; Gidengil et al. 2006; Nevitte et al. 2000). As Blais (2005) concluded, "we miss something important if we do not examine the group bases of party support. In the Canadian case, we miss the fact that the Liberals have won most elections and that they have won in great part thanks to the strong support of Catholics and Canadians of non-European origin" (p. 834). This begs a question, of course: does a loss of support among these two groups of voters help to explain the Liberals' subsequent defeats? In other words, have the effects of these two characteristics changed? The distribution of social background characteristics may have remained much the same in 2008 as it was eight years earlier, but this stability is not necessarily true of their effects.

The second bloc of variables considers voters' fundamental values and beliefs. Canadians typically do not have a very clear grasp of concepts like "left" and "right" (see Gidengil, Blais, Nevitte et al. 2004). But this does not mean that the public lacks coherent views about the appropriate balance between the state and the market. Indeed, these views have proved to matter to people's choice of party (Blais et al. 2002; Gidengil et al. 2006; Nevitte et al. 2000). The potential electoral relevance of basic values and beliefs goes beyond the questions that define the traditional left-right dimension. It is possible that a "new" left-right dimension has emerged, one that revolves around moral questions and gender roles. Then there are people's views about such fundamental matters as the appropriate relationship between Canada and the United States as well as the place of Québec in Canada. Religiosity, views about racial minorities, and beliefs about the nature of politics in Canada can each be added to the list. Fundamental values and beliefs are not immutable, so we need to ask whether changes in their distribution have played a role in the parties' changing electoral fortunes. Changes in the identity of the governing party suggest that beliefs about the nature of politics in Canada may be particularly critical in this regard. However, the relevance of values and beliefs for understanding electoral dynamics is not contingent on changes in their distribution. How much any given value or belief matters to vote choice can vary from election to election depending on the context and the nature of the campaign. Some campaigns may resonate with one set of values, while other campaigns may activate quite different ones.

Party identification is the third bloc considered in the model. The assumption here is that people's party attachments are influenced by their fundamental values and beliefs, as well as by their social background characteristics. Indeed, we would argue that this anchoring in social identities and in values and beliefs is what limits the flexibility of people's party ties, and it is a contention that receives support from findings about the ideological nature of partisanship in the United States (Bafumi and Shapiro 2009). Introducing party identification to the models before economic evaluations, issue attitudes, and leader evaluations makes an assumption about the direction of causality. Given the debate about the applicability of the concept of party identification in Canada (see Chapter 4), some readers may question this particular choice of causal ordering. This is where the 2004–2006–2008 panel data come in particularly useful. These data make it possible to answer an important question: how responsive are Canadians' party attachments to short-term electoral forces? Indeed, these elections offer a particularly useful opportunity to revisit the applicability of the concept of party identification to voting behaviour in Canada. If Liberal partisanship could withstand the sponsorship scandal in 2004 and the new revelations about the extent of corruption that emerged in the run-up to the 2006 election, then the case for the applicability of Michigan-style party identification in Canada would be more credible. And, of course, the prospects for the Liberal Party would look brighter. To minimize the possibility of reverse causation (see above), we rely on the campaign measure of party identification rather than on the post-election measure.

The sponsorship scandal was not the only short-term force that might have swayed voters. In fact, there are three types of short-term forces that have been highlighted in the literature: perceptions of the economy, issue attitudes, and evaluations of leaders. Economic evaluations are the fourth bloc of variables introduced into the model. They follow after party identification because partisans are apt to evaluate the performance of the incumbent through the filter of their party attachment (Nadeau et al. 2000). A performance that is good enough for partisans of the incumbent party may be judged more harshly by partisans of the challengers. This is one reason that simple reward-and-punish models may not perform well empirically. How well these economic voting models perform may also depend on objective economic realities. Economic conditions changed between 2000 and 2008. Did this play a role in explaining parties' changing fortunes? The weight of the cumulative research evidence is that voters are readier to blame the incumbent party when the economy is doing badly than they are to give it credit for better times. The governing party does not necessarily reap the electoral rewards when the economy has been doing well. But it may pay a price for poor economic performance. Thus, there is an intriguing possibility to explore: did the stock market crash help save the Liberals from an even worse defeat in 2008 by limiting the scope of the Conservative victory?

Issues are added to the model next. It is clear that perceptions of how the economy is doing can influence where people stand on the issues (Clarke and Kornberg 1992). From that vantage point, the 2008 election provides an inviting test case. In that election, the Conservatives characterized the Liberals' proposed green shift as just too risky an undertaking in a time of such economic uncertainty.

Issues typically matter more than economic evaluations (Blais et al. 2004), and some issues matter more than others. The sponsorship scandal was clearly a major liability that limited the scope of the Liberals' victory in 2004 (Gidengil et al. 2006). Did the revelations that emerged during the Gomery Commission hearings inflict even greater damage on the Liberals' chances in 2006? In 2008, Stéphane Dion and the Liberals made the "green shift" the centrepiece of their campaign: did it help them, or did it hurt them? The answers to those questions depend upon how public opinion is distributed. Even a high-profile issue may matter little to the election outcome if opinion is evenly divided because the votes of those on each side will be self-cancelling. Note that we use voters' positions on the issues to assess their effects. Like Miller and Shanks (1996), we are persuaded that "measures based on structured questions concerning voters' opinions usually provide a more appropriate assessment of...electoral 'relevance'...than do voters' own explanations for their vote preferences" (p. 211).

The final bloc of variables consists of evaluations of the party leaders. We use evaluations as measured in the campaign because post-election measures can be contaminated by the outcome of the election. Voters' reactions to the leaders typically have a powerful influence on their vote choice, but this does not necessarily translate into a substantial impact on vote shares (see Blais et al. 2002; Johnston 2002). Leader evaluations are likely to have the most impact on an election outcome when one leader is much more—or much less—popular than the others. An important part of the Conservatives' campaign strategy in the 2008 election was to target

Dion and portray him as a weak leader. Thus, the conditions may well have been in place for leadership to be a significant factor in explaining the scope of the Liberals' defeat in 2008.

The analytical approach adopted here necessarily simplifies a decision calculus that is inherently complex and almost certainly varies from voter to voter.[4] But the goal is not to account for every individual vote choice; it is to identify which factors were most important to voters overall. The main aim of the entire enterprise is to shed light on what lay behind the parties' changing fortunes between the 2000 and 2008 elections and to delineate the major fault lines that prepared the ground for the electoral upsets of 2011. Our multistage explanatory model is well suited to this task.

Notes

1 Note, though, that Clarke and his colleagues (2004) treat the social-psycho-logical model as a variant of the sociological approach.

2 It is worth noting, though, that Fiorina actually found a good deal of stability in party identification and concedes that there is a strong inertial component to voting. The flexibility or stability of Canadians' party attachments will be the subject of Chapter 4.

3 Details of the estimation strategy can be found in Appendix A.

4 For example, individual vote choices will be influenced by the context in which voters decide and by the available options.

CHAPTER TWO

THE CHANGING SOCIAL BASES OF PARTY SUPPORT

S ocial background characteristics may seem like an odd place to begin the search for an explanation of changing party fortunes. According to conventional wisdom, social cleavages in vote choice are weak in Canada (Clarke et al. 1979). Indeed, Mark Franklin (1992) characterizes Canada as an "historical decline" country where social cleavages have effectively ceased to structure vote choice. Then there is the criticism that was aimed at the Columbia model (see Chapter 1), namely, that the distribution of social background characteristics changes too slowly to explain electoral dynamics, at least in the short term (Kanji and Archer 2002; Campbell et al. 1960). Certainly, people are much more likely to change their vote from one election to the next than they are to change their religion. What this criticism overlooks, though, is the possibility that the *effects* of social characteristics on vote choice can change from one election to the next. This chapter argues that election outcomes cannot be adequately understood unless the role of social background characteristics is taken into consideration. People's social backgrounds *do* affect their choice of party. Moreover, the changing effects of social background factors turn out to be a crucial component of electoral dynamics.

Social Cleavages Old and New

As John Meisel (1975) long ago observed, Canada presents "a cornucopia of intriguing anomalies" when it comes to the role of social background characteristics in structuring vote choice (p. 253). Prime among these has been the fact that regional and religious cleavages "supersede class almost entirely as factors differentiating the support for national parties" in Canada (Alford 1963, xi). Almost 50 years ago Alford reached the conclusion that Canada was a case of "pure non-class voting" (1963, x–xi). Subsequent attempts to prove Alford wrong have been unable to provide any compelling evidence that Canadians vote along class lines (Gidengil 2002). To understand why the absence of a class cleavage in voting seems so anomalous, we need only recall Harold Lasswell's (1936) classic definition of politics. If politics is about "who gets what," then there are good reasons to suppose that people's material circumstances should influence their choice of party. The fact that they do not do so in Canada has been explained in large part by the strength of other cross-cutting cleavages, particularly religion and region.[1]

The finding that religious identities have been such a strong determinant of vote choice in Canada has been particularly puzzling. Indeed, it has struck some observers as an anachronism, akin to "a moderately interesting, but strikingly peculiar, houseguest who has overstayed his welcome" (Irvine 1974, 570). The puzzle is easy to state: Canada has no counterpart to Europe's Christian democratic parties, and religious issues have long been absent from party platforms, and yet religious affiliation has, for many years, been one of the best predictors of vote choice. Indeed, the fact that Catholics have traditionally been much more likely than Protestants to vote Liberal was a critical ingredient in the Liberal Party's former record as "one of the four most successful parties in contemporary democracies" (Blais 2005, 821).

The puzzle has defied explanation. The religious cleavage could not be explained away by other social background characteristics that are associated with being Catholic or Protestant, such as language, social class, or ethnic ancestry (Irvine 1974). William Irvine suggested an alternative explanation that focused on the role of childhood socialization. Parents could be passing on both their religious affiliation and their party preference without their children making any conscious connection between the two. However, the rate of intergenerational transmission of party loyalties would have to differ across groups in order for group differences in party vote shares to persist across generations (Johnston 1985). Either Catholic parents were more successful in passing on their party loyalty or, more likely, their influence was being reinforced by forces in the larger community. And there is evidence, at the individual level, that the relationship between being Catholic and voting Liberal is strongest in constituencies where Catholics are more numerous (Bélanger and Eagles 2006).

Just how these larger societal forces operate remains somewhat unclear.

Liberal leaders have often been Catholic and so have many local Liberal candidates, but these facts do not account for the traditional propensity of Catholics to vote Liberal. Issue attitudes do not explain the relationship either. Catholics do not typically differ much from non-Catholics on most issues, and, when they do differ, the differences should work in the opposite direction—to weaken the relationship between religious affiliation and vote choice (Blais 2005). For example, Catholics are more likely than non-Catholics to oppose both abortion and same-sex marriage, yet it seems that disagreement with the party's stance on moral issues did not dissuade Catholics from voting Liberal, at least in 2004 and 2006 (Stephenson 2010). Catholic voting patterns become even more perplexing when we consider the fact that it is the most religious Catholics who have traditionally proved to be the Liberals' strongest supporters (Blais 2005).

The decline in Liberal fortunes since the 2000 election suggests that it may be time to bid the unwanted guest farewell. If Catholics have served as the bedrock of Liberal success, then it is reasonable to ask whether the Liberal defeats in 2006 and 2008 indicate that Catholic support has crumbled. And, if the religious cleavage between Catholics and Protestants has weakened, is it possible that "moral issue disagreement" has finally caught up with the party (Stephenson 2010, 97)? If it has, then religious Catholics should be the most inclined to have defected to the Conservatives. An alternative possibility is that Catholics have remained loyal, and non-Catholics have been deserting the party.

The persistence of regional cleavages is a long-standing feature of the Canadian political landscape. In the 2008 election, the Conservative vote ranged from a low of 30 per cent in Atlantic Canada to a high of 52 per cent in the West. The Liberals, meanwhile, fared the worst in the West with only 16 per cent of the vote and best in Atlantic Canada with a 35 per cent share. The NDP vote was regionalized as well. Twenty-six per cent of Atlantic Canadians voted for the NDP compared with only 18 per cent of Ontario residents. These regional figures mask even greater interprovincial variation, especially for the Conservatives, whose share of the vote ranged all the way from a mere 17 per cent in Newfoundland to 65 per cent in Alberta.

Precisely what these regional differences mean has been more difficult to pin down. When Canadians were asked to define their region, there turned out to be a good deal of disagreement even among respondents within the same province (Clarke et al. 1979). One interpretation of that finding is that regions are mere analytical categories; they hold little real meaning to their residents. According to this region-as-artefact thesis, the regionalization of the vote might be more plausibly explained by regional differences in the social make-up of the population. From this perspective, the fact that the Liberals poll higher in Ontario than they do in the West might be attributable to the fact that there are more Catholics, say, in Ontario than there are in the West. However, the evidence does not support this interpretation. Even allowing for variations in the social composition of Canada's regions, the regional differences in party support patterns remain. The reason is simple: people sharing the same social background characteristics tend to vote differently depending on where they live. A Catholic in western Canada is much less likely to vote Liberal than his or her counterpart in Ontario or Atlantic Canada. These patterns reflect regional grievances that have deep historical roots, but they also appear to reflect differences in voters' priorities and interests. In the 1990s, for example, while Ontario voters were preoccupied with the government's role in job creation, Western voters were more concerned about fiscal issues (Gidengil et al. 1999).

Regional cleavages seem entrenched, but it is worth noting that Canadians did not divide as sharply along regional lines in the 2008 election as they did in the 2000 election. In the 2000 election, one Ontario resident in two voted Liberal, compared with only one Westerner in four. The pattern of Alliance support was the mirror image: one Westerner in two voted Alliance, compared with only one Ontario resident in four. By 2008, the Liberals had lost ground in Ontario and the West alike. Meanwhile, the Conservatives had achieved what the Alliance could not, namely an electoral breakthrough in seat-rich Ontario. Indeed, in 2008, they outpolled the Liberals in the province (and continued to do so in 2011).

These shifting patterns raise an important question about the role of social background characteristics: how successful have the Conservatives been in broadening their support? In 2000, there was a striking contrast between the Alliance and the Progressive Conservative vote. Aside from its support in Atlantic Canada, the Progressive Conservative Party lacked a clearly defined social base (Blais et al. 2002). To the extent that it appealed to voters, that appeal typically cut across social divisions. The Alliance vote, by contrast, was clearly rooted in Canada's cleavage structure. The party fared best among Westerners, Protestants, rural voters, married couples, people of northern European ancestry, and men.

The most consequential of these factors was gender. Like the Reform Party, the Alliance held much less appeal to women than to men (Gidengil et al. 2005). The gender gap (outside Québec) was 11 points in 2000, and the party's lack of appeal to women was one reason that the Alliance could not defeat the Liberals in 2000 (Blais et al. 2002). The gender gap on the left was a mirror image of the gender gap on the right: in 1997 and 2000 alike, women were more likely than men to vote NDP. The emergence of this "modern gender gap" (Inglehart and Norris 2003) is not unique to

Canada: women were once to the right of men in many western democracies, but they are increasingly to be found to men's left. Surprisingly, given the transformations in gender roles and in women lives and experiences over the past half century, structural and situational factors are little help when it comes to explaining sex differences in vote choice. Explanations focusing on women's increased labour force participation or the feminization of poverty have failed in Canada, as elsewhere, to account for gendered patterns of voting. Indeed, far from explaining away these patterns, structural and situational factors only help us to understand why the sex differences are not larger still (Erickson and O'Neill 2002; Gidengil et al. 2005). In particular, the fact that women tend to be more religious than men has served to limit the size of the modern gender gap. The failure of female-centred explanations to account for the sex differences in vote choice is not so surprising once we recognize the role of men's changing behaviour in driving the process of gender realignment (Gidengil 2007).

The roots of the modern gender gap lie much more in the realm of values and beliefs than in structural and situational factors. The three most important value dimensions for understanding gendered patterns of voting are views about free enterprise, Canada's relationship with the United States, and social conservatism. Women tend to be a little more sceptical than men of the workings of the market, they are less likely to favour close ties with the United States, and they are more open to diverse lifestyles and sexual mores. Although these differences should not be overstated, they do compel us to ask whether the Conservatives have been more successful than the Alliance in attracting as many women as men to the party, these value differences notwithstanding.

Attitudinal factors were also central to explaining the so-called marriage gap in support for Reform and the Alliance (Wilson and Lusztig 2004). Married men and married women alike were more likely than their single counterparts to vote for these parties because they took more socially conservative positions on abortion, gay marriage, women's roles, and other issues relating to traditional morality. Thus, it is worth exploring whether the marriage gap has narrowed in the wake of Stephen Harper's efforts to moderate his party's image.

Contrary to stereotype, people who live in villages and rural areas are no more traditional in their views than residents of towns, medium-size cities, or big-city suburbs: "The intolerant rural hick is a straw man" (Cutler and Jenkins 2001, 385; see also Walks 2004). It is possible that the urban-rural cleavage is giving way to an inner city-suburban cleavage. Inner-city residents tend to have less traditional views about gender roles, sexual mores, and lifestyles than their suburban counterparts, especially those residing

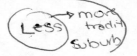

Less → more tradit suburb

23

in the "outer" suburbs (M. Turcotte 2001; Walks 2004). This difference might explain why the Conservatives were able to capture seats in suburban Ontario ridings in 2008 and to capitalize on that breakthrough in 2011.

Surprisingly, more is known about what factors explain differences in voting patterns across different types of community than about the voting behaviour of Canadians of non-European ancestry. Visible minority Canadians, a growing segment of the Canadian population, have traditionally been even more likely than Catholics to vote Liberal (Bilodeau and Kanji 2010; Blais et al. 2002; Nevitte et al. 2000), but the reasons for this are far from clear. Focusing on immigrants from non-traditional (i.e., non-European) source countries, Antoine Bilodeau and Mebs Kanji (2010) propose an issue ownership explanation for these voters' propensity to vote Liberal. They suggest that these immigrants have favoured the Liberal Party because of its stance on issues like immigration and multiculturalism. They go on to argue, though, that the Liberal Party's ownership of these issues may have diminished. Certainly, views about immigration and aid to racial minorities and developing countries were only minimally helpful in explaining why so many Canadians of non-European origin were voting Liberal in the 2004 election (Blais 2005). Moreover, these voters were supporting the party despite the fact that they were more opposed to abortion and same-sex marriage than other Canadians: "The bottom line is that we still do not have a good understanding why non-European Canadians so strongly support the Liberals" (Blais 2005). That was the case in the 2004 election. Since then, the Conservatives have been working strenuously to enhance their appeal to these voters. So it is important to ask, did the Liberals' subsequent decline mean that these visible minority voters were ceasing to be the bedrock of Liberal support? Their social conservatism suggests that the answer could be "yes."

The Liberals: A Party in Decline

Outside Québec,[2] Liberal dominance in 2000 owed a good deal to the support of two key groups: visible minorities and Catholics. By 2008, however, the Liberals could no longer count on the same degree of loyalty from those two segments of the population.

In 2000, visible minority voters voted overwhelmingly Liberal (see Figure 2.1). According to our estimations, even allowing for other social background characteristics, the probability of voting Liberal was fully 44 points higher in 2000 if a voter belonged to a visible minority.[3] Between 2000 and 2004, the visible minority vote dropped a massive 23 points (see Figure 2.1). The main beneficiary in that election was the NDP. The Liberals did not lose any further ground in 2006, but, in 2008, they lost another

Figure 2.1 *The Shrinking Liberal Core—Visible Minorities*

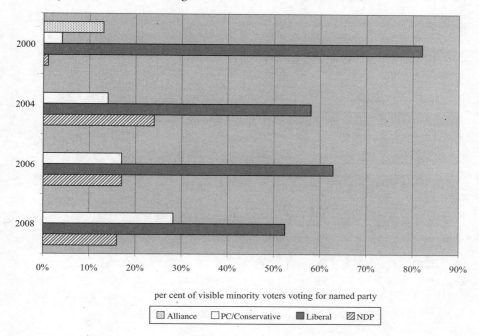

per cent of visible minority voters voting for named party

▦ Alliance   ☐ PC/Conservative   ■ Liberal   ▨ NDP

10 points. And, in that instance, it was the Conservatives who benefited. But even in 2008, the probability of a Liberal vote was still 26 points higher among visible minority voters. Without their support, the Liberal vote share would have been at least two points lower in 2008.[4]

The Liberals' loss of support among Catholics was more consequential. Catholic support outside Québec dropped a full 22 points between the 2000 and 2008 elections (see Figure 2.2). In 2000, one Catholic in two was a Liberal voter; by 2008, barely one Catholic in three was voting Liberal. The biggest drop occurred between 2004 and 2006, and the major beneficiary was the Conservative Party. In 2004, the Liberals had a 17-point advantage over the Conservatives among Catholic voters, but, in 2006, Catholics were as likely to vote Conservative as they were to vote Liberal. In 2008, they clearly preferred the Conservatives to the Liberals. It may be premature, though, to declare the traditional religious cleavage moribund: even in 2008, Catholics (32 per cent) were more likely than Protestants (19 per cent) to vote Liberal. But for their support, the Liberal vote share in 2008 would have been almost one and a half points lower.[5] Still, the import of the loss of Catholic votes since the 2000 election is clear: in 2000, Catholic support had boosted the Liberal vote share by almost four points.

Figure 2.2 *The Shrinking Liberal Core—Catholics*

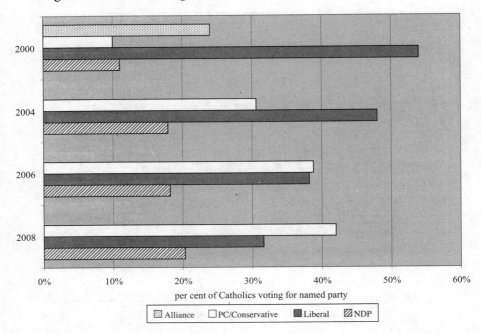

per cent of Catholics voting for named party

▨ Alliance ☐ PC/Conservative ■ Liberal ▨ NDP

Religious Catholics were no more likely than secular Catholics to desert the Liberals. Thirty-two per cent of Catholics who said that religion was very important in their lives voted Liberal in 2008, compared with 29 per cent of those who said religion was not very important or not important at all. And the less religious Catholics were actually more likely (47 per cent) to vote Conservative than their more religious counterparts (40 per cent). Evidence from the 2004–2006–2008 panel confirms the lack of any relationship between personal religiosity and Catholics' propensity to vote Liberal.[6] The same holds for moral traditionalism. There is no evidence indicating that Catholics who held more traditional views on questions of morality were any more likely to desert the party than their socially liberal counterparts. Similarly, whether a Catholic opposed same-sex marriage, or wanted to limit access to abortion, made little or no difference to their odds of deserting the Liberals.

The problem for the Liberals was not "issue disagreement" (see Stephenson 2010). The problem was the sponsorship scandal. The scandal resonated more powerfully with Catholics in 2006 in the wake of the Gomery Commission hearings (see Introduction) than with other voters.[7] Catholics who believed that there had been a lot of corruption under the Chrétien Liberals, who were angry about the scandal and the way that it had been handled, and who doubted Prime Minister Martin's ability to prevent a similar scandal in the future[8] were significantly less likely to be still voting Liberal in 2008. Our estimates suggest that, but for negative views about the sponsorship scandal, the Liberal's share of the Catholic vote in 2008 would have been 2 points higher. The Liberals might have paid a higher price had party identification not worked to keep Catholics loyal to the party. Catholics who identified with the Liberal Party during the 2004 campaign were significantly more likely to keep on voting Liberal in 2008.

There was a clear age gradient to the decline in Catholic support for the Liberals. In 2000, 55 per cent of Catholics aged 18 to 34 voted Liberal; by 2008, that figure had slumped to a mere 16 per cent. Fully 50 per cent of young Catholic voters voted Conservative in 2008, and another 28 per cent voted NDP. That young voters should be least attached to "their" party comes as no surprise given that party identification typically strengthens with age (Campbell et al. 1960). Still, the loss of support in this age group does not bode well for the Liberals' chances of winning back the Catholic vote.

As Catholic support dropped, secular voters became more important to the shrinking Liberal vote. But for their votes, the Liberal vote share would have been almost 2 points lower in 2008. However, this simply reflected the fact that secular voters were less likely than other voters to desert the party. It did not result from any growth in Liberal support on the part of secular voters.

Francophones (outside Québec) remained the most loyal component of the Liberal core. In 2000, the probability of voting Liberal was 9 points higher for voters whose first language was French. That figure had increased to 16 points by 2008. But two caveats are in order. First, the increase in the probability of this group voting Liberal was somewhat illusory; it reflected the fact that support had dropped to such a low point among voters whose first language was not French. And even francophone voters were less loyal than they had been in 2000: the Liberals' share of their vote dropped from 57 per cent in that election to 44 per cent eight years later. Second, voters whose first language is French are a very small minority of the electorate outside Québec. Consequently, their support has only a modest impact on the overall Liberal vote totals. Still, without their support, the Liberals would have lost almost one more point in 2008.

The Liberal vote remained highly regionalized in 2008. Some of the variation in vote shares across the country is attributable to differences in the sociodemographic composition of the regions: controlling for other social background characteristics did cause the regional differences to

Figure 2.3 *The Union Vote*

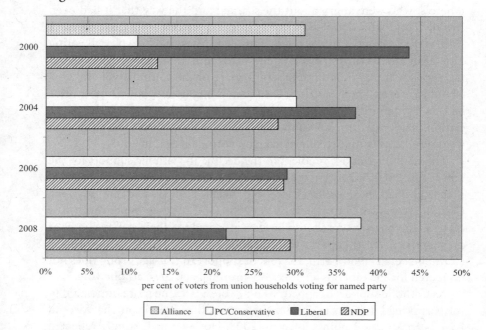

per cent of voters from union households voting for named party

☷ Alliance ☐ PC/Conservative ■ Liberal ▨ NDP

shrink somewhat. But the regional differences were not artefacts: even controlling for a variety of social background characteristics, the effects of region remained both strong and statistically significant. Lack of appeal in the West was clearly a serious drag on Liberal fortunes in all four elections. If the Liberals had fared as well in western Canada as they did in Ontario in 2000, their vote share would have been almost 8 points higher, other things being equal. By 2008, the party had lost ground in Ontario, but the fact that Westerners were even less likely to vote Liberal still cost the party 6.5 points. Greater appeal in Atlantic Canada than in the rest of the country did little to compensate for these shortfalls given the much smaller population base of that region.

A final sociodemographic factor that contributed to the decline in Liberal fortunes was a substantial loss of union votes between the 2000 and 2008 elections (see Figure 2.3). The party saw its share of the vote from union households cut in half, dropping from 44 per cent in 2000 to only 22 per cent in 2008. In 2000 and 2004, other things being equal, living in a union household made little difference to the odds of voting Liberal. That changed in 2006. Lack of appeal to voters from union households cost the Liberals over 2 points in both the 2006 and 2008 elections.

The Conservatives: On the Road to a Majority

The key question to ask about the Conservatives is clear: Have the Conservatives succeeded in broadening their support beyond the former Reform/Alliance core? Based on voting patterns in the 2008 election, the answer in two key respects is "yes." As noted already, the Conservatives made significant inroads in Ontario between 2004 and 2008. At the same time, they narrowed the urban-rural or, more precisely, the suburban-rural divide. As a result, both Westerners and rural residents came to form a smaller part of the party's—expanded—support base. In 2000, only 31 per cent of urban residents voted Alliance, compared with fully 45 per cent of rural Canadians. By 2008, the Conservatives were winning 40 per cent of the urban vote. Given that there are many more urban than rural voters, the growth in urban support was vital to the party's success.

The Alliance vote in 2000 had a strong ethnic flavour. Canadians of northern European ancestry were much more likely to vote for the party than other Canadians. Fifty-three per cent of these voters opted for the Alliance in 2000, compared with only 31 per cent of voters who did not claim northern European ancestry. The support of that group boosted the Alliance vote by almost a point. A similar pattern characterized Reform voting in 1997 (Nevitte et al. 2000). No such pattern was evident in Conservative voting in the three elections held between 2004 and 2008. Once other social background characteristics were taken into account, being of northern European ancestry ceased to be a significant predictor of vote choice. That finding provides another indication of the party's broadened appeal.

Still, there are two important exceptions to this pattern of narrowing divides in Conservative voting. Fundamentalist Christians were an important source of support for Reform and the Alliance alike. In 2000, half of all Christians who believed that the Bible is the literal word of God voted Alliance. In 2008, the Conservatives attracted the support of fully 63 per cent of these fundamentalist Christians.[9] The Liberals paid the electoral price; the Conservatives outpolled the Liberals by a substantial margin of 47 points among Christian fundamentalists. Without their votes, the Conservative vote share would have been over 3.5 points lower, and the Liberal vote over 2.5 points higher in 2008. Fundamentalist Christians proved to be just as important to the Conservative vote in 2008 as they had been to the Alliance vote in 2000.

Married people were an even more important source of Conservative votes, a pattern that was very much in evidence for the Alliance in 2000 and for Reform in both the 1993 and 1997 elections. The "spouse in the house" phenomenon remained strikingly stable (Wilson and Lusztig 2004). Had it not been for the support of married voters, the Alliance vote share would

Figure 2.4 *The "Modern Gender Gap"*

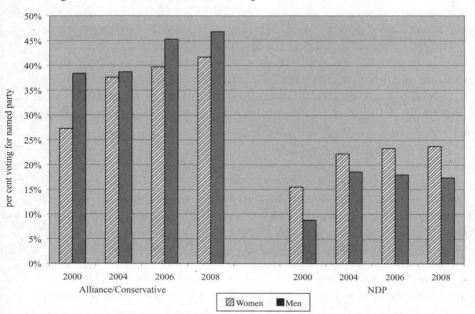

have been as many as 7.5 points lower in 2000. Their support boosted the Conservative share of the vote by 6.5 points in 2008. Had the Conservatives fared as well among voters who were not married, they might well have secured a majority in that election.

The Conservatives have been somewhat more successful in narrowing the gender gap (see Figure 2.4). In the 1993 federal election, the gender gap in Reform voting outside Québec was 11 points. Support for the new right rose among women and men alike in the following two elections, but the gender gap held steady at 11 points. In 2000, 38 per cent of men voted Alliance, compared with only 27 per cent of women. The failure to appeal to more women cost the party an estimated 5.5 points and was a key factor in its failure to break through in Ontario: "If the party had been able to do as well among Ontario women, it would have managed to make the inroad it was aiming for" (Blais et al. 2002, 93). And, we might add, the Alliance would have won the fight for the right.

In 2004, it seemed that the Conservatives had succeeded in eliminating the gender gap: women were as likely as men to vote for the new party. But the disappearance of the gap proved to be only temporary. The gap re-emerged in the 2006 election, and it persisted in 2008. Even if one controls for a variety of social background characteristics, women were less likely than men to vote Conservative. That cost the party over 3 points in both elections and may possibly have been the difference been a Conservative minority and a Conservative majority. That said, the gender gap in Conservative voting in 2008 was half the size of the gender gap in Reform and Alliance voting.

The NDP: A Party on the Rebound

Three groups of voters have been consistently important to the NDP's electoral fortunes: those who profess no religion, members of union households, and women.[10]

Traditionally, the NDP has attracted more support from people who have no religious affiliation. Even in 2000, the party could count on the support of 22 per cent of these voters. The probability of an NDP vote in this group was fully 16 points higher than it was among those who belonged to one religion or another, and, but for their support, the NDP vote share would have been over 2.5 points lower in that election. These secular voters remained a mainstay of the NDP vote. But the NDP has no lock on this segment of the population: in the three elections held between 2004 and 2008, secular voters divided their support almost equally among the NDP, the Liberals, and the Conservatives. One reason the NDP was not able to increase its support among these voters turns out to be their growing attraction to the Green Party (see Chapter 9).

Historically, union households have also been a mainstay of support for the NDP (Archer 1985). Even during the previous high point of NDP success in the 1980s, though, the party never attracted a plurality of the votes of this group.[11] The Liberals typically used to fare best among union households. Still, the collapse of the union vote is one of the keys to understanding why the NDP fared so poorly in the 1990s. Indeed, in the 2000 election, even the Alliance outpolled the NDP by more than two to one among union households (see Figure 2.3).

Regaining the union vote was critical to the NDP's resurgence. In 2004, the party doubled its share of the union vote, eating into Liberal support and attracting almost as many votes from union households as the new Conservative Party. But the NDP failed to increase its share of the union vote in the next two elections. Stalled at 29 per cent, the NDP trailed the Conservatives by almost 9 points among union households in 2008. That said, belonging to a union household remained one of the best predictors of an NDP vote. The probability of voting NDP was 14 points higher for voters from union households; had it not been for their support, the party's vote share would have been 3.5 points lower in 2008.

The party's support rebounded in part because of gender: women returned to the party sooner and in greater numbers than their male counterparts. That shift represented a reversal of the pattern that prevailed in the 1960s and early 1970s, when women were less likely than men to vote for the NDP. Women's support began to increase in the late 1970s, and, by the time of the 1979 federal election, the NDP was doing equally well among women and men. That pattern persisted through the 1980s, and, when the party's support collapsed in the 1993 federal election, it collapsed among women and men alike. But women were more likely than men to return to the party in the next election. That gender gap in NDP support persisted (see Figure 2.4). Even allowing for other social background characteristics, the probability of voting NDP was 5 points higher for women than for men in 2000. This figure rose steadily to over 7 points by 2008. These increments were not very large, but they were consequential. Sex, after all, is the "fault line of maximum potential cleavage," dividing the electorate almost 50/50 (Jennings 1988, 9). Were it not for its greater appeal to women, the NDP's vote would have been over 2 points lower in 2000 and almost 4 points lower in 2008. And if men had been as likely as women to vote for the party, the NDP's vote share would have been almost 4 points higher in 2008. The implication is clear: just as the Conservatives needed to enhance their appeal among women, the NDP needed to attract more men to the party. There is one important asymmetry, though, in the gendered patterns of support for these two parties: the Conservatives came close to attracting the support of half the male voters in 2008, but the NDP managed to attract only a quarter of the female vote (see Figure 2.4). Women were more likely than men to vote NDP, but many more women voted Conservative than voted NDP.

The NDP's electoral support in 2008 represented a mirror image of the Conservatives' in two other respects. First, the NDP fared worst among fundamentalist Christians, and, second, it did especially poorly among people who were married. Had marital status not mattered, the NDP vote share would have been fully 6 points higher in 2000.[12] This "marriage gap" persisted in 2004, even as support for the NDP grew, and it continued through the 2008 election. If the NDP had done as well among married people as it did among those who were not married, its vote share would have been at least 5 points higher in 2008.

Change and Continuity

Social background characteristics have turned out to be an important part of the explanation for the parties' changing electoral fortunes between 2000 and 2008. The shifting voting patterns had implications for the composition of each party's vote. The Conservatives clearly achieved some success in broadening their electoral base. Thanks to the party's gains in Ontario, its support base had become less regionalized and more urban by 2008. And compared with the Alliance vote, Conservative support was less sex-differentiated. However, the party's distinctive religious profile may yet prove to be a constraint on its ability to close the gender gap. Despite the growth in Catholic support, among Conservative voters Protestants outnumbered Catholics in 2008 by a margin of more than two to one, and almost a third of Conservative voters were Christian fundamentalists believing in a literal interpretation of the Bible. The presence of so many socially conservative voters is likely to hamper efforts to attract more women to the party, given that women tend to have more liberal attitudes than men when it comes to sexual mores and newer lifestyles.

The big losers, of course, were the Liberals. Losses of support among Catholics, visible minorities, and union households were important contributing factors to the decline in the Liberals' electoral fortunes between 2000 and 2008. The most important change relates to the voting behaviour of Catholics. Coming out of the 2008 election, Catholics still made up a larger proportion of the Liberal support base than of the Conservative base, but the party was no longer distinctively Catholic; in 2008, the Liberal vote was made up of an almost equal number of Catholics and Protestants. Based on his analysis of CES data from 1965 to 2004, André Blais (2005) concluded that "the Liberal party would *not* dominate in Ontario in the absence of the strong support it enjoys among Catholics and visible minorities" (p. 834). The loss of Catholic votes to the Conservatives since 2000 is thus critical to understanding why the Liberals have gone from dominance to decline. The shifts among Catholic voters may well signal the disappearance of Canada's traditional religious cleavage. But religion has not become any less important to vote choice in Canada. Rather, the traditional religious cleavage is being displaced by a new religious cleavage that pits Christian fundamentalists and other religious conservatives against more secular voters.

Despite the loss of visible minority votes, the Liberal base remained the most ethno-racially diverse of the three parties. Indeed, the increase in the number of visible minority voters and the decline in the Liberal vote overall meant that members of visible minorities actually accounted for a slightly larger share of the Liberal vote in 2008. They remained, though, very much a minority among Liberal voters. The loss of union votes had a more dramatic impact on the Liberal base. In 2000, over a third of Liberal voters came from union households; by 2000, that figure had dropped to just over a fifth.

By 2008, the NDP had succeeded in regaining much of the support that it had lost in the years running up to the 2000 election. The party's support base was distinctive in two key respects in 2008: NDP voters were more secular than were Liberal or Conservative voters and they were much more likely to come from union households. However, despite the party's electoral gains—and its steadfast advocacy for a strong social safety net—it was no closer to becoming the natural home for the "have-nots" in Canadian society.

It is unusual for an explanation of vote choice in an advanced industrial state to have made no mention of class, but there is little inkling that class factors were finally emerging to play a role in Canadians' vote choice. Social class was represented in our vote choice models using educational attainment.[13] Levels of formal education had some significant effects on vote choice, but the effects were inconsistent. Having less than a high school education increased the odds of an NDP vote in 2004 and 2008, but not in 2000 or 2006. Being a university graduate increased the odds of voting Liberal in 2008, but not in the three earlier elections. Sector of employment did not have a consistent effect on vote choice either: other things being equal, public sector workers were more likely to choose either the NDP or the Liberals over the Conservatives in 2006. But employment sector made no difference to how people voted in the other three elections. Despite years of electoral flux, voters' material circumstances were still having little effect on their choice of party. When it came to choosing a party, region and religion continued to trump social class.

This chapter began with the observation that many analysts are sceptical that social background characteristics can help to explain short-term electoral dynamics. And it is certainly the case that the sociodemographic makeup of the Canadian population shifted only marginally between 2000 and 2008. Nonetheless, the evidence presented here indicates that the *effects* of social background characteristics on vote choice can change over a relatively short period. Indeed, their changing impact during this crucial period has provided some important insights into the fading fortunes of the Liberal Party and the corresponding increase in the Conservative vote. These changes undoubtedly helped to pave the way for the shifting of Canada's electoral landscape in 2011.

Notes

1 An alternative explanation for the weakness of the class cleavage in voting attributes the emphasis on regional cleavages to elite manipulation (Brodie and Jenson 1988; Ogmundson 1975).

2 As explained in the Introduction, Chapters 2 to 8 focus on vote choice outside Québec.

3 See Appendix A for details of how vote choice probabilities were estimated.

4 Appendix A provides details of how the impact on party vote shares was calculated. Note that being foreign born, adhering to a non-Christian religion, and having neither English nor French as a first language do not significantly affect vote choice, once belonging to a visible minority is included in the model.

5 Canadians who adhere to a non-Christian religion have been even more likely than Catholics to vote Liberal. However, this is largely explained by the fact that they are more likely to belong to a visible minority. Once a control is included for this factor, the effect of affiliating with a non-Christian religion is not statistically significant.

6 Liberal vote choice in 2008 was regressed on Liberal vote choice in 2004, and factors that might have explained why Catholics who voted Liberal in 2004 failed to vote Liberal in 2008 were added as independent variables. The analysis is restricted to Catholics. To correct for panel attrition, we estimated a Heckman selection model with second stage probit. The selection variables were 18 to 34 years old and political knowledge (as indicated by ability to name the party leaders when interviewed after the 2004 election). Neither political interest nor education was a significant predictor of attrition, once political knowledge was included.

7 The impact of the scandal on the odds of voting Liberal in 2006 was much stronger for Catholics than for other voters: when an interaction between being Catholic and views about the scandal was added to the vote models used to estimate the impact of issues (see Chapter 6), the effect was both strong and statistically significant for the choice between the Liberals and the Conservatives and for the choice between the Liberals and the NDP.

8 These four items were combined to form a scale. For more on the effects of the sponsorship scandal, see Chapter 6.

9 Twenty-one per cent of voters outside Québec believed in 2008 that the Bible is the word of God and is to be taken literally word for word.

10 We are using membership in a union household rather than union membership because the latter information was not collected in the 2000 CES. The 2004, 2006, and 2008 CES data indicate that being a union member has only a slightly stronger effect on voting NDP than merely belonging to a household with at least one union member. For example, in 2008, 32 per cent of union members voted NDP, compared with 29 per cent of voters from union households.

11 The highest level of union support for the NDP recorded in the CES surveys was 28 per cent in 1980.

12 Note that this is net of age. In other words, the marriage gap cannot be explained away by the fact that married voters tend to be older.

13 Educational attainment was used rather than household income because there was a good deal of missing data on the income measure, reflecting the reluctance of some respondents to reveal their income. Income and educational attainment are strongly related. As a check, we compared the cross-tabulation of education and vote choice with the cross-tabulation of income and vote choice. The pattern turned out to be very similar.

CHAPTER THREE

VALUES AND BELIEFS

The changing demographics of the parties' support raise a variety of questions about the role of ideological orientations in explaining the parties' shifting electoral fortunes. Did the growth in Conservative support mean that the party was expanding beyond its traditional right-wing constituency? Or had the size of that constituency grown? Were the NDP's prospects for growth constrained by the size of the potential constituency for a left-wing party, or was the problem instead that the NDP was competing with the Liberals for the same left-of-centre constituency? Did the fact that the Liberals lost core supporters to both the Conservatives on the right and the NDP on the left indicate growing ideological polarization in recent elections? The answers to these questions are critically important for understanding the outcome of the 2011 election.

Notions of left and right do not exhaust the universe of potentially relevant ideological orientations. People have a variety of fundamental values and beliefs that can influence their vote choice in a variety of direct or indirect ways. These orientations might influence citizens' party attachments, their positions on the issues of the day, and their perceptions of the party leaders (Barnea and Schwartz 1998; Feldman 1988; Feldman and Zaller 1992; Kinder 1983; Knutsen 1995a, 1995b; Van Deth and Scarbrough 1995). Religion, for example, can be a source of abstract principles that have political relevance. Communal outlooks can matter too, and so can beliefs about the way that the political system operates. Early Canadian election studies paid little attention to values and beliefs. But more recent investigations demonstrate that a consideration of values makes for a more complete understanding of why Canadians vote the way they do (Blais et al. 2002; Gidengil et al. 2006; Nevitte et al. 2000). These findings lend considerable weight to the notion that value orientations and beliefs serve as templates that guide complex decisions (Blais et al. 2002; Sniderman, Brody, and Tetlock 1991).

This chapter explores the role fundamental values and beliefs played in explaining the changes in the parties' electoral fortunes between 2000 and 2008. One possibility is that the shifts reflected changes in Canadians' underlying values and beliefs. Another possibility is that the value architecture connecting citizens to political parties changed. The latter change might have happened in at least two ways: the salience of particular values and beliefs in the vote calculus could have changed or voters' perceptions of which party is most in tune with their basic values and beliefs could have altered.[1]

Telling the Left from the Right

The notion that parties' ideological orientations could influence voters' choice of party and contribute to an understanding of electoral dynamics might seem to fly in the face of the conventional wisdom about Canadians' capacity for ideological thinking. We do not typically think of Canadian voting behaviour as being ideologically motivated. After all, many Canadians seem to lack even a minimal grasp of the concepts of "left" and "right."

This first became evident when respondents in both the 1965 and 1968 Canadian Election Study were asked to place each of the political parties, as well as their ideal party, on several party image scales. Included among these dimensions was the left-right scale. The response patterns revealed several anomalies (Kay 1977). Party identifiers placed their own party farther to the right than did those who identified with the other parties, and each party's own identifiers typically placed their ideal party to the right of centre. Even NDP supporters, on average, placed their ideal party slightly to the right of centre. Every party, including the NDP, consistently received more votes among those who perceived the party to be "right wing" rather than "left wing," and this tendency was accentuated when the party was perceived to be both "right wing" and "for the working class." Respondents were so consistent in their behaviour that these ratings cannot be just dismissed as random responses to meaningless questions. Ogmundson (1975) supplies one possible explanation for this puzzling pattern of findings: perhaps some respondents interpreted the term "right" to mean "correct" or "honest," "legitimate," or "in the right." And from that standpoint who would not want their ideal party to qualify as "right"? Ogmundson's point was that the terms "left" and "right" are very abstract notions. And when people are presented with terminology that they do not grasp, they simply latch on to the one word they do understand.

The 1984 Canadian Election Study asked Canadians just what the terms "left" and "right" meant to them. It turned out only 40 per cent of Canadians were willing and able to define the terms, and some of those who did venture definitions appeared to have only a vague understanding; others were downright confused (Lambert et al. 1986). Moreover, people's self-placements on a left-right scale often seemed to be unrelated to their positions on the issues of the day. Despite all the commentary in the media at the time of the 2000 election about the "fight-for-the-right" and the "demise of the left," there was little to suggest that comprehension of left-right terminology had improved since 1984. Only one respondent in three correctly identified the NDP as being on the left and the Alliance as being on the right (Gidengil, Blais, Nevitte et al. 2004).

It would be a mistake, though, to infer from this evidence that traditional left-right ideology is largely irrelevant to vote choice in Canada. Difficulty in defining and using left-right terminology does not necessarily mean that people fail to think about political issues and personalities in ideologically coherent ways. Relying on voters' ability to understand and use left-right terminology appropriately implies a narrow view of what qualifies as an ideological understanding of politics. Moreover, asking people to locate themselves and each of the parties along a left-right scale implies that notions of left and right can be captured by a single dimension. However, evidence from publics in several advanced industrial states seems to suggest that there are now two left-right dimensions; a traditional left and right, and a new left and new right. The traditional left-right cleavage revolves around opposing views about the free enterprise system and the appropriate balance between the government and the market. The left tends to be more sceptical of the workings of the capitalist system, and this scepticism is reflected in enhanced support for redistribution and a greater willingness to rely on the state to provide a social safety net. The new left-right cleavage revolves around opposing views about traditional morality and so-called family values. The new right tends to favour a more traditional view of gender roles and to look askance at feminism. The new right also tends to be opposed to alternative lifestyles and sexual orientations.

An alternative analytical strategy for assessing whether people think about politics in ideologically coherent ways is to determine whether their fundamental values and beliefs cluster together in ideologically meaningful ways. It turns out that many Canadians do organize their ideas in ways that are both ideologically coherent and consistent with the existence of two distinct left-right dimensions (Nevitte et al. 2000). Equally important, where people stand on the two dimensions has provided useful clues for understanding why they vote as they do (Blais et al. 2002; Gidengil et al. 2006; Nevitte et al. 2000). Building on this work, we consider two indices that correspond to these two dimensions.[2] The *market liberalism* index captures people's attitudes toward free enterprise and government intervention in the market. Respondents who are persuaded of the merits of the free enterprise system and who prefer less government intervention in economic affairs score higher on the market liberalism index than those who are more sceptical about the workings of the free enterprise system and therefore think that governments should be more involved in the economy. This core economic outlook, which corresponds closely to the traditional left-right dimension, has had a significant impact on peoples' vote choices in a variety of national settings (Dalton, Flanagan, and Beck 1984; Inglehart and Klingemann 1976; Knutsen 1995b). The second index taps the new left-right dimension. *Moral traditionalism* encompasses views about the role of women, feminism, and beliefs about gays and lesbians. People who are more conservative in these respects score higher on the moral traditionalism index than those who hold more liberal views. This value dimension has had a significant impact on electoral behaviour in Canada and elsewhere (Blais et al. 2002; Gidengil et al. 2006; Lusztig and Wilson 2005; Nevitte 1996; Nevitte et al. 2000).

Beyond Left and Right

Thinking about the influence of values and beliefs means going beyond "left" and "right," however these terms are defined. It implies a broader view of what it means to "think ideologically." Values and beliefs encapsulate people's conceptions of what is desirable and can serve as a template for evaluating the political parties, the issues, and leaders of the day. If a party or its leader is perceived as being likely to promote those values, they will be evaluated more favourably and vice versa. Similarly, voters will evaluate issues according to the extent to which those issues resonate with their own beliefs and value commitments.

Personal religiosity can be a powerful influence when it comes to evaluating the political world. There is evidence that Canadians, like their counterparts in other advanced industrial states, have become increasingly secular over the course of the last three decades (Bibby 1979, 2008; Nevitte 1996). Even so, there is also clear evidence that personal religiosity—the extent to which religion is important in one's life—continues to have a significant effect on people's electoral choices (Esmer and Pettersson 2007).

Communal outlooks are important as well (Blais et al. 2002: Gidengil et al. 2006; Nevitte et al. 2000). Views about the appropriate relationship between Canada and the United States have long been a source of division in Canada's political life (Ayres 1996; Banting, Hoberg, and Simeon 1997; Clarkson 2002; Gidengil, Blais, Nadeau et al. 2004). The salience of these views increased with the advent of the Canada-US Free Trade Agreement in 1988 (Johnston et al. 1992) and its subsequent expansion into the North American Free Trade Agreement. Accordingly, we consider a *continentalism* index that captures respondents' views about the benefits (or not) of free trade with the United States, whether ties between the two countries should be closer or more distant, and feelings about the United States. Higher scores indicate that respondents favour a close relationship with the United States. The second long-standing source of division outside Québec is how far the rest of the country should go in accommodating that province (see, for example, Johnston 1992; LaForest 1995; McRoberts 1997; Resnick 1990; Taylor 1993). Consequently, we also consider an *accommodating Québec* measure that captures respondents' views about how much should be done for Québec. The third communal outlook relates to respondents' orientations toward racial minorities. Race is a feature of Canada's multicultural landscape that is becoming increasingly important, and it is arguably one that has received insufficient attention (Kymlicka 1995, 1998; Thompson 2008). The *racial outlook* measure captures how much respondents think should be done for racial minorities.

The final two dimensions under consideration concern different axes of political discontent. The *political disaffection* index taps into respondents' evaluations of the working of the political system in general. Those who are located at the higher end of the index are more distrustful of politicians, political parties, and the political system generally. They see themselves as being "outside" of the political mainstream in the sense that they do not think that their interests are adequately represented, and they feel relatively powerless. Once again, there is evidence that this kind of political disaffection can have an impact on electoral outcomes both in Canada (Bélanger and Nadeau 2005; Roese 2002) and in other advanced industrial states (Bélanger 2004; Dalton 1999; Nye, Zelikow, and King 1997). The other dimension of political discontent concerns regional grievances. A long-standing feature of the Canadian political landscape, these grievances have had significant electoral repercussions (Clarke et al. 1979; Gibbins 1980; Gibbins and Berdahl 2003; Gidengil et al. 1999; Henry 2001; Simeon and Elkins 1974). The *regional alienation* dimension reflects respondents' evaluations of whether the federal government has treated their province worse than others.

Table 3.1 *Basic Values and Beliefs, Outside Québec, 2000–2008 (voters only)*

Year	Market Liberalism	Moral Traditionalism	Religiosity	Continentalism
2000	−0.04	−0.12	0.34	0.13
2004	−0.05	−0.24	0.16	0.12
2006	−0.09	−0.25	0.15	0.15
2008	−0.06	−0.28	0.13	0.12

This list of politically relevant values and beliefs is not exhaustive, but it does capture those dimensions that have been shown to be particularly pertinent to the Canadian setting. There are two questions to explore here: How much impact did these outlooks have on voters' choice of party in the four elections held between 2000 and 2008? And, more important, does a consideration of these kinds of outlooks help us to understand the parties' changing electoral fortunes?

Value Stability and Change
It may be tempting to attribute the electoral dynamics between 2000 and 2008 to shifts in Canadians' basic values and beliefs, but there are good reasons to be cautious about that interpretation. After all, the conventional wisdom is that values, unlike opinions about the issues of the day, tend to be very stable. Socialization theorists have repeatedly demonstrated that people generally acquire their core values and beliefs early in the life cycle, during their formative years, and that, once these outlooks are internalized, they tend to be resistant to change over the life course (Dalton 1988; Inglehart and Baker 2000). And there is a substantial body of evidence that supports that expectation both in Canada (Nevitte 1996) and elsewhere (Abramson and Inglehart 1995). This does not mean that all values and beliefs are static, though. Rather, value change tends to be gradual because it is driven mostly by such factors as population replacement and structural change, which are themselves gradual processes. There is evidence of short-term peaks and troughs in value trajectories, but these period effects typically occur in response to such exogenous factors as a depression or war (Inglehart 1997), and reversals of this kind tend to be short lived. There is another potential source of value change in the Canadian context that may be more long lasting: high levels of immigration contribute to greater value diversity (Kanji and Bilodeau 2006; White et al. 2008).

Accommodating Québec	Racial Outlook	Political Disaffection	Regional Alienation
−0.22	0.14	0.01	0.14
−0.21	0.25	0.02	0.16
−0.20	0.04	−0.04	0.17
−0.23	0.09	−0.06	0.22

Note: The column entries are mean values. All of the items run from −1 to +1. See Appendix B for details of question wording.

The 2008 campaign coincided with the stock market crash and the onset of a recession, but this did not appear to influence Canadians' views about the free enterprise system (see Table 3.1). This is not to say that Canadians enthusiastically embrace the workings of the free market. On the contrary, respondents expressed a good deal of ambivalence about the workings of the free market, and scores on the market liberalism index were slightly negative on balance throughout the period.

When it came to questions of morality, there was less ambivalence. Respondents holding traditional views on morality were in the minority, and their numbers dwindled over the course of the decade.[3] This finding is consistent with trends reported elsewhere (Andersen and Fetner 2008; Hall and Rodriguez 2003; Inglehart and Norris 2003; Nevitte and Cochrane 2007). Levels of personal religiosity also declined over the same period. In both cases, the drop between 2000 and 2004 is particularly striking. Even so, the average respondent reported that religion was at least somewhat important in his or her life in 2008.

Sentiments toward Québec and beliefs about Canada's relationship with the United States remained remarkably stable. Attitudes toward racial minorities, on the other hand, proved to be quite volatile: they were quite positive in 2004 but had become more ambivalent on balance by 2006. Surprisingly, levels of political disaffection proved to be quite stable, despite the prominence of the sponsorship scandal in both the 2004 and 2006 campaigns. Indeed, if anything, Canadians' views about politics and politicians became a little less negative over this period. The fact that levels of political disaffection seemed impervious to short-term forces suggests that there is an important long-term component to citizens' evaluations of the workings of the political system. Regional alienation, by contrast, seems to have increased steadily since 2000.

Values, Beliefs, and Social Background Characteristics

One reason basic values and beliefs tend to be fairly stable is that they are rooted in people's social identities. A closer examination of the data indicates that three social background characteristics—gender, region, and the rural-urban divide—are particularly important influences on Canadians' values and beliefs. There are clear differences between men and women on all of the dimensions considered. Women are less likely than men to be market liberals. And they are less traditional than men in their moral outlooks. Women also expressed lower levels of political disaffection and regional alienation. They were less likely than men to want closer ties with the United States, and they were more likely to want to do more for Québec. Women consistently reported higher levels of religiosity than men, and they expressed more positive views toward racial minorities. These gender differences were not large (typically around five points), but they were consistent across multiple value domains, they were statistically significant throughout the decade, and they are consistent with findings reported elsewhere (Gidengil 1995; Gidengil et al. 2003; Norris 1988).

There were also consistent regional differences. Typically, Atlantic Canadians and Westerners differed the most, with Ontarians occupying the middle ground. Western Canadians, for example, turn out to be the most supportive of market liberalism and moral traditionalism. Atlantic Canadians were the least supportive on both dimensions. Western Canadians were the least inclined to want to do more for Québec, while Atlantic Canadians were the most inclined to do more. Western Canadians were the least positive about Canada's ties with the United States; Atlantic Canadians and Ontarians alike were typically more positive, though these differences had disappeared by 2008. Atlantic Canadians reported the highest levels of religiosity and showed the most support for racial minorities. Western Canadians, by contrast, reported the lowest levels of religiosity and were much less inclined to do more for racial minorities. These differences were not substantial, but they were consistent.

The pattern is somewhat different for political dissatisfaction. In 2000, levels of Western political disaffection were significantly higher than those found in either Atlantic Canada or Ontario, but, by the time of the 2008 election, political disaffection had decreased appreciably in the West. Moreover, by 2008, evidence of "Western alienation" seems to have virtually disappeared (Gibbins 1980, 1982; Gibbins and Berdahl 2003). During the same period, there were correspondingly sharp increases in levels of regional alienation among Ontarians. In 2000, Ontarians' levels of regional alienation were significantly lower than either their Western or Atlantic Canadian counterparts. By 2008, levels of alienation in Ontario were closer to those found among Westerners. Regional alienation in Atlantic Canada remained at levels that matched those found in the West at the beginning of the decade. Thus, by the time of the 2008 election, levels of alienation in Atlantic Canada were much higher than those found in either Ontario or the West. It is surely no coincidence that these shifts in Ontario and western Canada occurred in tandem with the change from a Liberal government to a Conservative one.

There were also differences between urban and rural voters on most of these value dimensions at the beginning of the decade. But by the end of the decade, many of these differences had virtually disappeared. Urban and rural Canadians were essentially alike when it came to market liberalism. And there was evidence of a gradual convergence between urban and rural voters on the moral traditionalism dimension: rural respondents were consistently more inclined to hold morally traditional values at the start of the decade. By 2008, however, those differences had disappeared. Similarly, rural voters exhibited higher levels of political disaffection in 2000, but those differences had also disappeared by 2008. Urban voters were slightly more inclined than their rural counterparts to favour a closer relationship with the United States and to want to do more for Québec. But urban and rural dwellers had converged on the Québec dimension by the 2008 election. At the beginning of the decade, urban dwellers typically exhibited somewhat lower levels of religiosity and somewhat more positive racial outlooks. But, by 2008, both urban and rural respondents held similar outlooks on both of these dimensions.

Values, Beliefs, and Vote Choice

There was little evidence of aggregate change in Canadians' views about the free enterprise system between the 2000 and 2008 elections. Consequently, it is difficult to attribute the improvement in the Conservatives' electoral fortunes to any growth in the size of the pro-free market constituency. Throughout the period, those in favour of leaving market forces to work unfettered remained in the minority, and, if anything, the Conservative party was hurt by its support for a limited role for government in the economy. The vote in Canada may not be sharply differentiated along class lines (see Chapter 2), but the traditional left-right divide remains one of the keys to understanding vote choice. In all four elections, voters who were sceptical of the workings of the free enterprise system were much more likely to support the NDP over other political parties: the probability of voting NDP was typically 16 to 20 points higher for market sceptics.[4] By contrast, those who were persuaded of the system's benefits had much higher odds of voting for the right, and these odds increased over the course of the four elections. Other things being equal, the likelihood of voting Alliance in 2000 was 11 points higher for someone who was strongly pro-market compared with someone who was ambivalent about the workings of the market.[5] By 2008, that figure had increased to 21 points. The effects of views about market liberalism on the propensity to vote Liberal were much weaker.[6]

Despite this evidence of increasing polarization, the estimated impact on the parties' vote shares remained modest. This finding may seem paradoxical, but it reflects the distribution of opinion. A given value orientation, or core belief, can only affect the election outcome if it has a significant impact on individual vote choice *and* if opinion is skewed in one direction or the other. In all four elections, the balance of opinion toward market liberalism was only slightly tilted in the anti-market direction (see Table 3.1), and this circumstance necessarily constrained the impact on party vote shares. The net beneficiary in all four elections was the NDP: had this factor not mattered, the party's share of the vote would have been over 2.5 points lower in 2000, almost 2 points lower in 2004, over 3.5 points lower in 2006, and 2 points lower in 2008. These gains came at the expense of both the Liberals and the Conservatives (and the Progressive Conservatives in 2000).

Opinion was more skewed on the moral traditionalism dimension, so the gains and losses proved to be bigger. Moral traditionalists were much more likely to vote Alliance in 2000 and Conservative thereafter. No other value or core belief had such a consistently powerful effect on the probability of voting Alliance. Other things being equal, the propensity to vote for the Alliance in 2000 was fully 29 points higher for someone who held very traditional views on moral questions, compared with someone who was ambivalent. The problem for the Alliance was that moral traditionalists were in the minority, so the party's perceived social conservatism reduced its share of the vote by over 1.5 points. Moral traditionalism was a less important factor in Conservative voting: in all three subsequent elections, the probability of voting Conservative was about 20 points higher for those scoring highest on the moral traditionalism index. Moral traditionalism, nonetheless, proved to be a greater drag on the party's vote share because the balance of opinion shifted in the socially liberal direction. But for this, the Conservatives' vote share might have been over 4.5 points higher in 2004, almost 5 points higher in 2006, and almost 6 points higher in 2008.

The relative importance of the moral traditionalism dimension to Liberal and NDP voting fluctuated across the four elections, and so did the impact on their vote shares. In all four elections, the two parties were in competition for the socially liberal vote. In 2000, they benefited more or

less equally at the expense of the Alliance. The NDP was the major beneficiary in 2004 (5 points) and 2006 (almost 3.5 points). But, in 2008, the
support of socially liberal voters boosted the Liberal vote share by an estimated 3.5 points, compared with less than 2.5 points for the NDP.

Personal religiosity had much less of an impact on vote choice in all four
elections. Religious people were more likely to vote Alliance in 2000 and
Conservative in the next two elections. More secular people, meanwhile,
were more inclined than other voters to vote NDP. However, these effects
were modest, and, in 2008, religiosity did not significantly affect people's
choice of party. In 2000, the Alliance vote share received a modest boost of
about 1.5 points, but the effects of religiosity in subsequent elections were
much smaller. In 2008, religiosity made virtually no difference at all.

Orientations toward continentalism, by contrast, proved to be consistently important. Voters who favoured a closer relationship between
Canada and the United States were significantly more likely to vote Alliance in 2000 and Conservative in the next three elections. Those wanting
more distant ties had significantly higher odds of voting NDP in all four
elections. The probability of voting Alliance in 2000 was 15 points higher
for people with the highest scores on the continentalism index, compared
with those who were neutral; the estimated effect on NDP voting was of
a similar magnitude for those who scored lowest on the index. By 2008,
the impact on vote choice had increased: the comparable estimates were
25 points for the NDP and fully 31 points for the Conservatives. Given
that the balance of opinion was clearly tilted toward a closer relationship
between the two countries, the parties of the right turned out to be the
main beneficiaries. The estimated contribution to the Alliance vote share
in 2000 was 2 points. The Conservatives benefited by more than 4.5 points
in 2004, 4 points in 2006, and almost 4 points in 2008. It was the Liberals,
though, not the NDP that paid the electoral price: 3.5 points in 2004 and
around 3 points in the following two elections.

Views about accommodating Québec became progressively more
important to the Conservative vote during the course of the three elections.
The increasing importance of these views is in striking contrast with the
lack of any significant effect on Alliance voting in 2000. One of the most
important constraints on the Reform vote in 1997 was the perception that
its leader, Preston Manning, posed a threat to national unity (Nevitte et
al. 2000). Neutralizing the Québec question in 2000 was a major achieve-
ment for the Alliance under Stockwell Day. However, with the merger of
the Alliance and the Progressive Conservatives, views about accommodating Québec began to exert more influence on people's vote choice. People
who wanted to do less for Québec were significantly more likely to vote

Conservative in the next three elections, and they were correspondingly less likely to vote Liberal in 2004 or 2008 and NDP in 2006. Because the balance of opinion favoured doing less for Québec, this helped the Conservatives and hurt the Liberals and the NDP. Had views about accommodating Québec not mattered in 2008, the Conservative vote share would have dropped over 3.5 points, while the Liberals would have gained almost 2.5 points, and the NDP would have picked up slightly more than 1 point. The importance of these views to the Conservative base outside Québec, however, operates as a potentially important constraint on the party's ability to increase its support within the province (see Chapter 10). This limitation became abundantly clear in the 2011 election.

Racial outlooks mattered much less throughout the period. To the extent that there was a discernable pattern (and there was none in 2004), those who favoured doing less for racial minorities were more inclined to gravitate to the Conservatives. Those who favoured doing more for racial minorities, by contrast, had higher odds of voting NDP. The implications for party vote shares were generally trivial, though the NDP did gain slightly more than 1 point in 2008 at the expense of both the Conservatives and the Liberals.

Perhaps the most intriguing findings concern political disaffection and regional alienation. In 2000, those who were more politically disaffected and regionally alienated were significantly more likely to vote Alliance; in 2004, they were more likely to vote Conservative or NDP. In both elections, they were significantly less likely to choose the Liberals. But there was a striking change in 2006. In that election, the Conservatives ceased to benefit from the votes of both the politically disaffected and the regionally alienated. And in 2008, the pattern reversed: the politically disaffected and the regionally alienated became significantly *less* likely to vote Conservative. In 2008, higher levels of political disaffection worked to increase the likelihood of an NDP vote, while regional alienation boosted support for the Liberals. One possible explanation for the changing impact of political disaffection on the Conservative vote may well have to do with incumbency effects. People tend to be more satisfied with the way the political system is working when the political party they support holds office; the "outs" are typically more dissatisfied (Anderson and Guillory 1997; Gabriel 1995; Nevitte and White 2008). The shifting polarity of the effects of regional alienation might in turn reflect the regional concentration of support for the Liberals and Conservatives. After all, the evidence indicates that regional alienation grew in Ontario and declined in the West.

Striking as these patterns are, their impact on party vote shares turns out to be quite modest. The impact was strongest in 2008, but the effects were offsetting: satisfaction with the workings of the political system boosted the Conservative vote share by a little over 1 point, but growing regional alienation cost the party almost 1.5 points (almost wholly to the Liberals' benefit).

Values, Beliefs, and Electoral Dynamics

Three main findings emerge from this chapter. First, no evidence suggests that the size of the constituency for a right-wing party has grown. This is the case whether "the right" is defined in terms of market liberalism or moral traditionalism (see Table 3.1). Indeed, between 2000 and 2008, the potential ranks of the new right constituency shrank as views about moral questions became less traditional, on average. Second, there were pronounced shifts in the effects of political disaffection and regional alienation on vote choice. In 2000, disaffection and regional alienation boosted support for the Alliance. The same was true of the propensity to vote Conservative in 2004. But, by the time of the 2008 election, political disaffection had become more strongly associated with an NDP vote and regional alienation worked to the benefit of the Liberals, not the Conservatives. In all likelihood, these changes reflect both incumbency effects and the persistence of regionalism in Canadian politics. Last, voting was clearly polarized around three value dimensions: market liberalism, moral traditionalism, and continentalism. But these dimensions produced very different support patterns. Both market liberalism and continentalism pitted the Conservatives against the NDP, whereas moral traditionalism pitted the Conservatives against the NDP *and* the Liberals. In these respects, the NDP and the Liberals were competing for the same left-of-centre constituency.

The dynamics described in this chapter could have significant implications for the potential for growth of each of the three largest political parties outside of Québec. One implication is that there are few reasons to be optimistic about the prospects for the continuing growth of the Conservative Party. There has been no surge in public enthusiasm for free market values, so the Conservatives would find it difficult to expand their support base by appealing to voters' free market sentiments. Nor is there much reason for Conservative Party optimism when it comes to the trends in public attitudes toward moral traditionalism. Morally traditional voters are typically more inclined to support parties of the right. But the ranks of the moral traditionalists are shrinking. The effect of religiosity tells a similar story: those with higher levels of personal religiosity were significantly more likely to vote Conservative. The problem was that the importance of religion in Canada is declining.

The similarity in the pattern of the effects of values on support for the

Alliance and the rebranded Conservatives is striking. This similarity is most evident for the market liberalism, moral traditionalism, and continentalism dimensions. The impact of all three dimensions on the likelihood of a Conservative vote in 2004 more closely mirrored the pattern of effects for the Alliance vote in 2000 than the Progressive Conservative vote in that election. Moreover, the Conservative vote, like the Alliance vote, was much more strongly affected by basic values and beliefs than was the case for the Progressive Conservative vote. There is one striking exception, and it poses a strategic dilemma for the Conservatives. Views about Québec had little or no effect on the probability of voting Alliance, but voters who were less sympathetic to Québec became increasingly likely to support the Conservatives. The implication is clear: a Québec—Western Canada Conservative coalition of the type that gave the Progressive Conservatives two majority victories under Brian Mulroney would be difficult to reconstruct.

The shifts in the effects of political disaffection and regional alienation also have important implications for the Conservatives. Like Reform and the Alliance, the Conservatives were the beneficiaries of political disaffection and regional alienation when they carried the mantle of leading the Loyal Opposition. But the disaffected and alienated became markedly less likely to support the Conservatives after they formed the government. Moreover, the ranks of the regionally alienated have swollen in vote-rich Ontario and remain stubbornly persistent in Atlantic Canada.

The sea changes in the effects of political disaffection and regional alienation offer a ray of hope, perhaps, for any Liberal Party effort to rebuild its support, particularly in Ontario. Yet the electoral fate of that party, at least as far as values are concerned, has become increasingly entangled with the NDP. The competition between the two parties became much more pronounced between 2000 and 2008. Most notably, the Liberals and the New Democrats were in increasing competition for the hearts of those who are less traditional in their moral outlooks. Indeed, by 2008, Liberal voters and NDP voters were virtually indistinguishable on the moral traditionalism dimension. They also looked very similar when it came to views about accommodating Québec, doing more for racial minorities, and regional alienation. And Liberal voters were also closer to NDP voters on the market liberalism index than they were to Conservative voters. Coming out of the 2008 election, the Liberals confronted a dilemma. On the one hand, they may have been in a better position to reap the "opposition dividend": the longer political parties are in power, the larger are the ranks of people who have reason to be irked by the government of the day. Yet the Liberal Party had to compete with the NDP for voters who occupy a similar value space.

The implication for the NDP was clear: the main constraint on the party's growth during these years was the competition for the left-of-centre vote not the size of that constituency. Indeed, the new left constituency grew between 2000 and 2008. Winning the competition for these voters would be critical to increasing the party's support and surpassing the Liberals.

Certainly, one upshot of the shifts over the four elections was that Conservative voters became increasingly differentiated from those supporting the other two parties. The challenge facing the Conservatives was to soften their image as market liberals and moral traditionalists. The challenge facing the Liberals and the New Democrats was how to compete successfully for voters who increasingly occupy the same, or a similar, value space. In 2011, it seems, the NDP came out on top. However, the present fragmentation on the left may be as problematic for the Liberals and the NDP as the fragmentation on the right was for the Progressive Conservatives and Reform during the 1990s.

Notes

1 Changing salience and changing perceptions are likely to reflect the parties' campaign strategies and patterns of media coverage. Exploring these possibilities would require detailed data on party platforms and press releases, as well as on media content.
2 See Appendix B for details of scale construction.
3 Cross-election comparisons of moral traditionalism are complicated by the fact that the index consists of different items in 2000. Questions about sympathy for feminism and gay marriage had to be substituted for questions concerning feelings about feminists and gays and lesbians because respondents were not asked to express their feelings about these groups in the 2000 Canadian Election Study. However, whether we substitute the gay marriage item for feelings about gays and lesbians in 2004, 2006, and 2008 or drop any item about feminism, the key finding concerning a drop in moral traditionalism holds.
4 Note, though, that the estimated effect reached a high of 27 points in 2006.
5 By "ambivalent," we mean someone who scored zero on the −1 to +1 scale. All of the estimated effects reported here use zero as the reference category.
6 The estimated impact was greatest in 2000 at 19 points, dropped to only 5 points in 2004, and climbed back up to 13 points in 2008.

CHAPTER FOUR

PARTY LOYALTIES

Social background characteristics and fundamental values and beliefs matter because they help to anchor people to political parties. But there is a good deal of variation when it comes to how strongly Canadians are attached to their political parties. Some voters are staunch partisans: they have a more or less standing decision to vote for "their" party. Others lack any sort of partisan tie: they approach each election afresh. Still others fall somewhere in between: they are predisposed to support one party or another, but they can be induced to defect from "their" party and vote for another one depending on the issues of the day or how they feel about the party leaders. To win an election, political parties face two key challenges. First, they must be able to mobilize their core supporters to vote for the party, and, second, they need to maximize their appeal to those who lack meaningful party ties. To understand each party's changing electoral fortunes in the four elections held between 2000 and 2008, then, three questions need to be answered. Is the party's partisan core growing or shrinking? How many core supporters ended up voting for the party? And how did the party fare among non-partisans? Answering these questions makes it easier to understand how the Conservatives managed to win a majority in 2011 while the Liberals suffered an even worse defeat than they had experienced in 2008.

Party Identification: A Contested Concept in Canada

The starting premises, of course, are that a substantial number of Canadian voters do have meaningful attachments to political parties and that we can reliably estimate the size of a party's partisan core. But the nature of partisanship in Canada has been contested (Gidengil 1992); it cannot simply be taken for granted.

Party identification occupies a central place in the Michigan school's social-psychological model of vote choice (see Chapter 1). It is a feeling of closeness or attachment to a political party. Just as people may identify with a religious, racial, or ethnic group, they may identify with a particular political party. Party identification can have a direct impact on vote choice: some voters will simply vote on the basis of long-standing party loyalty. But it can also have an indirect effect on vote choice because it shapes people's economic evaluations, positions on issues, and perceptions of the party leaders. Accordingly, people who identify with a party will tend to vote for that party *unless* there are powerful short-term forces pulling them toward another party. But even if they vote for a different party, they should retain their party identification. This is the crucial point: if party identification changed along with the vote, we would have to wonder whether people really do have party attachments that are independent of their current party preference.

John Meisel (1975) argued that a Michigan-style conception of party identification as an enduring psychological attachment was "almost inapplicable in Canada." Based on the analysis of CES data from the first two federal elections studied (1965 and 1968), he concluded that party identification appeared to be "as volatile in Canada as the vote itself" (p. 67). Subsequent panel analyses,[1] using data from the 1974, 1979, and 1980 elections, seemed to confirm the instability of Canadians' party attachments (LeDuc et al. 1984). Thus Harold Clarke and his colleagues (1984) reached the conclusion that the "keynote of partisanship in Canada was its flexibility" (p. 56). That conclusion was tempered, though, by their recognition of a group identified as "durable partisans." To qualify as a "durable partisan," survey respondents had to identify very strongly or fairly strongly with their party, report that they had identified with the same party across time, and identify with the same party at both the federal and provincial levels. Respondents who failed to meet all three criteria—intensity, stability, and consistency—were classified as "flexible partisans." Flexible partisans were thus either weak in the intensity of their partisanship, variable in their partisanship over time, or inconsistent between the federal and provincial levels. The category also included those who did not identify with any party on the assumption that these were people in transition from one party to another.

It is possible, though, that this partisan typology overstates the flexibility of Canadians' partisan ties. A person with a strong, stable party attachment does not qualify as a durable partisan unless he or she identifies with the same party at both the federal and provincial levels. This consistency requirement has attracted some criticism. In what sense is it "inconsistent" to identify with different parties at the federal and provincial levels or to identify at one level but not the other? Having different party attachments at the federal and provincial levels may be less a matter of inconsistency than a case of dual identifications in a highly decentralized federal system, especially given that some provincial political parties have no federal counterparts. As Donald Blake (1982) argued, assuming that the identification at each level is meaningful, we have no reason to expect that "inconsistent" identification between levels will make for unstable voting behaviour within either level. In fact, at both levels, intensity of party identification appears to be at least as important a determinant of partisan stability and vote choice alike as split identification between levels (Blake 1982; Clarke and Stewart 1987). For some people, federal and provincial politics may represent two quite separate political arenas. Federal and provincial elections typically take place at different times, and the issues that dominate elections at each level are likely to be different, given differences in the responsibilities of the two levels of government. Moreover, the parties themselves lack close ties between the federal and provincial levels. Indeed, parties sharing the same name may occupy different locations on the ideological spectrum. This is exemplified by the ease with which some prominent politicians have moved between parties. Québec premier Jean Charest is a case in point: he moved from the leadership of the federal Progressive Conservatives to the leadership of the Québec provincial Liberals. Bob Rae, the former NDP premier of Ontario also changed partisan labels with no apparent discomfort, and so did Ujjal Dosanjh, the former NDP premier of British Columbia. Both former premiers were elected to parliament as Liberals.

Moreover, some of the apparent instability in party identification in Canada may be attributable to a measurement issue: the traditional party identification question asked of survey respondents did not explicitly offer the option of not identifying with *any* political party (Johnston 1992). The absence of that response option may have encouraged some people to name the party they were voting for even though they lacked any meaningful sense of psychological attachment to that party. Under those circumstances, party identification would appear to be as volatile as the vote itself. In 1988, the survey response option "none of these" was added to the traditional question. The proportion of people qualifying as "non-identifiers" consequently increased. Analyses working with that revised question indicate that it is difficult to make sense of recent elections in Canada without

Figure 4.1 *Per cent of Panel Respondents Repeating the 2004 Campaign Response to the Party Identification Question*

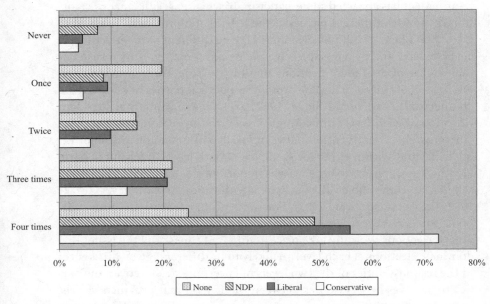

taking account of Canadians' party attachments (Blais et al. 2002; Gidengil et al. 2006; Nevitte et al. 2000). But without new panel data, the stability of those attachments is hard to determine. Before we assess the impact of party identification on the changing electoral fortunes of the parties in the four elections held between 2000 and 2008, then, it is important to establish first whether Canadians' attachments to political parties are indeed meaningful.

Is Party Identification Meaningful in Canada?

The 2004–2006–2008 Canadian Election Study included a panel component that makes it possible to revisit the stability of party identification in Canada. The context of these elections is particularly opportune for evaluating the stability of Canadians' party attachments. After all, these were circumstances under which there were good reasons to expect instability. If identification with the Liberal Party could withstand first the new revelations about the sponsorship scandal that emerged in the run-up to the 2006 election (see Introduction) and then the party's historic defeat in 2008, the case for the applicability of Michigan-style party identification in Canada would be more credible.

The place to begin is with party identification as measured during the 2004 campaign. Each respondent's response to the party identification question was tracked on four subsequent occasions: after the 2004 election, during the 2006 campaign, and after both the 2006 and 2008 elections. Fully half of the panel (50 per cent) gave the same response in all five interviews. A further one in five (19 per cent) repeated their 2004 campaign response in three of the four subsequent interviews. Conservative identifiers proved to be the most stable in their responses: almost three-quarters maintained the same identification through all five interviews (see Figure 4.1). But it was NDP identifiers, not Liberal identifiers, who were the least likely to remain true to their party: barely half repeated their answer each time they were interviewed. However, it was those who had replied "none" when first interviewed who were the least likely to repeat the same response. Only a quarter of those who said that they did not identify with any party when they were first interviewed can be considered "hard-core" non-partisans. Overall, that group accounted for about 8 per cent of the panel sample. Meanwhile, 42 per cent of the panel respondents qualified as stable partisans who maintained the same party identification across all five waves of the survey.

Predictably, partisan intensity and partisan stability are closely correlated (see Figure 4.2): 80 per cent of those who said that they identified very strongly with "their" party during the 2004 campaign continued to identify with the same party each time they were interviewed, compared with 60 per cent of fairly strong identifiers and only 33 per cent of not very strong identifiers. But there is evidence of a good deal of variation across different political parties: 92 per cent of very strong Conservative identifiers were unwavering in their replies, compared with only 71 per cent of very strong Liberal and NDP identifiers.

When people responded differently on different occasions, they were more likely to say "none" than to name another party. Seventy-nine per cent of those who indicated a party identification when interviewed during the 2004 campaign only ever named one party. Some of these respondents (34 per cent) occasionally answered "none," but they never named a different party. Assuming that people who answer "none" are in transition from one party to another (as Clarke and his colleagues' typology did) may therefore overstate the flexibility of Canadians' party ties. That said, 19 per cent of identifiers did name more than one party, but very few—less than 2 per cent—named more than two parties. The more strongly people identified with a party when first interviewed, the less likely they were to name another party subsequently: fully 93 per cent of very strong identifiers only ever named one party, compared with 76 per cent of fairly strong

Figure 4.2 *Per cent of Panel Respondents Repeating their 2004 Campaign Response to the Party Identification Question by Strength of Identification*

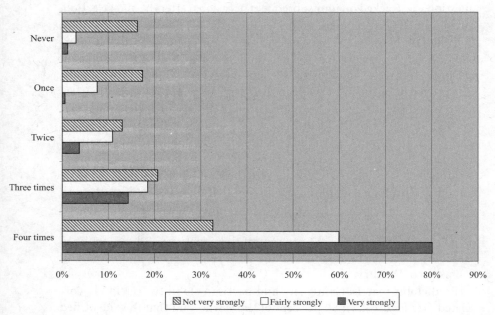

identifiers and 60 per cent of those whose identification was not very strong when first interviewed. Once again, the NDP seemed to have the least loyal partisans: one in three named another party, compared with only one Liberal in four and one Conservative in seven.

The patterns of inter-party movement in the panel sample clearly favoured the Conservatives. Given the ordering of Canada's parties along the ideological spectrum (see Chapter 3), it is not surprising that, when Conservative identifiers did name another party, they mostly chose the Liberals. More surprising, perhaps, is the evidence indicating that Liberal identifiers were more than twice as likely to name the Conservatives (18 per cent) at least once as they were to name the NDP (7 per cent). More surprising still is the finding that NDP identifiers were almost equally likely to name the Conservatives (16 per cent) as the Liberals (18 per cent). But the variations are clearly not symmetrical. Few Liberal (7 per cent) or Conservative (4 per cent) identifiers ever named the NDP, and fewer still (less than 2 per cent) named the Greens. Predictably, NDP identifiers (4 per cent) were more likely to name the Greens when they named another party.

These inter-party movements among the panel respondents raise

Figure 4.3 *Consistency between Post-election Party Identification and Reported Vote (panel respondents only)*

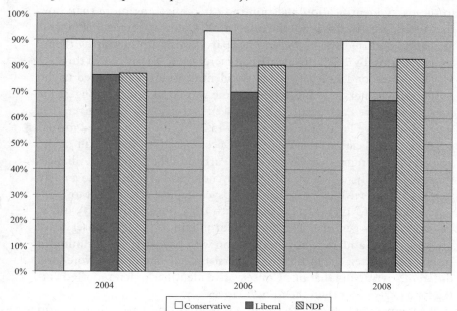

another question: to what extent does party identification travel with the vote? In the original Michigan conception, a person's vote in a given election is a product of the interaction between his or her long-standing predisposition to support a particular party and the short-term attitudinal forces peculiar to that particular election (Campbell et al. 1960). If the pull of short-term forces—such as the issues of the day or the leaders' personalities—is sufficiently strong, a voter may be persuaded to opt for a different party. It is this tension between the long-standing predisposition to support a given party and the short-term attractions of particular personalities or issues that makes the concept meaningful (Miller 1983). The key point is that the sense of party identification should endure even when people vote for a party other than the one with which they identify. If party identification really does represent a meaningful psychological attachment, it should not change along with the vote. Thus, the acid test is whether party identification remains intact even when people temporarily "defect" and vote for a different party for short-term reasons.

Figure 4.3 matches panel respondents' reported vote choice with their party identification as reported in the same post-election interview. If the correspondence between party identification and vote choice was too close, then there would be reason to question whether people's responses to the party identification question indicated anything more than how they voted. Clearly, this is not the case. In 2004, almost a quarter of Liberal identifiers reported voting for another party, while still declaring themselves Liberals. By 2008, this figure had increased to nearly one in three.

The correspondence between party identification, as measured in the post-election interview, and reported vote was consistently strongest for the Conservative Party. Indeed, it may seem suspiciously high, given that the Conservative Party was a new party in 2004. It only achieved formal status as an official political party in December 2003, as a result of the merger of the Progressive Conservative Party and the Canadian Alliance. Can people really form a meaningful psychological attachment to a party that is brand new? But if people have a psychological attachment to "parties of the right," then identification with the Conservative party might be construed as genuine. The key test for judging whether Conservative identification—and, indeed, identification with any party—is meaningful is to see how often the identification persists even when people vote for a different party. Note that one Conservative identifier in ten reported voting for a party other than the Conservatives.

The panel data suggest that many Canadians do have a meaningful attachment to a political party. The case of Liberal partisanship provides a particularly revealing example. The revelations of wrongdoing in the run-up to the 2006 election may have swayed the vote of Liberal partisans, but it did not necessarily shake their attachment to the party. Green and his colleagues characterize the typical American as a "tethered partisan," never straying far from his or her long-term party attachment (Green, Palmquist, and Schickler 2002, 57). Many Canadian partisans might be on a similarly short tether: they might answer "none" on occasion, but only one in five were willing to name another party. Predictably, the stability of party identification reflects the intensity of attachment: the weaker the identification, the less stable the attachment and the greater the propensity to switch parties. In the analyses that follow, then, we consider as partisans those whose identification was fairly strong or very strong (see also Blais, Gidengil et al. 2001).

The Liberals Lose Their Partisan Advantage

The first task is to estimate the size of each party's partisan core. One of the key challenges for parties during election campaigns is to get their partisans to vote for them. Accordingly, we focus on party identification as measured during the course of the campaign. The Liberals began the 2000

Figure 4.4 *The Distribution of Partisanship*

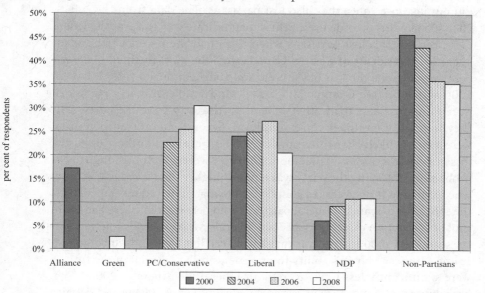

Note: Those who identified very strongly or fairly strongly with a party in the campaign survey are considered partisans.

campaign with a significant head start over the competition (see Figure 4.4): they had as many partisans as the Alliance and the Progressive Conservatives combined and four times as many partisans as the NDP. To win the election, the Liberals simply had to mobilize their partisans and do at least as well as the competing parties among non-partisans.

When the parties of the right merged in late 2003, that Liberal head start evaporated. The merger of the Alliance and what was left of the Progressive Conservatives gave the new Conservative Party almost as many partisans as the Liberals. And the number of Conservative partisans grew with each successive election. By the time of the 2008 campaign, almost one voter in three self-identified as a Conservative. The NDP also enjoyed net gains: the proportion of NDP partisans almost doubled between 2000 and 2008. Despite the unfolding of the sponsorship scandal in the run-up to the 2004 campaign, the proportion of Liberal partisans remained surprisingly stable. Nor did further revelations of corruption cause the Liberals to suffer any *net* loss of partisans in 2006. But, by 2008, the proportion of Liberal partisans had dropped by almost a quarter, and Conservative partisans clearly outnumbered Liberal partisans by a margin of three to two. Indeed, the Conservatives had almost as many partisans as the Liberals and NDP combined.

It is clear from these findings that, between 2000 and 2008, the Liberals did not just lose votes, they also lost partisans. The data from the 2004–2006–2008 panel provide useful clues that indicate why this was the case.[2] First, the Liberals lost partisans where they had the fewest partisans to begin with: residents of western Canada were the most inclined to desert the party. Despite the loss of Catholic and visible minority votes between 2004 and 2008 (see Chapter 2), Catholic and visible minority partisans were no more likely than other Liberal partisans to leave the party. But they were no more likely to remain loyal. Second, moral traditionalists were no more likely than others to defect. The same held for those opposed to same-sex marriage. Views about abortion were a factor, though. The probability of leaving the party was 8 points higher than average for those who wanted to limit access to abortion. But what mattered most of all was the sponsorship scandal. Liberal partisans who believed that there had been a lot of corruption under the Chrétien Liberals, who were still angry about the scandal in 2006 and the way that it had been handled, and who doubted Prime Minister Martin's ability to prevent a similar scandal in the future were significantly less likely to remain Liberal identifiers in 2008.[3] The probability that someone who was a Liberal identifier in 2004 would remain a Liberal identifier in 2008 was 38 points lower if they held those views.

Worse yet, Liberal partisans clearly became less likely to vote Liberal between 2000 and 2008 (see Figure 4.5). In 2000, 86 per cent of Liberal party identifiers ended up voting Liberal. That figure had dropped to 73 per cent by 2008. In 2004, and again in 2006 and 2008, Liberal identifiers were the least likely of any party's identifiers to vote for their party. This comes as little surprise given the nature of the short-term forces in these three elections. The sponsorship scandal in 2004, the new revelations of corruption in 2005, and Leader Paul Martin's decision to distance himself from the party label by campaigning as "team Martin" may have encouraged many Liberal partisans to defect on election day. A lacklustre leader and an unpopular environmental policy may have had the same effect in 2008. NDP identifiers also showed more willingness than Conservative identifiers to vote against their party in these elections. Some NDP supporters may have voted strategically rather than "wasting" their vote (see Chapter 9). But even NDP partisans demonstrated greater loyalty than their Liberal counterparts, despite those strategic incentives.

To compound their problems, the Liberals lost their advantage among non-partisans (see Figure 4.6). In 2000, the Liberals easily outpolled their closest rival, the Canadian Alliance, by a margin of four to three. In 2004, the Conservatives clearly had an edge over the Liberals, and they maintained that edge as the Liberals' appeal to non-partisans diminished.

Figure 4.5 *Vote Choice by Campaign Partisanship*

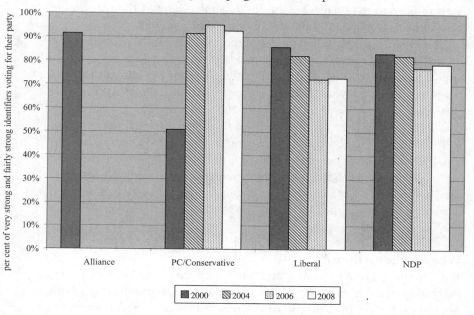

Figure 4.6 *The Vote Choices of Non-partisans*

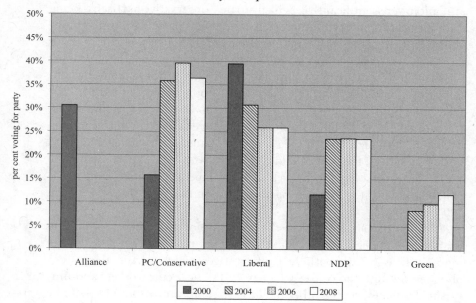

Significantly, in both the 2006 and 2008 elections, the Liberals barely managed to outpoll the NDP. Overall, the Liberals' share of the vote among non-identifiers dropped 14 points between 2000 and 2008.

The Liberals clearly failed on two important fronts: they were less successful than other parties in mobilizing their partisans, and they lost their appeal to non-partisans. The only positive news for the Liberals was that many of those who voted against the party still identified with it when they were re-interviewed following the 2008 election. The Conservatives, by contrast, were successful on both of those same fronts: they successfully mobilized their core supporters, and they appealed to non-partisans. Finally, the partisan core of the NDP almost doubled in size between 2000 and 2008, as did its share of the vote among non-partisans. Nonetheless, the NDP remained at a competitive disadvantage: the NDP had only half as many partisans as the Liberals in 2008 and a third as many partisans as the Conservatives.

Who Are the Partisans?

But who were these partisans, and what anchored them to their party?[4] A striking piece of evidence to emerge concerns the importance of ethnocultural factors in differentiating Conservative and Liberal partisans. The probability of identifying with the Conservative Party in 2008 was 19 points higher for Christian fundamentalists, while their probability of being Liberal identifiers was 13 points lower. Those with no religious affiliation were significantly less likely to be Conservative partisans. Being Catholic was a much weaker predictor of Liberal partisanship: the probability of identifying with the Liberal Party was only 6 points higher for a Catholic. Membership in a visible minority group was a more robust predictor of Liberal partisanship: the probability of those from a visible minority identifying with the party was 12 points higher in 2008. And their probability of identifying with the Conservatives was 15 points lower. Unfortunately, for the Liberals, there were still relatively few visible minority voters. Although French-speaking Canadians were much less likely to be Conservatives, the party could count on a core of loyal partisans in the West. Westerners were much less likely to be Liberal identifiers, and, as the panel data show, the Liberals' partisan base in the West shrank between 2004 and 2008.

Ethnocultural factors were the most important predictors of partisanship in 2008, but other factors mattered too. Married people were more likely to identify with the Conservatives, which mirrors the pattern observed for vote choice (see Chapter 2). Public sector workers and university graduates, on the other hand, were significantly more likely to be

Liberal partisans. But those in the 18 to 34 years of age group were significantly less likely to identify with the Liberals, a finding that does not bode
well for the future of Liberal partisanship.

NDP partisans came disproportionately from two groups. The probability of identifying with the party was 11 points higher for members of
union households, and it was 14 points higher for those with less than a
high school education. Women and people with no religious affiliation
were also significantly more likely to identify with the NDP, but these
effects were weaker.

There was a clear age gradient to partisanship: those aged 55 and over
were much more likely to have a party affiliation than those aged 18 to 34.
The probability of identifying with a party was 17 points higher for the
older age group compared with the younger age group. Westerners were
more likely to identify with a party, and French-speaking Canadians were
more likely than other respondents to be non-partisans. These effects,
though, were weaker.

The single most powerful predictor of non-partisanship was political
disaffection. The more frustrated people were with politics and politicians,
the less likely they were to identify with any party in 2008. The difference
in the estimated probability of being a partisan between people scoring
highest and lowest on the political disaffection index (see Chapter 3) was
huge—a massive 45 points.

Party identification is firmly rooted in fundamental values and beliefs.
The archetypal Conservative partisan in 2008 was a moral traditionalist
who favoured a more limited role for the government and a closer relationship with the United States.[5] The typical Conservative partisan also
favoured a tougher stance toward Québec. The probability of identifying
with the Conservative Party was 18 points higher for staunch moral traditionalists compared with those who were ambivalent. The comparable figures for the market liberalism and continentalism indexes were 16 points
and 28 points, respectively. Meanwhile, the estimated probability of being
a Conservative partisan was 12 points higher for someone who favoured
doing much less for Québec compared with someone who was content
with the status quo. These findings illustrate once again the challenge that
the Conservative Party would face if it decided to try to rebuild a Québec–
Western Canada electoral coalition of the sort that won the Progressive
Conservatives such a decisive victory in the 1984 election (see Chapter 3).

Neither Liberal nor NDP identification was as strongly anchored in
fundamental values and beliefs. And that finding may go some distance
toward explaining why identification with both of those parties proved to
be less stable. In 2008, a Liberal partisan was first and foremost someone

who rejected traditional stances on questions of morality. The probability of Liberal partisanship was 10 points higher for someone who strongly rejected moral traditionalism than for someone who was ambivalent. And an NDP partisan was, above all, someone who was sceptical about letting market forces work unfettered and who wanted to distance Canada from the United States. Being very sceptical of the workings of the free market, as compared with being ambivalent, increased the estimated probability of identifying with the NDP by 18 points. The comparable figure for the continentalism index was almost identical. These findings underline yet again one dilemma facing the Liberals and the NDP. They both compete for the same left-of-centre constituency (see Chapter 3). When it comes to partisanship, the Liberals were clearly losing ground to the NDP in 2008 in the competition for the loyalty of those who favour a stronger role for governments and weaker ties with the United States. But the Liberals still had a decisive edge in attracting those who reject moral traditionalism.

Short-Term Shocks and Strained Loyalties

Many Canadians lack any strong and enduring sense of psychological attachment to a particular party. And Clarke and his colleagues' notion of flexible partisanship provides a useful conceptual tool for understanding what happened in 1993: how two of the three parties that made up Canada's traditional two-plus-one party system—the Progressive Conservatives and the NDP—could be brought to the brink of electoral oblivion. But both the "textbook theory" (Sniderman, Forbes, and Melzer 1974) in general and the "flexible partisanship" typology in particular seem to understate the importance of party identification in Canada.

Evidence from the panel sample indicates that party identification is quite stable, though certainly not immutable, among those who profess strong party ties. One reason for the stability of party identification, especially in the case of Conservative and Liberal identifiers, is that sociocultural factors such as religion, region, and ethnicity play an important role in tying citizens to their parties. And party identification is clearly distinguishable from vote choice. People who identify with a party do tend to vote for that party. But enough of them vote at odds with their stated party identification to establish that they have a party attachment that is independent of vote choice in a given election.

Close to one-third of Liberal identifiers voted for a party other than the Liberals in 2008 and yet continued to identify themselves as Liberal when interviewed right after the election. Thus, party identification is not as volatile as the vote itself. The pull of short-term forces in the 2004, 2006, and 2008 elections was sufficient to strain Liberal loyalties, but these forces were not powerful enough to cause many partisans to abandon the party altogether. There were defections, of course, as the aggregate distributions signal and the panel data confirm, but enough Liberals remained stead-fast—despite voting for a different party—to suggest a meaningful attachment. The more serious problem for the Liberals was that these partisans were neither as loyal nor as numerous as they once were. The effects of short-term shocks—like the sponsorship scandal—on partisanship may dissipate with the passage of time (Green, Palmquist, and Schickler 2002; Green and Yoon 2002), which may be a source of comfort to the Liberal Party. But there is an important proviso: parties and party leaders have to act to stem the haemorrhaging and bring defectors back to the partisan fold (Fiorina 2002). Otherwise, the cumulative effect of short-term shocks may be to erode a party's partisan core. A crucial question for the future of the Liberal Party in the wake of its disastrous defeat in the 2011 election is whether the party has lost partisans as well as voters.

Unlike the Liberals, the Conservatives and the NDP saw their partisan cores swell. Given the volatility of NDP partisanship, the challenge for the NDP, having supplanted the Liberals in 2011 as the Conservatives' main rival, is to consolidate its partisan base. Otherwise, its success in 2011 may prove ephemeral. Conservative partisans, on the other hand, demonstrated an impressive loyalty to their party. As the Liberal experience suggests, though, even loyal partisans are susceptible to the effects of short-term shocks.

Notes

1 Panel data are ideal for testing the stability of party identification. In a panel design, the same people are interviewed on more than one occasion. Re-interviewing people in two or more elections makes it possible to distinguish people who have durable ties to a particular party from those whose partisanship changes in tandem with their vote.

2 Liberal Party identification in 2008 was regressed on factors that might explain why former Liberal identifiers no longer identified with the party. The analysis was restricted to people who identified with the Liberal Party during the 2004 campaign. To correct for panel attrition, we estimated a Heckman selection model with second stage probit. The selection variables were 18 to 34 years old and political knowledge (as indicated by ability to name the party leaders when interviewed after the 2004 election). Neither political interest nor education was a significant predictor of attrition, once political knowledge was included.

3 These four items were combined to form an index. For more on the effects of the sponsorship scandal, see Chapter 6.

4 To answer this question, we estimated a multinomial model in which the dependent variable had four categories of identification as measured during the 2008 campaign: none, Conservative, Liberal, and NDP. The model was estimated in two stages. Social background characteristics were entered at the first stage, and then basic values and beliefs were entered at the second stage.

5 Note that these characterizations apply to people who identified with the party and not to everyone who voted for that party.

CHAPTER FIVE

DOES THE ECONOMY MATTER?

So far, the focus has been on those factors that are typically considered to be long-term influences on the vote. But what about short-term influences? These are the factors that change from election to election, what commentators typically rely on to account for changing electoral outcomes. The short-term factor whose impact on elections has been the most extensively examined is undoubtedly the economy. There is a rich literature on the relationship between the economy and the vote in Canada (see Anderson 2008, 2010; Clarke and Kornberg 1992; Gélineau and Bélanger 2005; Nadeau and Blais 1993, 1995; Nadeau et al. 2000) and in the United States (Ebeid and Rodden 2006; Erikson 1989, 1990; Erikson, MacKuen, and Stimson 2002; Fiorina 1981; MacKuen, Erikson, and Stimson 1992; Nadeau and Lewis-Beck 2001), as well as cross-nationally (Anderson 1995, 2000, 2006; Blais et al. 2004; Duch and Stevenson 2008; Hellwig 2001; Lewis-Beck and Stegmaier 2007; Nadeau, Niemi, and Yoshinaka 2002; Powell and Whitten 1993; Van der Brug, Van der Eijk, and Franklin 2007).

Drawing on rational choice theory (see Chapter 1), the economic voting hypothesis is based on a simple reward-and-punish model: voters reward the incumbent party for good economic times, and they punish the party for bad times. In theory, this reward-and-punish calculus enables voters to simplify a complex decision task. When deciding how to vote, they only have to consult their pocket books and decide whether they are satisfied or not with the government's economic performance. That calculus is a low-cost short cut; it saves voters the trouble of having to invest the time and effort to find out where the political parties stand on the issues of the day or to inform themselves about the party leaders. They do not even have to know about the incumbent government's economic policies, still less figure out whether they agree with them or not. Instead, they can ask themselves a simple question: Has the incumbent performed satisfactorily in managing the economy? And the question can be answered by referring to their own financial circumstances.

This model is appealingly simple, but, in practice, economic voting is a less straightforward matter. Nor, it turns out, is it as prevalent as one might suppose. This chapter examines whether changing economic circumstances can help to explain the changes in the parties' electoral fortunes between the 2000 and 2008 elections. These two elections frame a period that is particularly useful for exploring these economic effects. In 2000, Canada was enjoying economic good times; in 2008, the country was on the brink of a recession. This raises two questions. Did those good times contribute to Liberal dominance in the 2000 election? And did the economic downturn work to deny the Conservatives a majority in 2008?

The Not-So-Simple Economic Voting Calculus

The first caveat to note is that what counts is not necessarily the state of the economy itself but people's assessments of economic conditions. These assessments can be affected by several factors other than objective economic conditions. Notably, partisanship can serve as a lens through which people view economic performance, and it can induce distorted or selective perceptions. Partisans of the incumbent party are more likely than others to take a charitable view of the government's performance. In a country like Canada, economic disparities among regions can complicate matters further: unemployment may be going down in the country as a whole, but it might nonetheless remain unacceptably high in a depressed region. The larger point is that perceptions mediate the relationship between objective economic conditions and voting for or against the incumbent.

The Liberals' experience in 1997 drives home an important point: economic perceptions matter, but they do not necessarily accord with the facts (Nadeau et al. 2000). The unemployment rate dropped between the 1993 and 1997 elections, but job creation was not a winning issue for the governing Liberals in 1997 because many voters harboured negative perceptions about the unemployment situation. These negative perceptions hurt the Liberals and limited the scope of their victory. A huge majority of Canadians—over 80 per cent—believed that joblessness had not gone down during the Liberals' term in office. And nearly 40 per cent even thought that unemployment had gone up. These misperceptions had a significant impact and reduced the Liberals' margin of victory.

Perceptions matter, but there are different kinds of economic perceptions. Egocentric orientations refer to voters' evaluations of their own financial circumstances, whereas the term *sociotropic* refers to perceptions of the economic health of the country as a whole. The notion of economic voting as an information short cut presupposes that egocentric evaluations drive economic voting. According to this pocketbook hypothesis, all voters have to do is to ask themselves whether they are better off than they were. If they reckon that they are better off, they reward the incumbent party; if they think that they are worse off, they vote to defeat the incumbent. This notion of pocketbook voting seems straightforward enough, but, in practice, voters seem to be more concerned with the health of the economy as a whole. The evidence suggests that, although both egocentric and sociotropic perceptions affect the vote, sociotropic perceptions have greater explanatory leverage (Lewis-Beck and Stegmaier 2007). In other words, whether people think that the overall economy is in good shape or bad shape tends to matter more than the state of their personal finances. It could be that people tend to see themselves rather than the government as responsible for their own financial fortunes, in good times and bad. And so they do not use their own financial situation as a basis for judging government performance. As Clarke and Kornberg (1992) have shown, many Canadians seem to believe that the government has less of an impact on their personal financial condition than on the economy as a whole. The ethic of self-reliance may explain that difference: like Americans, most Canadians think that people who fail to get ahead have only themselves to blame.[1]

There is a second potential complication: voters can vote retrospectively or prospectively. When voters vote retrospectively, they evaluate whether economic circumstances (be they personal or national) have improved or deteriorated over the recent past, typically the past year. With prospective evaluations, voters consider future economic conditions; they ask themselves whether things will get better or worse in the future. The weight of the evidence suggests that retrospective evaluations are more important (Fiorina 1981; but see MacKuen Erikson and Stimson 1992), so we apply that perspective in this chapter. Prospective evaluations are less reliable because they tend to be contaminated by expectations about the outcome of the election: if you think your party is the best for managing the economy *and* you think your party is likely to win, you are going to be more sanguine about the economic outlook (and vice versa).

Finally, there is the question of assigning credit and blame. Attributions of responsibility for economic conditions play a key role in economic voting. Voters are only going to vote on the basis of how the economy is doing or the state of their personal finances *if* they attribute responsibility for those conditions to the incumbent party. Economic conditions do not necessarily have political relevance (Clarke and Kornberg 1992).

The Contingencies of Economic Voting

The contingent nature of economic voting is important. The model assumes that voters are as apt to reward as they are to punish. But the asymmetry hypothesis suggests that people are more inclined to punish the incumbents for a poor economic performance than they are to reward them for economic success. In the case of Canada, Clarke and Kornberg (1992) have shown that the more positively Canadians evaluate the state of the national economy and their own financial situation, the less likely they are to credit the government with responsibility. Two reasons have been offered to explain why incumbents do not necessarily reap the benefits of a strong economic performance (Norpoth 1996). First, the economy is much less likely to feature in the news when it is healthy, so the issue is simply less salient. Second, voters *expect* the government to manage the economy properly.

The political context can also affect the extent of economic voting. Voters need to have a clear and plausible alternative party to turn to if they are dissatisfied with the incumbent's performance (Lewis-Beck 1988). The economic voting model was developed in the two-party US setting where the choice is clear. In multi-party systems, deciding how to register discontent on election day is more complicated because there may be several plausible opposition parties. Thus, in this type of system, the reward-and-punish calculus will help voters decide only whether or not to vote for the incumbent. Once a decision not to vote for the incumbent is made, voters still face the challenge of deciding which opposition party to support. Voters also need to be able to attribute responsibility to the incumbent, and this, too, may be harder in a decentralized federal system like Canada's (Anderson 2006). It turns out that some voters hold provincial incumbents accountable for the state of the country's economy, at least if they are of the same partisan stripe as the party in power federally (Gélineau and Bélanger 2005).

From this perspective, the ideal political context for casting an economic vote would be a two-party system in a unitary state or in a highly centralized federal state. In such a setting, responsibility will be clear, and, with one party in government and only one party in opposition, it will be easier for voters to translate their economic judgments into partisan choices. Canada satisfies neither criterion: the decentralized nature of the

Canadian federal system makes it difficult to assign credit and blame, and three parties crowd the opposition ranks. Together, these factors may work to weaken the potential impact of economic voting in Canada.

Then there is the broader economic context to consider. Economic voting is likely to be weaker in a country such as Canada, whose economic well-being is heavily dependent on the economic performance of a dominant trading partner. Indeed, in the present global economy, variations in unemployment, inflation, or gross domestic product (GDP) in Canada may have more to do with decisions made by private investors in New York or London or Singapore than with the policies adopted by the federal government. The problem is a common one shared by small states that depend on trade in open markets (Katzenstein 1986). If the state of the economy is mostly affected by factors over which the Canadian government has little control, there is not much reason for voters to reward incumbents for good economic times or punish them when the economy turns sour.

Economic Conditions and the Vote

Any assessment of how much economic conditions actually mattered to the outcomes of the four elections held between 2000 and 2008 needs to start with the objective state of the economy. The three standard indicators are economic growth, inflation, and unemployment. Unemployment is usually construed to be the most politically salient indicator in Canada (Nadeau and Blais 1995). The mean (and median) unemployment rate at the time of the 16 elections held between 1962 and 2008 was 6.8 per cent. The unemployment rate was 6.5 per cent in November 2000, 7.3 per cent in June 2004, 6.6 per cent in January 2006, and 6.2 per cent in October 2008. So, the unemployment rate was slightly below the post-1960 mean in three of the four elections. However, the incumbent government was defeated in one of these three elections, which raises questions about the relationship between objective economic conditions and incumbent vote shares.

The standard way to estimate the strength of the relationship between the unemployment rate at the time of the election and the incumbent party's share of the vote is to perform a simple linear regression. The results are summarized in Figure 5.1, which plots the "best-fit" line for the 16 elections held since 1962. There appears to be a rather strong relationship between unemployment and how the governing party fares at the polls (for similar findings for the 1962–2006 period, see Anderson 2010). In effect, an increase of 1 point in the unemployment rate typically produces a decline of 2.3 points in the incumbent party's vote share. The implication is that, if the unemployment rate increases by 2 points, support for the governing party will typically decrease by almost 5 points.

Figure 5.1 *Unemployment and Federal Incumbent Vote Share, 1962–2008*

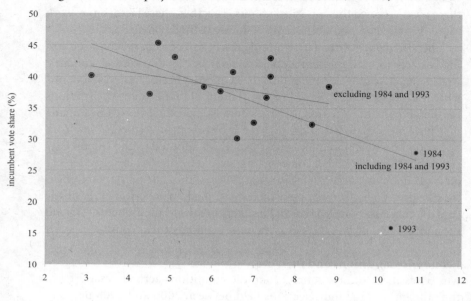

Note: The solid lines indicate best-fit lines as determined by an ordinary least squares regression analysis.

But there is another possible reading of the data. The unemployment rate at the time of the election exceeded 10 per cent in only two instances. And, in both elections, the incumbent party suffered a crushing defeat: the Liberals in 1984 and the Progressive Conservatives in 1993. Indeed, these are the only two elections in which the governing party received less than 30 per cent of the vote. Canadian voters clearly seem to punish governments when unemployment gets very high, but whether unemployment is 8 per cent or only 4 per cent does not seem to matter much. This becomes clear when the two elections with atypically high unemployment are dropped and the regression analysis is repeated. Now the "best-fit" line indicates a much weaker relationship: an increase of 1 point in the unemployment rate is associated with a decline of just under 1 point in the governing party's vote share, and this decline is not statistically significant.

It is impossible to be absolutely certain about which of these two interpretations is correct. But the individual level data for the 2000, 2004, 2006, and 2008 elections indicate that the second interpretation might be closer to the mark. As will become clear, voters' perceptions of the economy had only a weak impact on the vote in all four of these elections. These elec-

Figure 5.2 *Economic Perceptions*

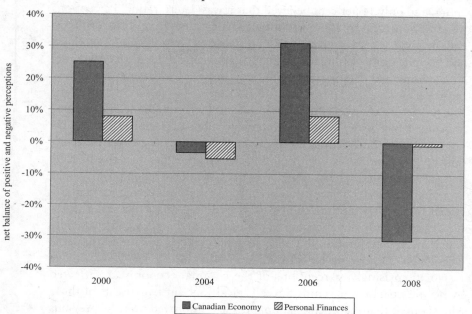

tions were held when the unemployment rate was quite typical, close to the median in recent Canadian history. Under such circumstances, it seems, the economy does not matter that much. It is only when unemployment rates cross a higher threshold that voters get into a punishing mood.

Changing Economic Perceptions

What matters to voting behaviour is how voters themselves think the economy has been doing. Did voters in the four elections between 2000 and 2008 think that the Canadian economy had improved or deteriorated? And did these voters believe that their personal financial situation had become better or worse over the previous 12 months?

Figure 5.2 presents the net balance of opinions on these two dimensions for each election. For instance, in 2000, 41 per cent of the respondents believed that the economy had improved while only 16 per cent thought that it had worsened (43 per cent responded that it was the same or that they did not know). This net difference of +25 for perceptions of the Canadian economy that year indicates that positive assessments outweighed negative ones by a margin of 25 percentage points. The outlook was equally rosy in 2006: 45 per cent thought that the Canadian economy was doing better, and only 14 per cent believed that it was deteriorating. Perceptions were more neutral in 2004; about half saw no change, and the rest were equally divided between positive and negative evaluations. But Canadians had become quite pessimistic by 2008: 45 per cent believed that the overall economy had deteriorated while only 14 per cent thought that it had improved.

The picture changes when perceptions of personal financial situations are considered. As we would expect, perceptions of personal finances do not change as much across elections as evaluations of the overall economy. In 2000 and 2006, positive evaluations outweighed negative ones by a modest margin. In 2004, negative evaluations outweighed positive ones by a smaller margin. The results for 2008 are worth inspecting particularly closely because the election coincided with the beginning of a major recession. Even so, only 24 per cent of respondents said that they had personally experienced deterioration of their personal finances, and about the same proportion (23 per cent) reported an improvement.

Not surprisingly, perceptions of the national economy are affected by people's personal circumstance. Typically, about two-thirds of those who thought that their personal finances had improved over the previous year also thought the national economy had improved. A similar pattern applies to those whose personal situation had worsened. But people do take notice of what is going on in the broader environment, irrespective of how they are doing themselves. In 2008, only one-third of those whose personal situation had improved were positive about the Canadian economy. Conversely, in 2000, only one-third of those whose personal finances had worsened thought that the Canadian economy was in a downturn.

Economic perceptions varied somewhat by region, though the overall mood was usually in the same direction (positive or negative) in all regions (note that we are not considering Québec here). Significantly, perhaps, it was in Ontario that economic evaluations were particularly rosy in 2000 and particularly gloomy in 2008. Westerners were the most upbeat in 2004.

Economic Perceptions and the Vote

If the economic voting model holds true to form, then the Liberals should have reaped the benefit of positive economic evaluations in 2000 and 2006. The Conservatives, by contrast, should have suffered from negative evaluations in 2008. It turns out that the economy had a strong effect on the probability of voting for the incumbent only in 2006. In 2004, economic perceptions simply did not matter; in 2000 and 2008, their impact was modest. The absence of any impact in 2004 is not surprising, given the net balance of positive and negative evaluations (see Figure 5.2).

Even though economic evaluations were quite positive in 2000, they do not seem to have contributed to the Liberal victory. For one thing, evaluations of the economy did not have a significant effect on the choice among the major contenders. Only perceptions of personal finances seem to have had some influence, and even then the impact of those evaluations was limited. Moreover, voters' perceptions of their personal financial situation were much more balanced than their perceptions of the country's economy, so their impact on the Liberal vote share turned out to be correspondingly small. All in all, then, economic perceptions were not particularly salient in the 2000 election.

Things were different in 2006. Economic perceptions were once again quite positive, and, on this occasion, they did help the Liberals. Everything else being equal, the propensity to vote Liberal was 7 percentage points higher when someone thought that the Canadian economy was getting better (and 7 percentage points lower when someone believed the opposite) than when someone saw no change in the state of the economy. As a consequence, the Liberals gained 3 percentage points because of these positive economic evaluations. The boost may seem modest, but the implication is clear: the Liberals would have suffered an even worse defeat in 2006 had they not been the beneficiaries of these positive economic perceptions.

There are good reasons to suppose that the economy might have mattered as much, if not more, in 2008. The election coincided with the onset of the most severe recession in the world economy since the Great Depression. Indeed, the prevailing view was that the Canadian economy was deteriorating (see Figure 5.2). Certainly, those who thought that the economy was taking a turn for the worse were less inclined to vote Conservative, but the effect was modest. The Conservatives lost only 1 point in 2008 because of those negative economic perceptions. But there is another part to the story that deserves serious consideration. Negative economic perceptions increased the likelihood that voters would opt for the Liberals over both the Conservatives *and* the NDP. The upshot was that the Liberals gained over 1.5 points. Again the implication is clear: the economic downturn likely spared the Liberals from an even more crushing defeat.

The Limited Influence of Economic Perceptions

If we take all of these results together, the larger point to make is that the economic voting model goes only a limited distance toward explaining the outcome of all four elections. The impact of economic perceptions on the vote was generally modest for three reasons. The first reason has to do with the

Figure 5.3 *Attributions of Responsibility for Personal Financial Situation*

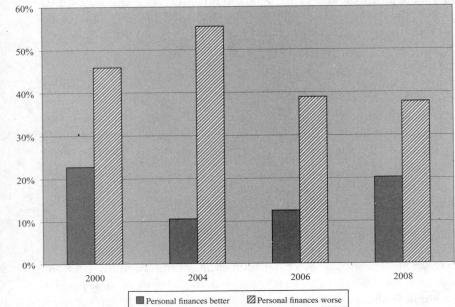

distribution of public evaluations about the economy. Typically, in these four elections, about half of the respondents did not see much change in their personal finances, and about 40 per cent said that the Canadian economy had neither improved nor deteriorated over the previous 12 months. There is no motivation for people to punish or reward the incumbent government if they reason that things are not going particularly well or badly. In short, public evaluations were not sharply divided over the state of the economy.

The second reason is that economic perceptions are themselves affected by partisan predispositions (Bartels 2002). In each of the first three elections, when the Liberals were the incumbents, Liberal partisans were much more likely to say that the Canadian economy was getting better. In 2006, for example, 58 per cent of Liberal partisans said that the economy was improving compared to only 40 per cent of non-partisans. Likewise in 2008, when the Conservatives were the incumbent party, Conservative identifiers were less negative in their assessments: only 36 per cent of them thought that the economy was worsening compared with 45 per cent of non-partisans. There are also signs of projection effects with respect to perceptions of personal finances though these effects are much weaker. In 2006, 31 per cent of Liberal identifiers reported that their personal situation had improved; the percentage among those with no party identification was 25 per cent. Furthermore, non-partisans, who are the most likely to be swayed by considerations such as the economy, were more likely than others to say that both their personal finances and the Canadian economy had stayed the same over the previous year. Fifty per cent of non-partisans reported no change compared with 45 per cent of partisans.

Finally, there is no reason for voters to reward or punish the incumbent party unless they believe that the government is responsible for whatever change has occurred. Respondents who indicated that their personal financial situations had gotten better were asked whether they thought that the policies of the federal government had made them better off or had not made much difference; conversely, those who responded that they were worse off financially were asked whether federal government policies had made them worse off or had made little difference. The same question regarding the responsibility of the federal government was asked of those who said that the Canadian economy had improved or deteriorated. The responses reveal some intriguing patterns. People were much readier to blame the government when their personal finances had changed for the worse than they were to credit the government with responsibility for any improvement. The asymmetry in attributions of responsibility was especially striking in 2004. On that occasion, over half of those whose personal finances had worsened blamed the government, while only 10 per cent of those whose finances had improved credited the government with the improvement (see Figure 5.3). Attributions were not as unbalanced in the other three elections, but the evidence of asymmetry was clear: typically about 40 per cent believed that the government bore some responsibility when their personal situation had changed for the worse, yet no more than 20 per cent were willing to credit the government for any improvement.

The asymmetry in attributions of responsibility was much less evident when it came to the state of the country's economy (see Figure 5.4). Indeed, there was little or no difference in the propensity to attribute credit or assign blame in either 2000 or 2006. The 2008 election, however, stands out as a clear exception to this pattern. Voters were much less prone to blame the government for the perceived deterioration in the country's economy. This election was the only one among the four in which fewer than 40 per cent of those who believed that the economy had changed for the worse laid the blame at the doorstep of the government. It seems that most voters were aware that the economic crisis had erupted in the American financial and

Figure 5.4 *Attributions of Responsibility for the Canadian Economy*

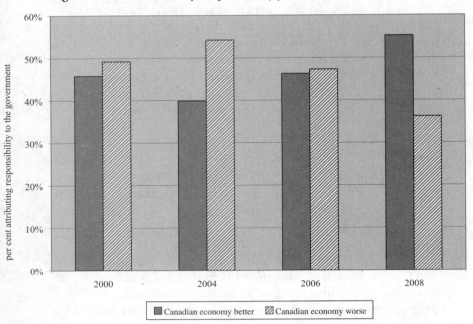

housing markets and reasoned, perhaps, that the Canadian government had very little to do with it. That interpretation might help to explain why the Conservatives avoided paying a bigger price for the economic downturn.

The role of attributions of responsibility in limiting the impact of economic perceptions on the vote becomes clear when support for the incumbent party is compared according to voters' perceptions of the economy and their willingness to assign credit or blame (see Figure 5.5). To limit possible distortions from the projection effects associated with partisanship, we excluded partisans from the following analysis. That strategy, of course, reduces the number of cases, so responses for all four elections are combined.

The largest group consisted of voters who saw no change in the Canadian economy. They made up 45 per cent of the sample of non-partisans. All in all, 34 per cent of the people in this group supported the incumbent party (the Liberals in 2000, 2004, and 2006, and the Conservatives in 2008), approximately the level of support observed in the total sample. The degree of support for the incumbent party was the same (34 per cent) among those who believed that the economy had taken a turn for the worse

Figure 5.5 *Incumbent Vote Share According to Economic Perceptions and Attributions of Responsibility to the Incumbent*

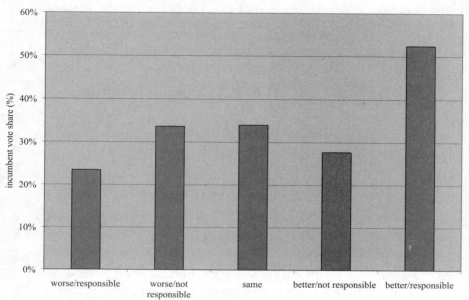

Note: Figure shows combined results for all four elections (2000, 2004, 2006, 2008).

but who did not blame the government for this state of affairs. Support for the incumbent party was actually slightly lower (28 per cent) among those who did not credit the government for what they thought was an improvement in the economy.

For those who believed that the government should be held responsible for the changing fortunes of the Canadian economy, the evidence was quite different. The incumbent party drew 52 per cent of the vote among non-partisans who thought that government policies were at least partly responsible for an economic upturn. But incumbents got only 23 per cent of the support of non-partisans who said that the government had something to do with a perceived downturn. The differences are substantial: the incumbent vote share was 18 points higher among those who gave the government credit and 11 points lower among those who assigned blame when compared to the vote share among those who saw no change in the economy. Note that the positive impact of a good performance seems even stronger than the negative effect of a bad performance among those who attribute responsibility. These effects, to be sure, are confined to small groups. Among non-partisans, only 11 per cent credit the incumbent party for improvements in the economy and only 10 per cent blame it for worsening conditions. The great majority of voters saw little change, or, when they did see a change, they were inclined to believe that this had little to do with the government.

Revisiting Conventional Wisdom

The economy is a classic valence issue (see Chapter 1): everyone wants a healthy economy. The conventional wisdom, in Canada as in the United States, is that the incumbent is likely to be re-elected in good economic times and to be defeated in hard times. In other words, the state of the economy is the best predictor of electoral outcomes. However, the findings reported in this chapter indicate that the net impact of both objective economic indicators and subjective economic perceptions on the outcomes of the four elections held between 2000 and 2008 was quite modest. The evidence presented here makes it difficult to argue that many voters relied on the state of the economy as a primary yardstick for judging the competence of the governing party.

The economy was clearly not a crucial factor in explaining Liberal dominance in the 2000 election. It was even less of a factor in accounting for the decline in Liberal fortunes in the next three elections. Indeed, economic conditions only explain why the Liberals did not suffer worse defeats in 2006 and 2008. The main reason is that most voters believed that the government of the day was not responsible for the ups and downs of either the national economy or their own financial situation. Regardless of whether GDP was going up or down or the unemployment rate was rising or falling, these objective conditions did not figure prominently in most voters' decision calculus.

Evaluations of the economy may not have mattered much to vote choice in these four elections. Recall, though, that the two worst electoral defeats suffered by incumbent governments in Canada in the post–World War II period occurred in 1984 and 1993 when the unemployment rate reached its highest levels. These two elections clearly indicate that when the economy is doing *very* badly, it becomes a prominent issue on the agenda, and voters are prepared to punish incumbents.

In that context, the 2008 election is especially interesting. At the time of the election, the unemployment rate was still relatively low, but Canadians realized, nonetheless, that the economy was headed for hard times. Even under those conditions, the Conservative government was not punished. It was not punished because it was not held responsible for the downward turn facing the economy. There were other clearly identifiable culprits to blame: the American housing and financial markets. As a consequence, even when economic concerns were paramount, no party clearly benefited or lost because of these concerns.

Note

1 However, Lewis-Beck (1988) has shown that pocketbook voting is weak in western Europe, too, despite the fact that western Europeans are more likely to believe that the government influences how they are faring financially.

CHAPTER SIX

THE ISSUES AND THE VOTE

The weakness of economic voting is unique neither to the elections held between 2000 and 2008 nor to Canadian elections more generally. An examination of economic voting in 11 Canadian, British, and American elections between 1987 and 2001 found that the economy mattered in all three countries, but issues typically mattered more than the economy for vote choice and party fortunes alike (Blais et al. 2004).[1] Some issues matter more than others, though. So the first task is to ascertain which issues had the most impact on voters' choice of party. And the next is to determine how these affected the parties' changing electoral fortunes.

Figuring out which issues mattered is important. In theory, at least, elections provide ordinary citizens with an opportunity to influence public policy. If people vote for the party whose positions on the major issues of the day are closest to their own views, then the party with the most popular issue positions should win the election. By that logic, political parties have a clear incentive to pay attention to citizens' concerns and opinions. The hope is that the party that best represents the majority point of view will be elected and will then act to advance that point of view once in government.[2] Indeed, elections are often interpreted by the media and by political elites as conferring a mandate. If Party A advocates policy X and Party A wins the election, then that victory is interpreted as a mandate to implement X.

Issue voting, though, is only one of several determinants of vote choice. People may choose instead to vote for the party whose leader they like the best, regardless of where the leader stands on the issues of the day. Alternatively, people may vote for "their" party without paying much attention to the party's positions on the issues in any particular election. There are three key conditions that must be satisfied in order for issues to matter to vote choices and electoral outcomes: the parties have to take clear stands on opposing sides, voters have to be aware of where each party stands on those issues, and the balance of opinion has to favour one side over the other (Campbell et al. 1960, 168–87). Only if all three conditions are in place will issues have the potential to affect the election outcome. If opinion is equally divided with as many voters in favour as there are opposed, the net effect on the parties' vote shares is likely to be minimal.[3] This is because a party will lose as many votes among those who oppose its position as it gains from those who are in favour.

No consideration of issues in the 2004 and 2006 elections can afford to ignore the sponsorship scandal (see Introduction). The scandal does not qualify as an issue in the strict sense of the term. That is, it did not deal with what actions the government should take to manage challenges facing the country. The sponsorship scandal was more about the past than the future, and it was not about policies as such. Rather, it was driven by concerns about the improper management of public funds. But, of course, voters care about scandals, so scandals can affect vote choice. The question we need to answer is, how much did it matter? To what extent was the decline of the Liberal Party attributable to the assignment of blame for the scandal and for how the scandal was managed?

Issue Voting

In his classic study, *An Economic Theory of Democracy*, Anthony Downs (1957) provided the most theoretically powerful explanation of why issues should matter. Downs's rational choice model assumes that voters compare the expected utility they would gain if Party A or Party B or Party C were to be elected (see Chapter 1). The expectation is that people will vote for the party that will maximize their utility. Voters compare the expected utility of voting for each party by considering the parties' positions on the most important issues of the election. Critics charge, though, that few voters are equipped to engage in this type of decision calculus. To vote on the basis of issues, voters have to inform themselves about the salient issues, form an opinion on them, find out where the parties stand, and then figure out which party is closest to their own viewpoint. But few voters pay much attention to politics, even when an election is underway, and many voters are poorly informed about the issues and where the parties stand on them (Gidengil, Blais, Nevitte et al. 2004). If voters are unaware of the parties' positions, it seems unlikely that issues would carry much weight in their choice of party.

Indeed, early voting studies came to the conclusion that there was little issue voting. In *The American Voter*, Campbell and his colleagues (1960) argue that "many people fail to appreciate that an issue exists, others are insufficiently involved to pay attention to recognized issues, and still others fail to make connections between issue opinions and party policy" (p. 183). More recent studies have taken a more nuanced position. In their analysis of the 2008 American presidential election, Abramson, Aldrich, and Rohde (2010) initially state that issues "were important in the 2008 election" (p. 166), though they later note, "Some voters may have projected the position they favoured onto the candidate they favoured. And it does appear that unless all the conditions for issue voting are present, issue voting does not occur" (p. 168). Finally, they concede that issues "cannot account for Obama's victory in the popular vote" (p. 168). Clarke and his colleagues (2004) reach a similar conclusion in their analysis of the 2001 British election. On the one hand, they observe that Labour was advantaged over the Conservatives by its relative proximity to many voters on the major issues (p. 123), but they also note later that "the issue proximity model trails all of its competitors, except for the social class and general socio-demographics models" (p. 124). Once again, issues are construed to play a role, but their effect is characterized as limited.

All issues, of course, are not the same. Carmines and Stimson (1980) introduce an important distinction between "easy" issues and "hard" issues. Easy issues are symbolic rather than technical; they deal with broad ends rather than specific means, and they have typically been on the political agenda for a long time. In the Canadian setting, the question of how much should be done to accommodate Québec qualifies as an "easy" issue. Free trade, by contrast, was a "hard" issue in 1988. The point is that "easy" issues are less demanding of voters, so even voters who pay little attention to politics can factor these issues into their voting decision.

The sponsorship scandal might have been easy for people to comprehend. Many people associate politics with corruption, so a scandal has a flavour of familiarity. It is a simple emotionally laden affair involving "bad guys," the kind of phenomenon that lends itself to a soft news approach (Baum 2002). The scandal was widely covered by the media. The report of the Auditor General, and her strong indictment of the sponsorship program, was *the* story of the week when it broke in 2004. In fact, it was the story of the month. *The Globe and Mail,* the *National Post* and the *Toronto Star* all reserved their front pages for the scandal on February 10, and stories continued to appear on the front page at least every other day for two

Figure 6.1 *The Impact of Views about Defence Spending and the Division of Powers on Vote Probabilities, 2000*

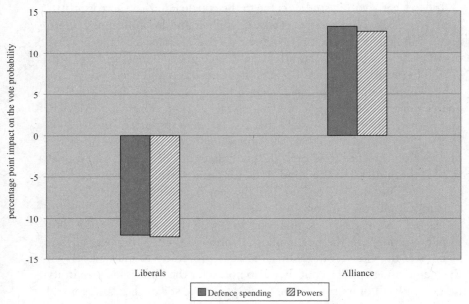

weeks. The scandal was also intensely covered during the 2004 election itself. It was one of the most frequently covered issues on television news, second only to health care. Indeed, there was a story about the scandal on one of the two main network evening news broadcasts on 25 of the 36 campaign days. Even voters who did not follow politics very closely might have been influenced by the scandal "issue."

Policy Issues and the Vote

The issues that were debated varied from one election to the next and so did their overall impact on parties' vote shares. According to the CES evidence, issues were least consequential in 2000. There were really only two issues that mattered in that election: the division of powers and defence spending (see Figure 6.1).[4] Voters who believed that the provincial governments should have more power were more inclined to support the Alliance, and so were those who favoured increased spending on defence. In both cases, these same voters were less likely to opt for the Liberals. The Alliance was on the winning side of both issues. Thirty per cent of voters wanted the provinces to have more power, and only 14 per cent wanted the provinces to have less power. Meanwhile, 38 per cent wanted to see

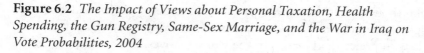

Figure 6.2 *The Impact of Views about Personal Taxation, Health Spending, the Gun Registry, Same-Sex Marriage, and the War in Iraq on Vote Probabilities, 2004*

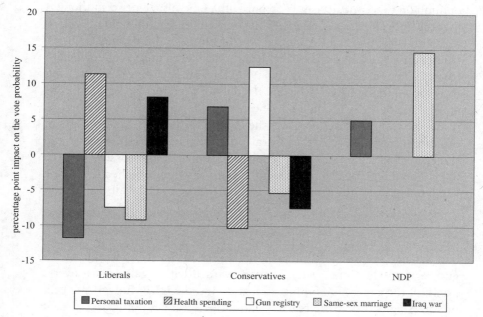

defence spending increased, and only 15 per cent favoured a reduction. So one reason the Alliance easily outpolled the Progressive Conservatives was that it took relatively popular positions on these two issues. Overall, issue voting in 2000 favoured the Alliance at the expense of both the Liberals and the Progressive Conservatives. Had issues not mattered, the Alliance vote share would have been 3.5 points lower, the Progressive Conservatives would have gained almost 1.5 points, and the Liberals would have gained 2.5 points.[5] On balance, the gains and losses on these issues seem rather modest. The implication is clear: Liberal dominance in 2000 cannot be attributed to the party's stand on the issues. We have to look elsewhere for an explanation of that outcome.

The eruption of the sponsorship scandal meant that the 2004 election took place in a very different context. The prominence of the scandal in that campaign might seem to leave little room for other issues to matter. Surprisingly, that turns out not to be the case. Five issues had an appreciable impact on the parties' vote shares in 2004. Two of these issues helped the Liberals: the war in Iraq and health spending (see Figure 6.2). Voters who thought that the Liberal government under Chrétien had made the right decision in keeping Canada out of the US war with Iraq were more likely to prefer the Liberals to the Conservatives. The balance of public opinion on this issue decisively favoured the Liberals: 78 per cent thought that the decision was a good one while only 18 per cent thought the opposite. This issue boosted the Liberal vote by almost 3 points, mostly at the Conservatives' expense. The Liberal gains were even greater on the health front. Eighty per cent of voters favoured increased spending on health, and this worked to the Liberals' benefit. Had it not been for this issue, the Liberals' share of the vote could have been over 4.5 points lower. Once again, it was the Conservatives who lost the most votes (an estimated 4 points). But three other issues cost the Liberals votes: tax cuts, the gun registry, and same-sex marriage. Together, the Liberals' stance on these issues cost the party over 3.5 points. Nonetheless, the gains easily outweighed the losses: had it not been for the sponsorship scandal (see below), the Liberals would have been the net winners on the issues in 2004.

The Conservatives were the net losers. Setting aside the scandal, the Conservatives had three winning issues in 2004: the gun registry, tax cuts, and defence spending. For their clear stance in favour of scrapping the gun registry, the Conservatives were rewarded with a gain of just over 2 points at the expense of both the Liberals and the NDP: fully 61 per cent of voters agreed that the registry should be scrapped; only 25 per cent were opposed.[6] With 36 per cent of voters favouring tax cuts and only 6 per cent wanting an increase, the Conservatives gained just over 1 point at the Liberals' expense on the issue of personal taxes. They also gained ground, just over 1 point, because of their position on defence spending, this time at the expense of the NDP. The balance of opinion in that case tipped more strongly in favour of increased defence spending in 2004: 55 per cent wanted increased spending while only 13 per cent supported cuts. However, the issue had less influence on people's propensity to vote Conservative, so the net gain was smaller than it had been in 2000. These gains were insufficient to offset the losses incurred on other issues. Had it not been for the sponsorship scandal (see below), the Conservatives would have lost almost 3 points as a result of issue voting.

Intriguingly, views about same-sex marriage had little impact on the probability of voting Conservative in 2004, and it had no impact on the party's share of the vote. Views about same-sex marriage had the most impact on the probability of voting NDP. There were more people opposed (37 per cent) than favourable to same-sex marriage (32 per cent), but the NDP still gained 1 point because it was the only party outside Québec clearly on the side of gays and lesbians. The net loser on this issue was actu-

Figure 6.3 *The Impact of Views about Corporate Taxation, Same-Sex Marriage, Environmental Spending, and Day Care on Vote Probabilities, 2006*

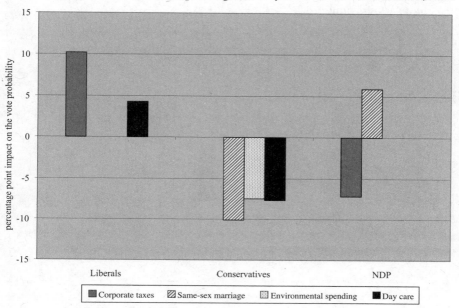

ally the Liberals: the issue attracted some voters to the NDP who might otherwise have voted Liberal. The NDP also picked up 1 point for its opposition to having private hospitals in Canada, mostly at the Conservatives' expense. Citizens clearly wanted a publicly funded health care system; 55 per cent opposed having private hospitals versus 38 per cent in favour. Views about private hospitals, however, did not do much to increase the probability of an NDP vote. Indeed, if anything, the NDP was a net loser on the issues. The larger point, though, is that a vote for the NDP was typically not motivated by voters' positions on the issues.

In 2006, only three issues (apart from the scandal) made much of a difference to each party's share of the vote: corporate taxes, day care and the environment (see Figure 6.3). The only winning issue for the Liberals was corporate taxes. Voters who wanted higher corporate taxes were more likely to vote Liberal, and many more voters wanted corporate taxes increased (41 per cent) than decreased (10 per cent). This issue reaped the Liberals almost 2 points. Surprisingly, it was the NDP rather than the Conservatives who lost more votes on this issue.

The Conservatives did not have a single winning issue in the 2006 election (except for the scandal). Worse, they lost votes on two issues. When

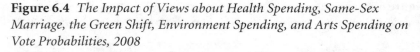

Figure 6.4 *The Impact of Views about Health Spending, Same-Sex Marriage, the Green Shift, Environment Spending, and Arts Spending on Vote Probabilities, 2008*

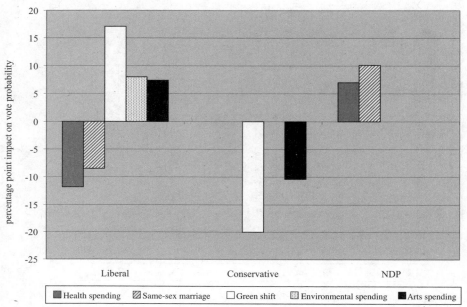

the Liberals proposed a national daycare program, the Conservatives countered by promising to pay money directly to parents to spend as they saw fit. That position may have appealed to the grass roots of the Conservative party, but it was not a position shared by the majority: 64 per cent of voters favoured funding a national daycare program. Only 31 per cent wanted the Conservative alternative. This policy stance cost the party an estimated 1.5 points; the Liberals were the main beneficiary on this issue. The other issue that hurt the Conservatives was the environment. The majority of voters (59 per cent) wanted to see an increase in spending on the environment, and this cost the Conservatives 2 points. This time it was the NDP that was the main beneficiary (with almost 1.5 points). The issue that had the strongest impact on the probability of voting Conservative was same-sex marriage, but it had little net impact on party vote shares because opinion was so evenly divided: 35 per cent of voters opposed same-sex marriage, 34 per cent were in favour, and 32 per cent were unsure or did not know. In 2006, as in 2004, the Liberal Party emerged as the net winner on the issues, setting aside the sponsorship scandal, and once again the Conservatives were the net losers. Had it not been for their positions on the issues, the Conservatives might well have increased their vote share by as many as 4 points. The Liberals, meanwhile, would have suffered an even worse defeat. Yet again, the net impact of issues on the NDP's share of the vote was minimal.

The pattern was very different in 2008 (see Figure 6.4). The Liberals were clearly the net losers (a net loss of 4.5 points), and the NDP were just as clearly the net winners (a net gain of almost 4 points). Issues had a negligible impact on the Conservative victory. In 2008, the scandal was more or less behind the Liberals, and attention now focused on the green shift. But that policy initiative was of no help in reviving the party's fortunes. The Conservatives successfully framed the green shift as a tax and argued that it was just too risky an undertaking in a time of economic uncertainty. The effect of framing the shift as a tax becomes clear when the responses of voters who received different versions of a question about the green shift are compared.[7] When asked whether the green shift would hurt Canada's economy, 46 per cent of voters agreed that it would. When the phrase "carbon tax" was substituted for "green shift," the figure rose to 60 per cent. The green shift thus ended up helping the Conservatives, boosting their vote share by over 2 points.[8]

The Liberals might have paid an even higher price were it not for the fact that this issue cost the NDP votes as well. The Liberals, the NDP, and the Greens (see Chapter 9) were all competing to attract the support of those for whom the environment was a priority. In the end, projecting an image of environmental concern did more for the Liberals than coming up with a detailed plan.[9] The Liberals won the competition for the votes of those who favoured spending more on the environment; this issue boosted the Liberal vote share by over 2.5 points at the expense of both the NDP and the Conservatives.

This focus on the environment may well have been misplaced. The environment was not a high priority issue for many voters. Improving health care was much more important, and, on that issue, the NDP enjoyed a decisive advantage in 2008. Voters who believed that health spending should be increased were more likely to choose the NDP or the Conservatives over the Liberals. This is a remarkable change from 2004 when these voters preferred the Liberals. In 2004, the health care issue garnered the Liberals over 4.5 points; in 2008, it cost them almost exactly the same amount. The health care issue benefited the NDP to the tune of just over 3 points in 2008, though the Conservatives picked up over 1.5 points as well.

The NDP was also the winner on the same-sex marriage issue. By 2008, the balance of opinion had shifted in favour of same-sex marriage: 34 per cent of voters supported same-sex marriage while only 27 per cent were opposed. It was a Liberal government under Paul Martin that had introduced legislation in 2005 legalizing same-sex marriage (see introduction), but it was the NDP that reaped the benefit of increased support, perhaps because the Liberal caucus was itself divided over the issue. Still, the net gain was modest (less than 1.5 points). Note, though, that it came at the expense of the Liberals not the Conservatives. Indeed, in 2008, the NDP and the Liberals were much more clearly competing for the votes of similar constituencies. Positions on the daycare issue illustrate the same point yet again. The Liberals benefited from their promise to introduce a nationally funded daycare program in 2006. In 2008, voters continued to prefer this option (by a margin of two to one) to the Conservative policy of paying money directly to parents. But, in this case, their votes went to the NDP rather than the Liberals, boosting the NDP vote share by over 1 point at the Conservatives' expense. Finally, it is worth noting one issue that had no net impact on the Conservatives' share of the vote. Voters who opposed the Conservatives' plan to cut funding to the arts were more likely to opt for the Liberals or the NDP, but this did not hurt the Conservatives because opinion on the matter was evenly divided: almost as many voters favoured cuts as wanted to see an increase.

The Sponsorship Scandal

The discussion so far has set aside any consideration of the possible effects of the sponsorship scandal. That scandal may well have been the most significant political event of the first decade of the twenty-first century in Canada. Recall that the 2004 election call followed by just a few months the release of the Auditor General of Canada's report, a report that documented many irregularities in the management of the program (see Introduction). And the 2006 election took place following the publication of the Gomery Commission findings, which concluded that there was evidence of serious corruption. The sponsorship scandal was thus central to both the 2004 and 2006 elections. Evidence already presented shows that some Liberal partisans fled the party because of the scandal (see Chapter 4). The question here is somewhat different: How many votes did it cost the party?

Canadians were clearly concerned about the sponsorship scandal (see Figure 6.5). Indeed, most voters said they were either very (42 per cent) or somewhat (41 per cent) angry about the scandal. When asked how much corruption there had been when Jean Chrétien was prime minister, 40 per cent said a lot and 45 per cent said some. Three quarters (75 per cent) of the voters believed that Paul Martin knew about the scandal before becoming prime minister, and two-thirds (66 per cent) of those who thought he did

Figure 6.5 *Reactions to the Sponsorship Scandal, 2004 and 2006*

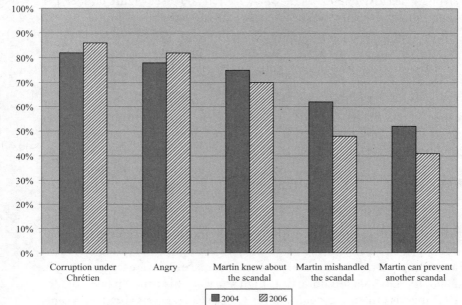

not know said that he should have known. Only 29 per cent indicated that Paul Martin had done a good job in dealing with the scandal, and 48 per cent lacked confidence that he would be able to prevent this type of scandal from happening again.

These were harsh judgments to say the least, and they hurt the Liberals. To probe the effects of the scandal, we use a sponsorship scandal index that combines responses to the questions about anger over the scandal, people's estimations of the amount of corruption under Chrétien, views about Martin's handling of the affair, and how much trust people had in his ability to prevent future scandals (see Appendix B). The propensity to vote Liberal decreased by 19 points among those who had negative perceptions on all four counts (compared with those who were neutral or ambivalent). And the probability of voting Conservative was 17 points higher. The scandal was clearly a crucial factor in the 2004 election. Our estimates indicate that the scandal cost the Liberals over 5.5 percentage points, almost entirely to the benefit of the Conservatives.

By the time of the 2006 election, Canadians had been exposed to the TV airings of the Gomery Commission hearings, and they had had the opportunity to read or hear about the commission's first report. It comes as no surprise to discover, then, that public reactions to the affair were as strongly negative in 2006 as they had been in 2004 (see Figure 6.5): 87 per cent thought that there was a lot or some corruption under Chrétien and 82 per cent were angry about it. However, following the release of the Gomery report (which absolved Martin of blame), the percentage who thought that Martin was aware of what was going on before he became prime minister did decline marginally from 75 to 69 per cent. More important, though, evaluations of Martin's handling became more forgiving: the percentage who thought that he had mishandled the affair dropped from 62 to 46 per cent, and the proportion who expressed little or no confidence in Martin's ability to prevent a recurrence of this type of scandal decreased from 48 to 38 per cent. So most Canadians were still angry about the sponsorship scandal in 2006, but they were somewhat more forgiving about Paul Martin's role in it.

The probability of voting Liberal in 2006 decreased by about 24 points when someone responded negatively to all four of the questions in the sponsorship scandal index; the probability of voting Conservative increased accordingly. But, because assessments of the scandal were less negative in 2006, the Liberals did not pay as high a price. This time, the net loss for the Liberals (and the net gain for the Conservatives) was about 3 percentage points. The impact of views about the scandal on Liberal vote losses were smaller in 2006, but they were still consequential: the 7-point Conservative lead over the Liberals outside Québec can be attributed almost entirely to the scandal. Had there been no scandal, the minority Liberal government would have been re-elected. As before, the NDP failed to reap any benefit at all.

The impact of the scandal might have been even greater were it not for a lack of awareness. Despite the near-saturation coverage in the media, it would be a mistake to assume that every voter knew about the Gomery Commission's revelations. Consider the state of knowledge about one of the Gomery report's key conclusions. During the 2006 campaign, respondents were asked what the report had to say about Paul Martin. Only a bare majority (53 per cent) knew that the report exonerated the prime minister; 41 per cent did not know (6 per cent actually thought that it blamed Martin). That lack of awareness suggests that the scandal may not have been an easy issue.

A second and more important factor that worked to diminish the scandal's impact was party identification. Voters clearly reacted to the scandal through the prism of their partisan attachments. In 2004, only 27 per cent of Liberal identifiers could be characterized as being very critical of the scandal and its handling (as indicated by a score above +.25 on the scandal

Figure 6.6 *Party Identification, Reactions to the Scandal, and the Liberal Vote*

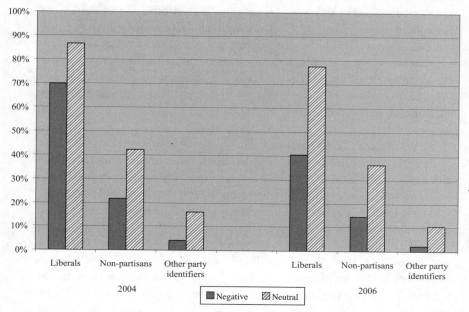

index) compared with 54 per cent of non-partisans and 72 per cent of other party identifiers. In 2006, reactions were less critical, but the partisan differences persisted: 16 per cent of Liberal identifiers were critical compared with 45 per cent of non-partisans and 65 per cent of other party identifiers. Liberal partisans, it seems, were much more prone to dismiss the affair as overblown by the media.

Regardless of their partisan stripe, those with negative perceptions of the scandal were clearly less likely to vote Liberal (see Figure 6.6). Even Liberal partisans were not immune to the effect of these perceptions, especially in 2006. A similar pattern holds for those who identified with one of the other parties: they were even less likely to vote Liberal if they were upset about the scandal and the way it was handled. The larger point, though, is that these voters were not likely to vote Liberal anyway, and this worked to reduce the impact of negative reactions. The Liberals suffered most among non-partisans. Non-partisans easily outnumbered Liberal partisans (see Chapter 4), and they reacted much more negatively to the scandal. The Liberal vote was 20 points lower among those with negative reactions.

The sponsorship scandal had an unequivocally substantial impact on the outcome of the 2004 and 2006 elections. No other issue cost the Liberals as many votes. Indeed, but for the scandal, the Liberals would have been the net beneficiaries of issue voting in both elections. At the same time, though, the scandal had relatively little effect on long-term partisan loyalties (see Chapter 4). The impact, rather, was mostly felt among non-partisans. Moreover, the scandal may not have registered with that segment of the electorate that pays little attention to politics. These voters may have been vaguely aware that there was a scandal, but this may not have been sufficient to persuade them to "throw the rascals out."

Issue Voting and Party Fortunes

The overall impact of issue voting also needs to be understood in a larger context. Consider the 2000 and 2008 elections. The Liberals were the net losers on the issues in 2000, but they won the election handily. In 2008, the Conservatives managed to win even though the issues garnered them few additional votes. These two experiences make it difficult to argue that the party with the most popular issue positions wins the election. Nonetheless, issues do matter. Recall that issue voting helped to keep the Liberals in power in 2004 by offsetting, at least partially, the damage done by the scandal. In 2006, issue voting saved the Liberals from a worse defeat. And part of the reason the Liberals suffered such a devastating defeat in 2008, clearly, was that they lost out on the issues.

With respect to the issues, the Liberals' biggest failure in 2008 related to health care. In 2004, that issue had clearly been a winning one for the party. In 2008, it cost them votes. The contrast between the two elections is striking. Health care is clearly one of the most salient issues for Canadians, and it is an issue that traditionally benefited the Liberals (see Nevitte et al. 2000). Voters who want more spending on health have usually been more prone to vote Liberal. But, in 2008, they turned to the NDP, perhaps because the Liberal message had shifted from social issues to the environment. The 2011 election drove home the point: the Liberals and the NDP are increasingly competing for the same voters. And on health in 2008, the NDP came out ahead.

Finding that the party that wins an election is not necessarily the one that best represents majority opinion is not a particularly optimistic conclusion. But that conclusion raises an important question: Why is this so? There are at least three plausible reasons. The first relates to the distribution of opinion. The same-sex marriage issue illustrates the point. That issue figured prominently in discussions of the Liberal decline, but its impact on the party's share of the vote was very modest because opinion was not skewed in favour of one side of the issue or the other. Second, there is the role of fundamental values and beliefs to consider (see Chapter 3). Issues come and go, but values and beliefs are more enduring. People react to the issues of the day through the lens of their normative beliefs. Once the effects of these values and beliefs are taken into account, the issues of the day have limited independent effects. Finally, people's partisan attachments influence their reactions to the issues. Partisans tend to like "their" party's positions, and that partisan prism works to constrain the independent effects of the issues. People can be shaken loose from their partisan moorings if they find themselves at odds with their party on an issue they really care about. But party attachments tend to be quite stable (see Chapter 4). To the extent that the issues of the day tap into more basic values and beliefs and parties prioritize the issues that matter to their core supporters, the impact of issues themselves will be correspondingly modest.

Notes

1 According to Michael Alvarez and his colleagues (2000), issue attitudes dominated in the 1993 election, but the economy trumped the issues in the 1988 election (Alvarez, Nagler, and Bowler 2000). This is a puzzling conclusion given the centrality of the free trade issue in 1988 (see Johnston et al. 1992). It likely reflects the fact that their focus was on explaining overall vote shifts between elections not the vote in a given election.

2 As Peter Russell (2008) has noted, since 1921, only three federal elections have resulted in "true" majorities—the party that won a majority of the seats also won at least 50 per cent of the popular vote. "False" majorities—the winning party wins the majority of the seats without winning most votes—call the notion of mandates into question.

3 Prima facie, it would seem that this criterion is only applicable to two-party systems. However, it may apply to multi-party systems as well to the extent that different issues play into the choice between different pairs of parties.

4 Our criterion for concluding that an issue mattered was whether it made a difference of more than 1 percentage point to the vote share of at least one of the parties.

5 There was no one issue that cost the Progressive Conservatives votes; their estimated net loss reflects the cumulative impact of several small issue effects.

6 Certainly, wanting to scrap the gun registry is not the same thing as opposing gun control. In 2004, 61 per cent of voters agreed with the rather strong statement that "only the police and the military should be allowed to have guns." The figure was almost identical in 2008.

7 The sample was randomly divided in two, with each random half receiving a different version of the question.

8 This may overstate the impact of the green shift: the question about the green shift mentioned the Liberals, which may have increased the risk of rationalization.

9 Note that the green shift had a trivial estimated impact on the Liberal vote share regardless of whether the environmental spending variable was included.

CHAPTER SEVEN

PARTY LEADERS—"THE SUPERSTARS" OF CANADIAN POLITICS?

L eader evaluations have been central to explanations of vote choice in Canada.[1] Here, as elsewhere (see, for example, Aarts, Blais, and Schmitt 2011; Bean and Mughan 1989; McAllister 1996), voters' choice of party often hinges on feelings about the party leaders (Bélanger and Nadeau 2009; Johnston et al. 1992). The powerful influence of leader evaluations on individual vote choice is clear, but it does not automatically translate into a similarly powerful impact on party vote shares (Gidengil and Blais 2007; Johnston 2002). Whether party leaders qualify as "the superstars of Canadian politics" is open to debate (Clarke et al. 1991, 89), but their popularity does not necessarily determine how their respective parties fare at the polls.

How much leaders matter to individual vote choice and election outcomes depends very much on both the relative popularity of the leaders and the electoral context (Gidengil and Blais 2007). Richard Johnston (2002) suggests that strong leader effects are most likely to be evident during periods of electoral volatility because voters have more need of the cues that leaders can provide. The four elections held between 2000 and 2008 would thus seem to have been particularly conducive to powerful leader effects. But to what extent did the leaders really matter to the outcomes of these four elections? How much of the Liberals' loss of support can be attributed to the increasing unpopularity of the party's leaders? What role did feelings about Stephen Harper play in the growing success of the Conservative Party? And did Jack Layton's personal popularity help to revive the NDP's flagging electoral fortunes?

Leader Evaluations, Vote Choice, and Electoral Dynamics

Party leaders have long occupied a central place in explanations of Canadian voting behaviour. Sixty years ago, James Mallory (1949) opined that the key to a party's electoral success was the leader's ability to capture the national mood. And indeed, the first full-length, survey-based study of voting behaviour in Canada, *The Diefenbaker Interlude,* took its title from the prime minister who dominated elections in the late 1950s and early 1960s (Regenstreif 1965).

The electoral importance of party leaders has been linked to the character of Canada's political parties. The traditional major parties have frequently been portrayed as brokerage parties competing for the median voter and rarely straying far from Canada's ideological centre. According to some analysts, "brokerage parties offer a particularly prominent position to the party leader" (Clarke et al. 1991, 89). This is because brokerage parties are less likely than parties with well-defined ideological positions to elicit strong and durable partisan ties. When political parties lack a clear and consistent ideological position, the leader plays a critical role in building a winning electoral coalition. The less ideological polarization and the less issue conflict, the more prone voters might be to resort to leader evaluations as a guide to their vote choice. There has been greater ideological differentiation between the parties since 1993, but there is no evidence to indicate that leader evaluations have become less important to vote choice (Gidengil and Blais 2007). This finding suggests that other factors contribute to the centrality of party leaders.

Feelings about party leaders can help people to figure out how to vote. Many citizens are "rationally ignorant" about politics (Downs 1957). Rather than expending the time and energy required to become informed about politics, they can turn to a variety of information short cuts to help compensate for their lack of knowledge (Popkin 1991; Sniderman, Brody, and Tetlock 1991). Voters may make inferences about how the leaders might perform as prime minister based on the leaders' personality traits or their conduct of the campaign. Even something as simple as the leader's own social background can help guide people's vote choice. Voters can use the leaders' backgrounds as a basis for inferring their issue positions or their ideological tendencies. And then there is "the simplest shortcut of all" (Cutler 2002), namely sociodemographic similarity. People are more likely to vote for a party if its leader comes from their region of the country, shares their mother tongue, or is of the same sex.

The way that party leaders are selected in Canada also increases their salience. The extra-parliamentary manner of selection gives Canadian party leaders more independence from their parliamentary caucus than their counterparts in some other Westminster-style political systems. As a result, voters might be more inclined to evaluate leaders independently of their parties (Johnston 2002), so the effects of leader evaluations may be stronger in Canada than they are in similar parliamentary systems that select party leaders by a simple vote among members of parliament (Graetz and McAllister 1987).

The way the news media cover elections also has the potential to enhance the prominence of party leaders. Matthew Mendelsohn's (1993, 1996) analysis of television news coverage of the 1988 and 1993 federal election campaigns found that leadership and the horse race provided the dominant news frames. Horse-race coverage is concerned with "who is ahead, who is behind, who is gaining, who is losing" (Joslyn 1984, 133). Thus, the horse-race and leader frames are almost interchangeable. Mendelsohn (1993) suggests that the horse-race frame provides a yardstick for evaluating the leaders: how well the leader runs the campaign becomes a basis for judging how well he or she will run the country. Perhaps the best evidence of how leader-centred media coverage has become is Mendelsohn's finding that a party will typically not receive any coverage in that night's news if the leader takes a day off from the campaign trail.

Televised debates between the party leaders also reinforce this focus on the leaders. The first televised leaders' debate took place during the 1968 campaign, but it was 1979 before the next debate took place. Since 1984, leaders' debates in both official languages have been a feature of every federal election campaign, with commentators eagerly waiting to see which leader will score the hoped-for "knockout blow." Leaders' debates can affect vote choice (Blais and Boyer 1996). Joe Clark's performance in the 2000 leaders' debate undoubtedly saved his party from electoral extinction (Blais, Gidengil, Nadeau et al. 2003). But the effects of the debates should not be overstated. John Turner was widely considered to have won the 1988 debate, but his party lost to Brian Mulroney's Progressive Conservatives. Jean Charest won the debate in 1997, and Joe Clark won in 2000, but neither "victory" could save their parties from defeat.

There are also reasons to be cautious about the impact of the media: leader-centred coverage does not necessarily make for a leader-centred vote. If leader-centred coverage enhances the salience of leader evaluations in voters' choice of party, then leader evaluations should carry the most weight with voters who pay the most attention to the news. But Anthony Mughan's (2000) research shows that leaders actually mattered least to television-dependent voters. And a cross-time, cross-national study of leader effects in seven countries (including Canada) found only a single instance when leaders mattered most to voters who watched the most news on television (Gidengil 2011). There is some evidence of a link between shifting media coverage and vote intentions. In their study of the 1988 election, Richard Johnston and his colleagues (1992) found that people evaluated Liberal Leader John Turner more favourably in the days following more positive news coverage and that support for the Conservative Party declined when the news was more favourable to him. And Matthew Mendelsohn and Richard Nadeau (1999) demonstrate a link between negative coverage of Kim Campbell and Conservative vote intentions. But, when the focus turns from vote intentions to actual vote choice, the impact of changing media coverage during the campaign seems to dissipate by election day (Dobrzynska, Blais, and Nadeau 2003). This finding may explain why increasingly personalized media coverage may not enhance the electoral importance of leader evaluations.

The leader-centred politics thesis claims that "election outcomes are now, more than at any time in the past, determined by voters' assessments of party leaders" (Hayes and McAllister 1997, 3). But evidence from Canada and elsewhere provides no ringing endorsement for this claim (Brettschneider and Gabriel 2002; Crewe and King 1994; Gidengil and Blais 2007; Holmberg and Oscarsson 2011; Kaase 1994). An analysis of the impact of leader evaluations on individual vote choice and party vote shares in eight federal elections held between 1968 and 2000 reports no increase in the electoral importance of leader evaluations (Gidengil and Blais 2007). Indeed, with the notable exception of the 1993 election, the net impact of leader evaluations on the parties' vote shares was typically quite modest.

For leader evaluations to influence election outcomes, one party leader must be markedly more—or less—popular than the other party leaders. If all party leaders have similar ratings, the net impact on party shares may be minimal. The same holds if opinion about a leader is evenly divided; the effects of leader evaluations will be self-cancelling. For every vote a party loses due to negative perceptions of its leader, it may gain a vote from those who view the leader favourably.

Leader Awareness

There is another prerequisite for leaders to matter: voters need to know who they are. The reality is that many voters have little interest in politics and pay little attention to political news, so their knowledge of politics is often quite modest (Converse 1964; Delli Carpini and Keeter 1996; Fournier 2002; Gidengil, Blais, Nevitte et al. 2004 ; Luskin 1987). How much citizens know varies depending on the topic, and some topics are more difficult than others. For instance, voters typically have a hard time identifying basic economic facts such as the rate of inflation or the unemployment

Figure 7.1 *Knowledge of the Party Leaders' Names (voters only) — Per Cent Giving the Correct Answer*

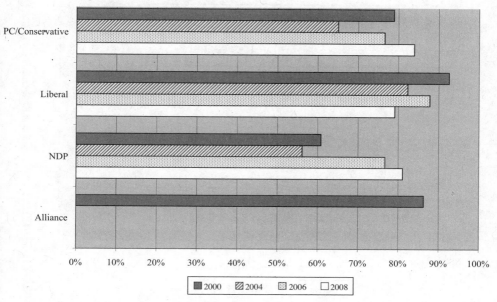

Note: The figures are derived from the campaign surveys.

rate. They also have difficulty recalling where the political parties stand on the issues of the day. Knowledge of political figures tends to be more widespread, but some political figures are better known than others: the more media coverage they receive and the greater their visibility, the more likely they are to be widely known.

Canada's party leaders tend to be relatively well known (see Figure 7.1). On average, four voters out of five were able to name the chief of the major federal political parties.[2] The only exception was the 2004 election when the figure dropped to two voters in three; all three parties had new leaders in that election. Party leaders who face the electorate for the first time tend to be less well known than returning ones. The list of federal election rookies includes Stockwell Day in 2000; Stephen Harper, Paul Martin, and Jack Layton in 2004; and Stéphane Dion in 2008. Leaders who survive their first federal election and return for further contests tend to garner more public recognition. Such was the case for Stephen Harper in 2006 and 2008, Paul Martin in 2006, and Jack Layton in 2006 and 2008. Incumbent prime ministers also tend to be better known than opposition leaders, presumably because they benefit from extra exposure. Thus, more voters were able to

Figure 7.2 *Average Ratings of Party Leaders (voters only)*

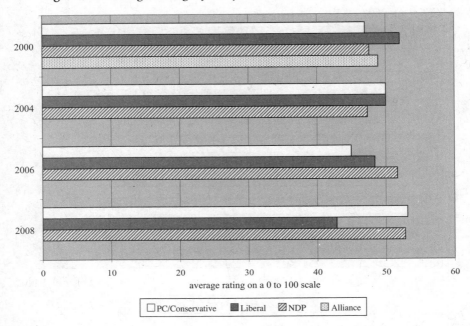

average rating on a 0 to 100 scale

☐ PC/Conservative ■ Liberal ▨ NDP ▦ Alliance

name Jean Chrétien in 2000, Paul Martin in 2004 and 2006, and Stephen Harper in 2008.

There are two noteworthy party stories. First, it took Stephen Harper three elections at the head of the Conservative Party to become known as well as Alliance Leader Stockwell Day was in 2000. Day's fundamentalist religious beliefs attracted a good deal of media commentary, culminating in an infamous report on CBC entitled "Fundamental Day" belittling those beliefs. Perhaps controversial leaders gain visibility more easily than less controversial ones. Second, the NDP leadership flew under the radar screen for many voters in both the 2000 and 2004 elections. But Jack Layton managed to match his rivals in the next two elections; heading up a third party, evidently, does not condemn a leader to anonymity. Indeed, in 2011, Layton led his party to second place, displacing the Liberals as the official opposition.

Feelings about the Party Leaders

None of the party leaders was particularly popular between 2000 and 2008 (see Figure 7.2).[3] Only three leaders received ratings that were positive on

Figure 7.3 *Leader and Party Ratings Compared (voters only)*

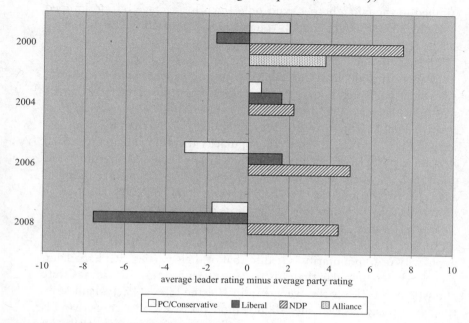

average leader rating minus average party rating

☐ PC/Conservative ■ Liberal ▨ NDP ▦ Alliance

Note: Ratings are measured on a 0 to 100 scale.

average: Jean Chrétien in 2000, Jack Layton in 2006 and 2008, and Stephen Harper in 2008. And, even then, their average ratings qualified as luke-warm, at best.

Leader evaluations clearly fluctuated, depending on both the particu-lar election and the person at the party's helm. According to the "fallen heroes" thesis, party leaders suffer a decline in popularity with each suc-cessive election (Clarke et al. 1991; A. Turcotte 2001). A new leader may temporarily raise average leader ratings, a honeymoon effect, but this effect typically wears off by the next election. This pattern holds regardless of the party and regardless of how popular (or not) the leader was in his or her first election as party leader. Only one leader managed to buck this trend in the nine elections held between 1965 and 1997 and that was Ed Broadbent, who led the NDP in the late 1970s and 1980s (Gidengil and Blais 2007). However, three leaders avoided the fallen heroes syndrome in the elections that took place between 2000 and 2008. NDP Leader Alexa McDonough proved to be more popular in 2000 than she had been at the time of the 1997 election, and her successor, Jack Layton, saw his popularity increase between the 2004 and 2008 elections. And, in 2011, commentators were referring to "Jack mania." In 2006, it looked as if Stephen Harper had succumbed to the fallen heroes syndrome when his average rating slumped to 45. By 2008, though, enough voters had re-evaluated the Conservative Leader to boost his average ratings by 8 points.

The most notable changes in leader evaluations concern the three Liberal leaders. In 2000, Jean Chrétien was the only leader to receive a positive average rating. Note, though, that his ratings exemplified the fallen heroes syndrome: between 1993 and 2000 his average ratings became less and less positive. Paul Martin proved to be less popular in 2004 than his predecessor had been, and he, too, saw his popularity dwindle during his second election as party leader in 2006. The popularity of Liberal leaders hit a low point in 2008 when Stéphane Dion received the lowest average rating of any leader in the four elections held between 2000 and 2008. His average rating was fully 10 points lower than those of his rivals.

Liberal Leader Michael Ignatieff's difficulty in connecting with voters in the 2011 election begs the question of the extent to which leaders' popularity or unpopularity is tied to that of their parties. Stéphane Dion was clearly less popular than his party (see Figure 7.3); his ratings were almost 8 points below the average rating for the Liberal Party. Paul Martin, by contrast, was evaluated slightly more positively on average than his party. A comparison of leader ratings and party ratings suggests that Jean Chrétien was not an asset to his party in 2000. The same held for Stephen Harper in 2006 and 2008. In all three cases, the leader ratings fell short of their respective party ratings.

The pattern for the NDP is different. In all four elections, the party leader was more popular than the party, which suggests that these leaders may have helped their party to do better than it might otherwise have done. But this comparison of leader and party ratings illustrates the potential limits of the extent to which a leader's popularity can affect a party's share of the vote. In all four elections, the average rating of the NDP was negative. Liking a leader does not necessarily enhance the odds of voting for his or her party, nor does dislike of the leader necessarily stand in the way of a party's electoral success.

What Lies behind Leader Evaluations?

But why are some leaders evaluated more favourably than others? One possibility is that people like leaders who resemble themselves (Cutler 2002). For example, Brenda O'Neill (1998) has shown that despite her party's massive loss of support in the 1993 election, Kim Campbell was able to attract some women to the Progressive Conservatives (see also Banducci and Karp

Table 7.1 *Explaining Leader Evaluations*

	Social background characteristics	Basic values and beliefs	Party identification	Leader traits
2004	.03	.15	.08	.31
2006	.06	.13	.14	.33

Note: The column entries are the average changes in R-square values obtained when each bloc of variables is added to a multistage model. One model is estimated for each party, for a total of three models for each election. The dependent variable for each model is the rating for the given leader on a 0 to 100 scale.

2000). NDP Leader Audrey McLaughlin had the same impact. Another possibility is that party leader evaluations reflect ideological or partisan affinities. A fiscal conservative, for example, is more likely to evaluate a Conservative leader favourably, just as someone who favours a greater role for the government is more apt to like the leader of the NDP. More basically, a partisan is likely to evaluate the party's leader more favourably than would a partisan of another party. But this is not an iron law. Deep dislike of a leader may prompt some partisans to defect.

These possibilities are explored through a series of multistage models. Blocs of variables were entered in sequence, beginning with social background characteristics, then basic values and beliefs, followed by party identification and finally voters' perceptions of leader traits. Table 7.1 shows the average gain in R-squared when each bloc of variables was added to the models. The results indicate which considerations are most important when it comes to explaining voters' evaluations of the party leaders.[4] Note that perceptions of leaders' traits were only available for the 2004 and 2006 elections. In both elections, voters were asked to rate the leaders' honesty and competence on a 0 to 10 scale.

Clearly, voters' social background characteristics are not very helpful in explaining how much voters liked—or disliked—a given leader (see Table 7.1). Still, there were some statistically significant effects. Stephen Harper's scores were somewhat higher among men, Westerners, Christian fundamentalists, married couples, and voters from non-union households. Paul Martin, meanwhile, was more popular with voters who were older and more educated, urban dwellers, visible minorities, Catholics, and those working in the public sector. Jack Layton did slightly better among the young, women, university graduates, atheists, and public sector workers.

Each party leader, in other words, had greater appeal among his party's typical clientele (see Chapter 2). Social background characteristics, however, explain only a small portion of the variation in the leaders' ratings.

Ideological outlooks and value judgments had a more powerful impact on leader evaluations. Once again, leaders typically had more appeal to the parties' usual supporters (see Chapter 3). The Conservative Leader was more popular among moral traditionalists, market enthusiasts, continentalists, and those for whom religion was important. The Liberal Leader received lower ratings from people who expressed moral traditionalism, political disaffection, and regional alienation. And the NDP Leader rated higher among those who were less traditional in their moral outlooks, more sceptical of the workings of the free enterprise system, opposed to closer continental integration, and desirous of doing more for Québec and for racial minorities.

There were also indications of partisan bias: identifying with a political party had a strong impact on assessments of the party leaders. Predictably, voters who were attached to a particular party were much more likely to evaluate that party's leader positively while those who identified with another party were significantly less likely to do so.

Above and beyond the effects of social background characteristics and of basic values and beliefs and party identification, perceptions about the personal virtues (or lack thereof) of party leaders drove their likability ratings. Studies of leader evaluations in several countries have shown that honesty and competence are the two most important personality traits (Bittner 2010). Both traits had a significant impact on voters' overall evaluations of the party leaders: the more honest or competent a leader was perceived to be, the more positive the evaluation.[5] Of the two traits, competence had the larger effect. A leader scoring +5 on the competence scale was rated 25 points higher than a leader who was perceived to be neither competent nor incompetent. The comparable figure for the honesty scale was 16 points.

All three leaders received rather lukewarm ratings on both traits (see Figure 7.4). All of the leaders' average scores hovered around the scale's midpoint on both dimensions. Voters were able to discriminate among the party leaders, but the differences in the leaders' average scores were generally quite small.

In 2004, during the sponsorship scandal, Martin was rated the least honest of the party leaders, but he was also perceived to be the most competent. That Layton was judged to be the least competent might help to explain why Martin's overall evaluations nonetheless ended up being more positive than Layton's (see Figure 7.2): perceptions of competence had

Figure 7.4 *Perceptions of Leader Traits (voters only)*

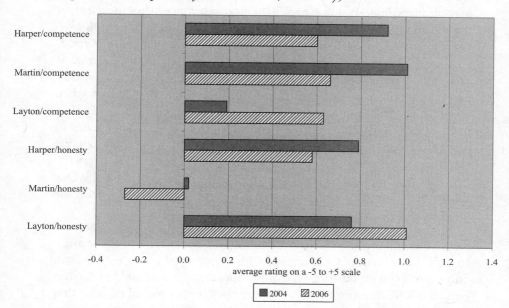

Note: Traits were rated on an 11-point scale. The average ratings have been centred on the neutral point.

a stronger impact than perceptions of honesty. That he was considered competent also helps to explain why Martin tied with Harper in overall popularity: people rated Harper as more honest than Martin, but not more competent.

Two years later, Harper received the lowest overall evaluations of the three leaders, and Layton came out on top (see Figure 7.2). The improvement in Layton's standing with voters was consistent with the improvement in his competence ratings. Moreover, Layton attained the highest score for honesty in 2006. Although Harper's scores dropped on both traits between the two elections, the drop was bigger for competence than for honesty. Martin's overall evaluations also declined in tandem with his ratings on both traits between 2004 and 2006. Note that Martin's honesty score implies that, on balance, he was viewed as being slightly dishonest. This perception may reflect fallout from the sponsorship scandal, even though the Gomery report cleared Martin of any blame (see Chapter 6).

Thus, leader evaluations are a function of both the voters' own characteristics (their social backgrounds, values and beliefs, and party attachments) and the perceived personality traits of leaders. These are the main reasons voters like or dislike a given leader. Moreover, changing perceptions of the leaders' honesty and especially their competence help to account for the ebb and flow of the leaders' overall popularity in these two elections.

In 2000, voters were not asked to rate each leader on these particular traits, but they were asked to say which leader they would describe as arrogant, as trustworthy, and as having new ideas. Chrétien was widely perceived as being arrogant: almost half of the voters named him when asked which leader was arrogant. Only 1 voter in 5 named Day, and only 1 in 20 named Clark. Hardly anyone picked McDonough. When it came to being trustworthy, on the other hand, voters were almost as likely to name Chrétien (17 per cent) as they were to name Day (18 per cent) or Clark (20 per cent). McDonough received fewer mentions (13 per cent).[6] Finally, Day (52 per cent) was the clear winner when it came to having new ideas; the other three leaders scored in single digits on that dimension.

Voters' responses to a series of statements about the leaders provide other clues about the perceived strengths and weaknesses of the leaders. In 2004, 56 per cent of voters agreed with the statement that "Paul Martin only cares about big business" but only 32 per cent agreed that "Jack Layton only cares about minorities." Forty-seven per cent endorsed the idea that "Stephen Harper is just too extreme." The latter perception proved hard to change. Indeed, in 2006, 53 per cent of voters shared this view of Harper. In 2006, voters were presented with this statement: "All Paul Martin cares about is staying in power." Sixty per cent agreed. However, only 24 per cent thought of Layton as someone "who cannot be trusted." In 2008, Harper continued to be dogged by the perception that he was just too extreme (46 per cent). Three elections as party leader had clearly done nothing to moderate his image. The Conservatives successfully painted Dion as a weak leader: fully 70 per cent of voters agreed with this statement. Given the importance of perceived competence in voters' overall evaluations, this view had to hurt the Liberal Leader. The Conservatives were much less successful, however, in persuading voters that all Dion cared about was the environment: only 16 per cent agreed. Even some Conservative supporters rejected that characterization.

Leader Evaluations and Vote Choice

Leadership clearly matters to individual vote choice. The more voters like a particular leader, the more likely they are to vote for that leader's party. The impact of leader evaluations clearly dwarfs the effects of social background characteristics, economic perceptions, and issue attitudes. Only basic values and beliefs and party identification rival the importance of leader evaluations for vote choice.

One way to illustrate the importance of leadership is to calculate the proportion of voters whose vote is consistent with their leader preferences. A staggering 90 per cent of people who rated Stephen Harper more positively than any other leader ended up casting a ballot for the Conservative candidate in the 2004, 2006, and 2008 elections. The figure for the Liberals was also very high: on average, four in five of those who liked the Liberal Leader best voted Liberal. Intriguingly, though, a substantial number of voters who ranked the NDP Leader first actually supported another party. On average, only 58 per cent of those who liked the NDP Leader best actually voted NDP in the four elections held between 2000 and 2008. Liking the leader did not necessarily trump other reasons that voters might have had to prefer a different party. Still, the larger point remains that a clear majority of citizens voted in line with their leader preferences in all four elections.

Leader Evaluations and Party Vote Shares

Leader evaluations can have a powerful effect on people's choice of party without necessarily making much difference to the outcome of the election. Thus, the crux of the matter is the bottom line: How much impact did leader evaluations have on the parties' share of the vote? Answering this question is crucial because fluctuations in the leaders' popularity are a potentially important source of electoral dynamics.

Overall, the effects of leader evaluations on vote shares were rather modest in the four elections held between 2000 and 2008. This was particularly true of the NDP. Alexa McDonough was much more popular than her party in 2000 (see Figure 7.3), but this added only a point to the NDP's share of the vote.[7] Conversely, when Jack Layton was the least popular of all the leaders in 2004, he only cost the NDP about 1.5 points. Layton was more popular in 2006, but the net gain was only about 1.5 points. Layton was evaluated positively in 2008 as well, but, on that occasion, he was no help to the NDP's bottom line. Recall that many voters who preferred Layton to the other leaders ended up voting for another party. The net impact of leader evaluations on NDP vote share was actually negative. Still, the leadership stakes only cost the NDP about 1 point. Overall, then, leadership evaluations were a minor determinant of the NDP's electoral fortunes. Perhaps these evaluations had a limited effect because, in these elections, the NDP was still not seen to be a real contender. It is possible that leader evaluations play a bigger role when the leader has the potential to become prime minister or leader of the opposition.

Where leadership evaluations really mattered was in determining the relative vote shares of the Liberals and the Conservatives. The one exception was the 2004 election when neither party's leader was any more popular than the other. The impact was typically greatest when one of the leaders was noticeably more—or less—popular. In 2006, Harper's unpopularity cost the Conservatives over 7.5 points. Two years later, when Harper was the most popular leader, he netted his party almost 5.5 points. The fact that Martin was more popular than Harper in 2006 added 6 points to the Liberals' bottom line. But in 2008, the Liberals were the big losers. Dion's low ratings hurt his party: had leadership evaluations not mattered, the Liberals would have gained over 4 points. It is worth noting, though, that Dion's unpopularity did not hurt the Liberals as much as Harper's unpopularity had hurt the Conservatives in 2006.

The Leadership Factor

In Westminster-style systems, party leaders are central to democratic politics. Canada is no exception. Party leaders are not only the main focus of media coverage during election campaigns, they preside over party organizations, parliamentary affairs, and government activities. Voters seem to recognize their crucial role. Most voters were able to identify the party leaders by name in the four elections held between 2000 and 2008. The incumbent prime minister was the best known of the party leaders, but awareness was also relatively high for the other leaders, especially if they had led their party in more than one election. Second, the vast majority of voters were able to indicate how they felt about the party leaders. And voters made discriminating judgments: some leaders were rated more favourably than others, and ratings changed over time. Third, leader evaluations were not simply the product of social background characteristics, ideological outlooks, or partisan biases. Judgments were driven, to a large extent, by perceptions about the personal traits of party leaders. And, finally, leadership certainly was relevant for vote choice. Leader evaluations were one of the most important determinants of individual voting preferences. People usually voted for the party whose leader they liked best.

That said, leader evaluations did not exert a correspondingly powerful effect on party vote shares in these four elections. They only mattered to the bottom line when one leader was more popular or unpopular than the others. Moreover, the leaders' popularity does not appear to have been the decisive factor in explaining the electoral dynamics that characterized this series of elections. The principal gains and losses experienced by the political parties between 2000 and 2008 did not coincide with the major shifts in leaders' popularity. The Conservatives made their biggest gain in 2006 when Harper's unpopularity actually hampered the party. The Leader's unpopularity hurt the Liberals in 2008, but their fall from grace in 2004 and 2006 must be attributed to something else. Indeed, the Liberals would have suffered a worse defeat in 2006 had Martin not been more popular than Harper. The NDP's electoral fortunes took a decided turn for the better in 2004, but the party might have done a little better had Layton been more popular. In short, the leaders' popularity was not the decisive factor in explaining the shifts in the parties' electoral fortunes between 2000 and 2008.

Notes

1 In the Canadian electoral system, of course, voters do not get to vote directly for a party leader. Instead, they vote for a local candidate. The presence of star candidates, or what Carty, Eagles, and Sayers (2003) have aptly termed "local heroes," can significantly enhance a party's support in certain ridings. The CES did not collect data on candidate evaluations in 2004, 2006, or 2008. A detailed analysis of the impact of local candidates on vote choice in the 2000 election suggests that the local candidate was a decisive consideration for 6 per cent of voters outside Québec and 2 per cent in Québec (Blais, Gidengil, Dobrzynska et al. 2003).

2 The figures reported here are based on the campaign interviews.

3 The figures are based on ratings provided during the campaign because post-election ratings tend to be confounded by awareness of the outcome. Respondents were asked the following: "Now the party leaders. Using a scale from zero to one hundred, where zero means you really dislike the leader and one hundred means you really like the leader, how do you feel about [name of leader in randomized order]? Use any number from zero to one hundred."

4 Leader evaluations were measured on a 0 to 100 scale.

5 Of course, we cannot rule out reverse causation: some voters may give a leader high marks for honesty and competence because they like the leader. However, the fact that the same leader can receive different scores for honesty and competence suggests that these scores are not simply a function of the leader's overall popularity. Note that voters were asked to evaluate the leaders' honesty and competence only in 2004 and 2006.

6 Note that the numbers do not total 100 per cent because some voters responded "none" and some did not know.

7 The estimates reported in this section were obtained by setting all of the leader coefficients to zero (leaving all other coefficients unchanged) and observing how much the average estimated probability of voting for a given party changed. In effect, we asked: what if leader evaluations had simply not mattered?

CHAPTER EIGHT

STRATEGIC CONSIDERATIONS

The working assumption, to this point, has been that voters vote "sincerely," for the party that they prefer. However, in a winner-take-all system like Canada's, it may be rational for some voters to vote strategically, for a party that is not their first choice. If their preferred party has no chance of winning in their riding, people might decide to vote for their second-choice party in hopes of defeating the party that they like the least (Cox 1997; Duverger 1954). Certainly, some people have voted strategically in Canadian elections in the past, but the scale of strategic voting, according to the evidence, is much lower than public commentary seems to suggest (Blais and Nadeau 1996; Blais, Nadeau et al. 2001b; Merolla and Stephenson 2007). However, the electoral context matters to strategic voting, and the electoral context has changed considerably since those studies were conducted. Weaker parties are hurt the most by strategic voting, so the relevant question to ask for the 2000 to 2008 period is whether the decline in the Liberal vote share made the party more susceptible to strategic defections.

Beginning with the 2004 election, a new set of strategic considerations could well have come into play. That election ushered in the longest period of minority government in Canadian history. The Liberals managed to hang on to power, but only by a thread, with a minority of the seats in parliament. In the following election, the Conservatives won more seats than the Liberals but not enough to form a majority government. In 2008, the Conservatives won again but fell short of a majority yet again. These were not the first elections to result in a minority government: 13 of the 28 federal elections held between 1921 and 2008 produced minority governments. However, most lasted less than 20 months (Docherty 2008). Only twice before had Canada experienced three minority parliaments in a row.[1]

Conventional wisdom has it that Canadians prefer majority governments (Cody 2008; Forsey 1964; LeDuc 1977). If so, we might expect that voters would be motivated to switch parties to reduce the likelihood of minority outcomes. Indeed, there is some evidence indicating that vote switching may have helped the Liberals secure a majority in the 1974 federal election (LeDuc 1977). However, that same study suggests that the experience of minority government between 1972 and 1974 weakened the preference for a majority outcome and diminished the willingness to switch parties in hopes of avoiding a minority. Much has changed since the 1974 election. The party system has shifted, new political parties have emerged, and there is greater ideological differentiation among parties and voters alike (see Chapter 3). The power of prime ministers and their inner circle has grown (Savoie 1999, 2008). Commentators bemoan the decline of parliamentary government, the lack of accountability, and the democratic deficit. All of these developments raise the possibility that Canadians may have come to see minority governments differently; a more negative view of minority governments perhaps even induces some to vote strategically to achieve a majority outcome.

Strategic Voting

The logic of strategic voting draws from the rational choice theory tradition (see Chapter 1). According to Anthony Downs (1957),

> A rational voter decides what party he [sic] believes will benefit him most; then he tries to estimate whether his party has any chance of winning...even if he prefers party A, he is "wasting" his vote on A if it has no chance of winning because very few other voters prefer it to B or C. The relevant choice in this case is between B and C. Since a vote for A is not useful in the actual process of selection, casting it is irrational. (p. 48)

When three or more parties compete in single-member constituencies under first-past-the-post electoral rules, supporters of the weakest parties face strong incentives to vote strategically. According to Maurice Duverger (1954), this type of electoral system exerts a strong psychological effect; it discourages voters from wasting their vote on a party with no chance of winning. According to Duverger, this effect works to favour a two-party system.[2]

Even so, empirical investigations of strategic voting in Canadian elections have found that most voters vote sincerely for their first-choice party even in the face of strong strategic incentives to do otherwise. The analytical approaches adopted by these studies varied, but, regardless of the approach used, the essential conclusion has been the same: there are only modest levels of strategic voting. Based on their study of the 1988 election, the election that turned on the ratification of the Canada–US Free Trade Agreement (Johnston et al. 1992), André Blais and Richard Nadeau (1996) estimated that 6 per cent of the electorate could be said to have voted strategically. Both the Liberals and the NDP opposed the agreement that had been negotiated by the Progressive Conservative government. Thus, there were powerful incentives for opponents of the agreement to cast a strategic ballot and vote for the party they perceived to have the best chance of defeating the Progressive Conservative candidate in their riding. Even under those conditions, fewer than 30 per cent of those facing a strategic choice opted for their second-choice party. It is not surprising, then, to find that there was much less strategic voting in the 1997 election; the incentives were weaker. Only about 3 per cent of voters voted strategically on that occasion (Blais, Nadeau et al. 2001b). Using an alternative analytical strategy based on an expected utility model, Jennifer Merolla and Laura Stephenson (2007) found even less evidence of strategic voting in the four elections held between 1988 and 2000.[3] Fewer than 3 per cent of the electorate cast strategic votes in these elections. Even among those with an incentive to vote strategically because their preferred party was perceived to have no chance of winning, only about 10 per cent apparently did so.

There are at least three possible reasons that relatively few voters cast a strategic vote.[4] First, there is partisanship. Every party has a core of loyal partisans who will stick with their party regardless of its electoral chances (Bowler and Lanoue 1992). The stronger the preference for their own party, the less willing these partisans will be to vote for any other party. The reason is simple: strong partisans are much less likely to have an acceptable second choice (Blais 2002). Moreover, partisans are apt to engage in wishful thinking: they tend to think that their party has some chance of winning in their riding even though the reality is that the party has no chance whatsoever (Blais 2002). Second, strategic voting requires a degree of political sophistication (Merolla and Stephenson 2007). Voters are more likely to reason that their vote may be "wasted" if they understand the workings of the first-past-the-post electoral system. Voters who are less politically sophisticated, or less politically aware, may also be more prone to overestimating their party's chances of winning. Finally, voters' willingness to forego their first choice in hopes of defeating the party they like the least is going to hinge on just how much they dislike that party. Unless they find the party with the best chance of winning to be totally unacceptable, voters may choose to stick with their first choice party (Blais, Nadeau et al. 2001b).

Preferences, Perceptions, and Vote Choice
The 2000 Canadian Election Study asked respondents to rate each party's chances of winning in their riding on a scale that ran from zero (meaning no chance at all) to 100 (meaning certain victory). The NDP's chances were rated the poorest: three-quarters of those who voted estimated the NDP's chances at less than one in three. Voters who liked the NDP best, though, were less pessimistic: only half gave the party such a poor chance of winning. Similarly, while almost two-thirds of voters rated the Progressive Conservatives' chances poorly, the number dropped to half among those who liked the party best. This same pattern held for all of the parties in all four elections: voters who liked a given party better than any of the alternatives tended to be more optimistic about its chances. This element of wishful thinking worked to constrain the potential amount of strategic voting that could occur even if all voters voted strategically when their preferred party was perceived to have no chance of winning.

Many voters, though, opted to vote sincerely, regardless of their preferred party's chances of winning their riding. In 2000, among voters who liked the NDP the best, fully two-thirds of those who considered the party's chances to be slim (less than one in three) nonetheless voted NDP; only one-third voted for a different party. A similar pattern held in the other three elections that took place during this period.[5] In all three elections, the NDP's chances were rated lowest among the three parties that won seats. Yet, three-quarters of voters who liked the NDP best in 2004 voted for the party, despite believing that it had no chance of winning their riding, and so did over two-thirds of their counterparts in both 2006 and 2008. This pattern held for the Progressive Conservatives in 2000 as well. Despite pessimism about the party's chances, over three-fifths of voters who liked the party best voted Progressive Conservative anyway.

The parties that had a realistic chance of forming the government or the official opposition—the Liberals and the Alliance in 2000 and the Liberals and the Conservatives in the next three elections—were typically given much better chances of winning the local race. This estimation was especially true for those who liked one or other of these parties the best. Consequently, fewer of their supporters faced a strategic dilemma. In any case, the vast majority of Alliance and Conservative supporters who thought that their party had little or no chance of winning voted for the party regardless of its chances. The figures ranged between 83 per cent and 92 per cent, depending on the election. Liberal supporters behaved the same way in 2000: 88 per cent voted Liberal even though they perceived the party's chances of winning their riding to be less than one in three. But, as the Liberal decline set in, the number of strategic defections increased.[6] In 2004, 17 per cent of voters who liked the Liberals best but thought the party had no chance of winning the local race chose to vote for another party. That proportion increased to 29 per cent in 2006 and to 37 per cent in 2008. If that trend continued, strategic defections may well have contributed to the party's devastating defeat in the 2011 election. That said, even in 2008, Liberal supporters remained quite sanguine about the party's prospects in their riding. They were most pessimistic in 2004, but, even in that election, three-quarters of voters who liked the Liberals best believed that the party had a chance of winning the local race.

In both absolute and relative terms, strategic defections may have cost the Progressive Conservatives and the NDP the most in the 2000 election.[7] These defections cost the Progressive Conservative Party as much as 19 per cent of its support among those who liked the party the best. The comparable figure for the NDP was 17 per cent. In each of the next three elections, the NDP took the biggest losses; they lost 11 per cent of their potential support in 2004 and 13 per cent in 2006 and 2008. By contrast, even in 2008, strategic calculations cost the Liberals only 6 per cent of the votes of those who liked the party the best. On balance, the scale of strategic voting in these four elections was quite modest. In 2000, 6 per cent of voters qualified as strategic voters. In 2004, 2006, and 2008, the figure was about 5 per cent.

Minority Governments

The number of voters who could potentially cast a strategic ballot is constrained by the competitiveness of the election. The potential pool of strategic voters is substantial only when there is a very close race between two parties. The pool is quite limited if there is no race at all (there is no doubt about the winner, so one's vote cannot make a difference) or if all parties are in the race (every party has a chance, so there is no reason to defect). When the logic of strategic voting is extended to the case of a minority government outcome, the number of voters who might vote strategically becomes much larger. Just how large that pool will be depends in the first instance on the distribution of opinion about minority government. Consequently, it is worth canvassing some of the arguments that have been made about the potential merits and drawbacks of minority government.

The last time Canada experienced three successive minority governments was in the 1960s. Spurred by overblown campaign rhetoric about the perils of minority government, Eugene Forsey (1964), one of the country's leading constitutional experts, set out to debunk the notion that "minority government...is necessarily bad: incompetent, weak, indecisive, if not worse" (p. 3). On the contrary, he argued, minority government should be viewed as an opportunity. His defence of minority government was two-fold. First, the lack of a majority may serve as a restraint on the governing party: "Having to get support from outside its own party may not only help a government to do good and sensible things but also prevent it from doing bad and foolish things" (p. 4). Second, minority government might encourage meaningful debate in the House of Commons and give some power back to individual members.

Faced once again with consecutive minority governments, a new generation of commentators took up these themes. Peter Russell (2008), for example, has argued that minority government has the potential to strengthen parliamentary democracy. Although he is mindful of the potential problems, he views minority government as preferable to the "false majority government" that results when a party wins a majority of the seats without winning a majority of the votes.[8] Russell's point is that prime ministers who lack a majority in the House are constrained by the need to build support for their policies. When governments can no longer take the confidence of the House for granted, they have to give at least some consideration to the views of the opposition parties. Minority governments thus "impose wider consultation, more humility, and more moderate rhetoric and policy than majorities do" (Cody 2008). As a result, policies are likely to end up being more reflective of majority opinion in the country. Commentators have also suggested that minority governments enhance accountability: a government that lacks a majority in the House can be called to account more effectively for its actions by opposition members (McCandless 2004).

There is not, however, a consensus among commentators on minority government. Some worry that minority governments place too much power in the hands of minor parties (Norton 2008) while others fear that the locus of responsibility for governmental actions may get blurred when policies are the product of legislative bargaining among the political parties (Jenkins 2008). Others think that the bargaining process encourages large budget deficits. Per-Anders Edin and Henry Ohlsson (1991), for example, concluded that negotiations in parliament constitute an important obstacle to deficit reduction. In their view, minority governments lack fiscal discipline. Indeed, we might expect minority governments to be tempted to reap short-term electoral gains by increasing spending. However, some studies have found that the type of government has no systematic effect on

Figure 8.1 *Views about Minority Government*

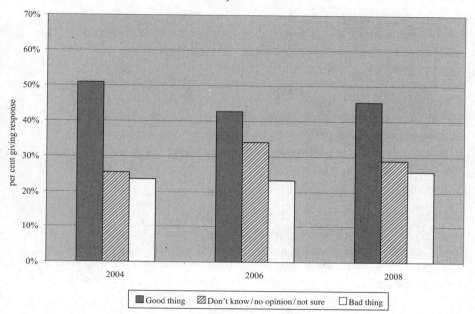

fiscal policy (de Haan, Sturm, and Beekhuis 1999). One study even suggests that, under certain circumstances, minority governments can be effective in cutting spending (Pech 2004).

Finally, minority governments may be good for small parties. As Howard Cody (2008, 28) observes, exerting influence on policy making is a small party's *raison d'être*. If the government needs a minor party's votes to stay in office and avoid an election, that party may enjoy much more influence than its share of the vote would warrant (Thomas 2007). Indeed, a study of electoral promises and minority governments in Spain concluded that the capacity of a small party to implement some of its policy proposals can be significantly enhanced when its support is required to maintain a minority government in power (Artés and Bustos, 2008).

Views about Minority Government

But what do voters think about minority government? Media commentary suggests that voters do not like minority governments (see Cody 2008). Support for that interpretation, however, is meagre at best. When asked during the closing weeks of the 2008 campaign whether they thought minority governments were a good thing or a bad thing, only one voter in

Figure 8.2 *Preferred Election Outcome (pre-election)*

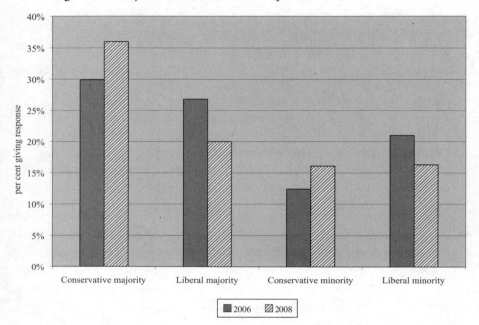

four thought that minority governments were a bad thing (see Figure 8.1). And, despite the experience of two consecutive minority governments, the distribution of opinion was little changed from 2004.[9] Voters in 2008 were a little less likely to think that minority governments were a good thing than they had been four years earlier, and they were a little more uncertain about the merits of this form of government, but the net shifts in opinion were small.

During the 2006 and 2008 campaigns, voters were asked which outcome they would prefer: A Conservative majority, a Conservative minority, a Liberal majority, or a Liberal minority. In 2006, voters preferred a Liberal minority to a Conservative minority; in 2008, they were evenly divided between the two options (see Figure 8.2). However, if the preferred partisan complexion of the government is set aside, what is striking is that, in both campaigns, one voter in three preferred a minority to a majority. Once again, the experience of minority government does not seem to have induced voters (at least in the aggregate) to re-evaluate the merits of minority government. The implication is that the Conservatives' majority victory in 2011 was probably not attributable to voters' dislike of minority governments.

Figure 8.3 *Hoped-for Election Outcome (post-election)*

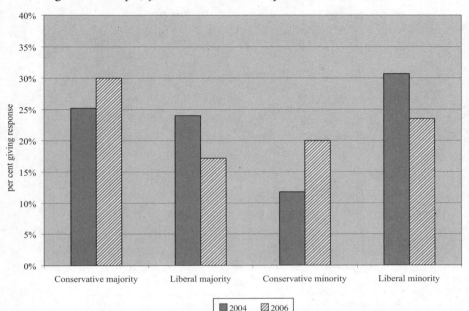

This pattern of responses mirrored those given in 2004 and 2006 when voters were asked which outcome they had personally been hoping for on election day. In 2004, 43 per cent wanted either a Conservative minority or a Liberal minority. In 2006, 44 per cent entertained the very same hopes (see Figure 8.3). To be sure, fewer voters were hoping for a Liberal minority in 2006, but the larger point remains: there is little evidence that, by 2006, support for the idea of minority governments had waned in the light of experience.

Finally, we can look at voters' satisfaction with the outcome of the election (see Figure 8.4). Voter satisfaction with election outcomes can be influenced by a variety of factors. For example, voters who voted for the winning party are going to be more satisfied than those who voted for a losing party (Anderson et al. 2005). And if their party's vote or seat shares increased, minor party supporters may be more satisfied than supporters of a major party that was on the losing side. Thus, views about minority government would not have been the only factors at play in determining whether voters were satisfied with the outcomes of the three elections that resulted in minority governments. Still, it would be difficult to argue that a third consecutive minority outcome induced a substantial drop in satisfaction in 2008 (see Figure 8.4).

Figure 8.4 *Satisfaction with the Election Outcome*

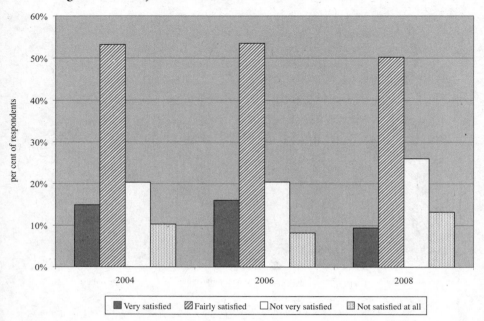

The Influence of Strategic Motivations, Values, and Economic Considerations

If the experience of minority government had little effect on voters' opinions, what factors influenced their evaluations of minority government? It is possible that age might have affected perceptions of minority government. After all, this was not the first time that older voters had experienced consecutive minority governments. But older voters were no more likely than their younger counterparts to think of minority governments as a good—or a bad—thing in 2008.[10] Indeed, social background characteristics did little to differentiate opinion on this question. In this regard, little appears to have changed since the 1970s (see LeDuc 1977). Only three characteristics had a significant independent impact on opinion about minority governments in 2008. Voters who professed no religion and voters from union households were more likely to think of minority governments as a good thing. Christian fundamentalists, by contrast, were more likely to think of them as a bad thing. As the analysis of social background characteristics and vote choice in 2008 shows (see Chapter 2), secular types were more likely to be NDP voters while fundamentalists were much more likely to vote Conservative.

As supporters of what was then Canada's perennial third party, NDP voters' opinions may well have been influenced by an appreciation of the possible legislative dividends that can accrue to smaller political parties in a minority government context. A similar logic applies to supporters of other smaller parties. Certainly, minor party supporters in general were more likely to think of minority governments as a good thing.[11] So, too, were partisans of the (then) two major political parties who expected their own party to lose the approaching election.[12] This attitude makes sense from a strategic perspective. For them, a minority outcome would be preferable to a parliament controlled by the competing major party. Understanding that minority government might be the best option for one's party under the circumstances is a calculation that requires some degree of political sophistication. Not surprisingly, then, the more voters knew about politics, the stronger these partisan effects.[13]

Political knowledge played an even more important role when it came to the impact of normative beliefs. Several commentators have suggested that minority governments are more responsive than majority ones (Finer 1975; Forsey 1964; Thomas 2007). Some voters seemed to share that view. Voters who said that "giving people more say in important government decisions" was an important goal to them personally were more likely to think of minority governments as a good thing.[14] This effect, though, was confined to voters who knew more about politics. Political knowledge is often taken as a good indicator of people's general political awareness (Zaller 1992), so it could be that these voters had been exposed to media commentary about the possible benefits of minority government. It is also possible that these voters had a better grasp of how Westminster-style parliaments work.

More pragmatic considerations also influenced views about minority government, and they did so regardless of whether voters were politically knowledgeable or not. Critics charge that minority governments tend to be indecisive, unstable, and short-lived. If they are right, minority governments might have negative consequences for the country's economic health. From that standpoint, it is not surprising to discover that voters whose priority was maintaining economic growth were significantly less likely to think of minority governments as a good thing.[15] Another criticism of minority governments is that they encourage fiscal irresponsibility. Governments may be tempted to increase spending in hopes of gaining sufficient support to achieve a majority victory in the next election. Not surprisingly, then, voters who wanted to see personal income taxes decreased were less likely to think of minority governments as a good thing.[16] Conservative partisans are more likely to want tax cuts, but controlling for Conservative partisanship did not cause the disappearance of the relationship between desiring tax cuts and being less likely to consider minority governments a good thing. In other words, a preference for tax cuts had a significant effect, regardless of voters' party identification.

Views about Minority Government and Vote Choice

The bottom line question, of course, is whether views about minority government had any effect on vote choice. In 2004, whether voters thought minority governments a good thing or a bad thing made little difference to their likelihood of voting for the party they liked the best. In 2006, by contrast, voters who thought of minority governments as a good thing were more likely (22 per cent) to vote for a party that was not their first choice than voters who had a negative view of minority government (15 per cent). There was a similar pattern in 2008: voters who thought of minority governments as a good thing were a little more likely (21 per cent) to opt for their second-choice party than voters who considered this type of government a bad thing (17 per cent). In 2006, though, voters who had negative views about minority government were no more likely to have settled for their second-choice party than voters who were unsure. In 2008, as well, the two groups were statistically indistinguishable. It seems, then, that positive perceptions of minority government may have induced some (but not many) voters to switch parties, while negative perceptions made little difference.

In all three elections, voters who thought of minority governments as a good thing were more likely to vote NDP and less likely to vote Conservative than voters who considered them to be a bad thing. In 2004 and 2006, they were less likely to vote Liberal as well. In 2008, though, with the Liberals' electoral fortunes in decline, voters who thought minority governments a good thing became more likely to vote Liberal. But simply comparing how vote choices differ according to views about minority government overstates the importance of these views. Clearly, people's views are influenced by partisan considerations. Conservative partisans were less likely to consider minority governments a good thing, and Conservative partisans were, of course, more likely to vote Conservative. The more nuanced question to ask is this: How much did opinion about minority government matter, once we take into account other influences?

To answer this question, we introduced views about minority government into the vote models. In all three elections, voters who considered minority governments a good thing were more likely to vote NDP than voters who were ambivalent or considered them a bad thing. But the effects were very modest, and the NDP reaped little electoral benefit. In all three elections, the party gained less than 1 point as a result of positive perceptions of minority government. The electoral payoff was so small because the voters who were most likely to think of minority governments as a good thing were likely to be voting NDP anyway. With the NDP gaining so little, the cost to the Conservatives or the Liberals was minimal.

Strategic Calculations and Electoral Dynamics

Rational choice theory argues that voters whose preferred party has little or no chance of winning should maximize their utility by switching to their second-choice party.[17] It turns out that relatively few voters followed this logic in the four elections held between 2000 and 2008. There were good reasons to expect to find an increase in the amount of strategic voting over this period. As the Liberals' electoral fortunes declined and the party found itself increasingly competing with the NDP for the same pool of voters, the strategic incentives became stronger for voters to opt for the party with the best chance of defeating the Conservatives in their riding. The Liberals did become more susceptible to strategic defections. But, the scale of the potential electoral damage was limited because the party's supporters were apt to overstate its chances of winning. To the extent that voters did vote strategically, it was the NDP that was the most vulnerable. Still, the majority of voters, even those whose preferred party had little or no chance of winning, chose to vote sincerely. In this respect, the behaviour of voters was no different from that of their counterparts in previous elections.

Views about minority government also made only a very modest difference to how people voted. Positive assessments of minority government outweighed negative ones, and there was little to suggest that the accumulated experiences with minority government caused many voters to rethink the matter. Their assessments reflected a mix of strategic motivations, normative beliefs, and economic considerations. Support for minority government was conditioned by partisan considerations: supporters of smaller parties tended to have more positive perceptions, as did major party supporters if they thought their party was going down to defeat. Support for minority government also reflected normative assessments of the implications for government responsiveness: voters who wanted a more meaningful say were more likely to think of minority governments as a good thing. Pragmatic considerations were also at play: concerns about the implications for the economy and for fiscal policy made for a more negative view of minority governments. That said, the net impact on party vote shares was very small, once all other influences on vote choice were taken into account. To the extent that views about minority government were rooted in partisan considerations, their *independent* impact on the parties' electoral fortunes was necessarily very limited.

Notes

1 The 1920s marked the first time that Canada had three successive minority parliaments. Note, though, that the minority government formed by Macken-zie King following the 1926 election was able to function as if it were a majority government thanks to the support of Liberal-Progressive, Progressive, Labour, and Independent MPs (Russell 2008, 24). Strictly speaking, there were four minority governments between 1921 and 1926 because Governor General Byng invited the Conservatives to form a minority government when Mac-Kenzie King's Liberals lost the support of the Progressives. The second time Canada had three minority parliaments in a row was in the 1960s. Diefen-baker's Progressive Conservative minority was replaced by two successive Lester Pearson–led Liberal minority governments.

2 Duverger also identified a mechanical effect whereby small parties are system-atically underrepresented in Parliament.

3 In this approach, it is the interaction between knowing their first choice will not win *and* having a large difference in utility between the second and third preferences that encourages voters to vote strategically.

4 These studies may slightly underestimate the degree of strategic voting. All these analyses are confined to support for one of the main parties and are thus unable to take into account strategic defection from minor parties. Furthermore, these studies all focus on the strategic desertion of one's preferred party. But there is the possibility that some voters stick with their preferred party partly because of strategic considerations; that is, they would desert their party if they thought that it were not a viable option.

5 Note that the question wording differed. In 2004, respondents were asked whether each party had a chance of winning in their local riding. In 2006 and 2008, respondents were asked which party had the best chance of winning in their local riding. They were then asked which party had the next best chance of winning, and, in 2006, they were also asked whether any other party had a chance of winning. Accordingly, caution is warranted in comparing parties' chances across elections.

6 Variations in question wording mean that the figures should be interpreted cautiously; they are not necessarily comparable across the four elections.

7 Possible strategic defections were identified using two criteria: (1) voting for a party that was not the preferred party and (2) the preferred party's chances of winning the riding were perceived to be slim or non-existent. The qualifier

"possible" is added because we do not have direct evidence regarding voters' motivations. The figures should be regarded as upper-bound estimates because there are no controls for other factors that might have induced voters to switch parties.

8 Notably, minority governments tend to be short-lived and encourage political parties to focus unduly on electioneering. They also risk politicizing the role of the governor general.

9 In 2004, respondents were asked this question: "There may be a minority government, would that be a good thing, a bad thing, or do you have no opinion?" In 2006 and 2008, the wording was slightly different: "Do you think minority governments are a good thing, a bad thing, or are you not sure?"

10 The findings in this section are based on a two-stage regression analysis. The dependent variable was opinion about minority government in 2008 recoded to run from +1 (a good thing) to −1 (a bad thing), with "don't know/not sure" responses coded 0. At the first stage, the model included only social background characteristics. Characteristics that were statistically significant at the $p < .10$ level were retained in the model. At the second stage, attitudinal variables were added. The models were estimated using ordered logistic regression.

11 A dummy variable was included in the attitudinal model, coded 1 for those who voted for the NDP, the Green Party, or a minor party.

12 A dummy variable was included in the model coded 1 for Liberal and Conservative identifiers who expected their party to lose the election.

13 Political knowledge was measured using a four-item index. Correct answers received a score of 1 and incorrect answers and "don't knows" were scored zero. The questions asked respondents to name their provincial premier, the Republican candidate for the US presidency, Canada's governor general, and a federal cabinet minister.

14 Respondents were presented with a list of four goals and asked, "Which goal is most important to you personally? One, fighting crime; two, giving people more say in important government decisions; three, maintaining economic growth; or four, protecting freedom of speech? And, which is the second most important to you, personally?" Respondents selecting "giving people more say" as their first priority received scores of 1, while those who selected it as their second priority were scored .5. All other respondents were scored 0.

15 Respondents selecting "maintaining economic growth" as their first priority were coded 1, while those who selected it as their second priority were coded .5. All other respondents were coded 0.

16 Respondents were asked, "Should personal income taxes be increased, decreased, or kept about the same as now?" One random half was explicitly reminded of the trade-off between spending and taxes. Depending on the ordering of the questions about taxes and spending, they were advised either

to "[k]eep in mind that spending more in one area means spending less in another area or increasing taxes" or "[k]eep in mind that cutting taxes means spending less in some areas."

17 It should be added, though, that, from a strict rational choice perspective, voters should be aware that the probability that their one vote will decide who wins the election is practically nil and thus conclude that the most reasonable option, if there is some cost in voting, is to abstain.

CHAPTER NINE

THE GREENS
AND THE PERILS OF BEING A
"SINGLE-ISSUE" PARTY

The fact that so many voters vote sincerely for their preferred party even when they realize that it has no chance of winning in their riding is good news for a small party like the Green Party. By the time the 2008 election came around, the Green Party of Canada had been in existence for 25 years. It officially registered as a political party in August 1983 and held its founding conference in November of that year (Sharp and Krajnc 2008). In 1984, the party ran candidates in just over a fifth of the country's ridings (see Figure 9.1); in the next three elections, Green candidates ran in about a quarter of the country's ridings. But in none of these elections did the Green Party attract the support of even .5 per cent of the vote. The Greens ran candidates in just over one-third of all federal ridings in the 2000 federal election, but still received less than 1 per cent of the vote.

In the 2004 election, the Green Party crossed two thresholds. First, the party crossed a candidate threshold: for the first time, the Greens ran a full slate of candidates across the entire country. The 2003 reform to the Canada Elections Act undoubtedly had something to do with the party's greater electoral presence. Now every vote was worth $1.75, so there was an incentive to run a candidate in every riding. As a result, the party qualified for about 1 million dollars of public funding annually (Haranda 2004). The Green Party also crossed a threshold of voter support, attracting the votes of over 4 per cent of the voting public. The party managed to attract only a slightly larger share of the vote in 2006, suggesting that the party might have reached some sort of plateau in voter support. But, in 2008, the

Figure 9.1 *The Green Party—Vote Share and Candidates Fielded, 1984–2011*

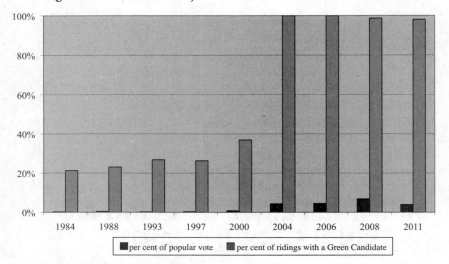

Source: Canada. Parliament of Canada (2011).

Green vote grew again, with the party taking almost 7 per cent of the total number of votes cast. With the Green Party of Canada routinely running a full slate of candidates and attracting the support of more than 900,000 voters, it is no longer credible to dismiss the party as an electorally inconsequential home to a marginal band of eco-enthusiasts. And, although the party's support dwindled significantly in 2011, it was successful in getting party leader Elizabeth May elected as the party's first member of parliament. The analysis of the Green Party in this chapter focuses on the 2008 election for the country as a whole[1] and explores three basic questions: Where did Green voters come from? Who voted for the Green Party, and what attracted them to the party? And why did the growth in Green support prove to be fleeting?

Alternative Explanations for Green Voting
Green parties have made significant inroads into the electoral landscapes of many advanced industrial states including Germany, Belgium, Austria, Australia, and Sweden. A variety of different theories have been proposed to explain Green parties' appeal. One line of speculation associates the rise of Green parties with significant value shifts that have reshaped citizens' priorities in several advanced industrial states. A prominent version of this line of speculation argues that, since the 1960s, there has been a genera-

tionally driven value shift away from preoccupations with physical and economic security and that these "materialist" outlooks have been gradually replaced by higher order, "postmaterial" orientations (Abramson and Inglehart 1995; Inglehart 1977). The contention is that concern about the environment is a part of a larger and emerging postmaterial value syndrome, one that places greater emphasis on the quality of life. Environmental concerns, of course, are not reducible to a single simple dimension. Important conceptual distinctions need to be made, for example, between "protective environmentalism," which focuses on keeping rivers and oceans clean, maintaining air quality, and limiting the clear-cutting of forests, and "recuperative environmentalism," which aims to reverse the polluted legacy of smokestack industrialism (Nevitte and Kanji 1995). There are vigorous debates about how closely these different types of environmental concerns are tied to the core of postmaterial outlooks (Blake 2002; McAllister 1994; Nas 1995; Offe 1987; Rohrschneider 1988). But there is credible cross-national evidence linking postmaterial outlooks to support for Green parties (Inglehart 1995; Rüdig, Franklin, and Bennie 1996).

This value change hypothesis is plausible in the Canadian setting. There is clear evidence that Canadians have become significantly more postmaterial in their outlooks. According to World Values Survey data, about 16 per cent of Canadians qualified as "postmaterialists" in 1981. By 2006, the figure had risen to 28 per cent. And during the same period, the proportion of materialists dropped from 26 per cent to just 10 per cent in 2006.

A second possible explanation for why Canadians might have voted for the Green Party comes from the "politics of disaffection" line of speculation. The argument in this case is that Green political parties provide an electoral home for those people who are dissatisfied with the political status quo and with traditional mainstream political parties. Rising levels of voter discontent have been linked to the emergence of third parties and "anti-party parties" of both the left and right in a variety of countries (Dalton and Weldon 2005). There is also evidence that people's ties to traditional political parties have weakened across most advanced industrial states (Dalton 1999; Dalton and Wattenberg 2001; Webb, Farrell, and Holliday 2002).

A third possible explanation for the increase in the Green Party's share of the vote is that the party was able to capitalize on an issue whose time had come. According to this interpretation, Green support grew between 2000 and 2008 because the environment had become a more important issue for Canadians. That line of speculation also seems to be plausible. In 2000, just over half (54 per cent) of Canadian voters said that "protecting the environment" was a very important issue to them personally in

Figure 9.2 *How 2008 Green Voters Voted in 2006*

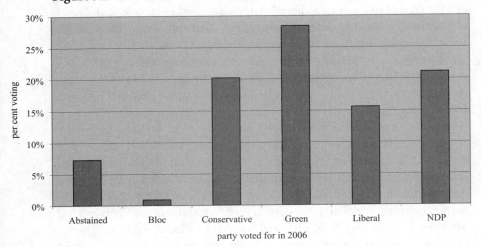

the election. By 2008, this figure had risen to almost two-thirds (65 per cent), and a similar proportion (67 per cent) thought that the government should be spending more on the environment. Indeed, Canadian levels of public support for the environment are among the highest found among citizens of any advanced industrial democracy (Nevitte 1996). But that same piece of evidence presents a puzzle: if such a decisive majority of Canadians believe that the environment and spending more to protect it are so important, then why has the Green Party not attracted more than 6.8 per cent of the votes?

The idea that the Green Party attracted more votes in 2008 because it was a party pressing the right issue at the right time certainly seems plausible (Lewis-Beck and Mitchell 1993). But rival parties are nimble at responding to changes in voters' priorities. As Bennulf and Holmberg (1990) note, "When environmental issues become permanent ingredients of politics, chances increase that the old established parties move in, adjust their policies and capitalize on the subject" (p. 181). And in the 2008 election campaign, the traditional political parties certainly acknowledged the increased salience of the environment among the Canadian public. The NDP, like traditional parties of the left elsewhere, claimed the environmental high ground. And, the launch of the green shift as a centrepiece of the Liberals' campaign was deliberately designed to demonstrate the party's environmental *bona fides* and to attract voters who cared about the environment.

Where Did Green Voters Come From?

In other advanced industrial states, Green parties have typically achieved electoral gains as a result of defections from the traditional parties of the left (Dalton 2009). One question to explore, then, is whether the increase in support for the Green Party of Canada between 2006 and 2008 came at the expense of the NDP. But it is also possible that the rising support for the Greens resulted from the mobilization of citizens who had not voted before.

When we compare how people voted in 2008 with how they reported voting in 2006, three intriguing findings emerge.[2] First, the Green Party clearly did provide an electoral home for some voters who had not voted in the previous election. But the scale of that mobilization of previous non-voters was quite modest. Just 7 per cent of those who voted Green in 2008 reported that they had abstained in 2006 (see Figure 9.2). Second, there is no support for the contention that the increased support for the Greens came mostly at the expense of the NDP. Rather, the Greens attracted relatively similar levels of support from former supporters of all three mainstream political parties. About one in five (21 per cent) of those who voted Green in 2008 reported that they had voted for the NDP in 2006. Almost as many were drawn from the former ranks of Conservative (20 per cent) and Liberal (16 per cent) voters. However, these shifts clearly hurt the NDP somewhat more than the other parties simply because the NDP had a smaller vote base than the other political parties in 2006.[3] The third finding is that the Green vote in 2006 proved to be relatively volatile, at least when compared to that of the mainstream parties. For example, of those who voted Conservative in 2006, 80 per cent reported that they voted for the Conservatives again in 2008. The comparable figure for both the NDP and the Liberals was 66 per cent. But only 46 per cent of those who voted for the Green Party in 2006 went on to vote for the Greens in 2008. And, as the 2011 election was to show, the 2008 Green vote proved to be just as volatile.

Even though the Green Party of Canada did not draw more heavily from the NDP than from other mainstream political parties for electoral support in 2008, there are other indications that the NDP was more vulnerable to defections to the Greens. One in four of those who voted NDP in 2008 named the Greens when asked for their second-choice party, compared with only one in five of those who voted Liberal. And NDP voters were more than twice as likely as Conservative voters to identify the Greens as their second-choice party (see Figure 9.3). Conversely, Conservative voters were almost three times as likely as NDP voters, and twice as likely as Liberal voters, to view the Green Party as "too extreme." However, all three

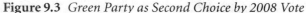

Figure 9.3 *Green Party as Second Choice by 2008 Vote*

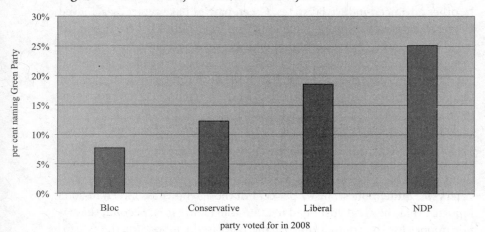

parties' voters were quite similar when it came to identifying the Greens as the party they would "never vote for": only a small minority ruled out the possibility of ever casting a Green vote.

The Bloc Québécois, meanwhile, was the least vulnerable to defections to the Greens in 2008. Hardly any of those voters who reported voting Bloc in 2006 opted for the Green Party in 2008.[4] More to the point, Bloc voters were the least likely to name the Greens as their second-choice party (8 per cent). Then again, few reported that they would "never vote for" the Greens (6 per cent), and fewer still thought that the Green Party was "too extreme" (2 per cent).

These findings raise two questions. First, if Green supporters were drawn more or less equally from the ranks of all three mainstream parties, what was it that attracted them to the party? And second, why were so few Bloc voters drawn to the party? Bloc voters, after all, were the least likely to find the Greens too extreme and the least likely to rule out the possibility of voting for them.

Who Supported the Green Party?

Green parties in Europe typically attract much of their support from the young and the well-educated (Bennulf 1995; Betz 1990; Birch 2009; Goerres 2008; Manning 2003; Rüdig and Franklin 1992). Age matters in Canada, too, but middle-aged voters were as likely as their younger counterparts to report that they voted Green in 2008.[5] One implication of that finding is that the rise of postmaterialist values may have some explanatory purchase. Voters in the 35 to 54 age group were socialized and matured to adulthood during an era of economic and physical security; they constitute the prototypical postmaterialist generation (Inglehart 1977). Voters aged 55 and over, by contrast, were significantly less likely to vote Green: had the Greens had as much appeal to older voters as they did to middle-aged and younger voters the Green vote share in 2008 would likely have increased by 1 point.

The impact of education on Green Party support is also consistent with the support base of European Green parties. University graduates were significantly more likely to vote Green in 2008.[6] Their support boosted the party's vote share by almost 1.5 points. This is a segment of the population that may be particularly likely to vote based on concern about the environment. In 2008, in contrast to the previous elections, the Liberals also benefited from the support of university-educated voters (see Chapter 2). The Greens gained even more from the support of secular voters. The probability of voting for the party was 8 points higher among those who reported no religious affiliation, and their support boosted the Green vote by almost 2 points. Secular voters have also been a mainstay of the NDP vote (see Chapter 2), so this tendency among secular voters is yet another indication that the NDP may be vulnerable to defections to the Green Party.

Surprisingly, the Green Party did significantly better among rural voters. The probability of voting Green was 5 points higher among rural residents than among their urban counterparts,[7] and their support contributed an additional point to the Green vote share. This particular finding is at odds with the patterns of support for Green parties in other advanced industrial states; in those settings, the Green vote is typically higher among urban dwellers (Bennulf 1995; Betz 1990; Manning 2003). What explains that particular difference is not entirely clear. One possibility is that rural voters are more aware of the extent of environmental degradation. However, the finding of greater rural support for the Greens is consistent with the earlier observation that the value divides that traditionally separated rural and urban Canadians seem to have faded since the 2000 federal election (see Chapter 3).

The Green Party did not fare as well in Québec despite the fact that Québec voters tend to be quite secular. Even controlling for the effects of a variety of other social background characteristics, Québec voters were significantly less likely to vote Green. Net of other factors, the probability of voting for the party was 5 points lower in Québec than in other parts of the country, and the party's lack of appeal in the province cost it at least 1 point.

Québec, of course, has its own dynamics when it comes to voting in federal elections (see Chapter 10). The presence of the Bloc Québécois, whose *raison d'être* is advancing the cause of Québec sovereignty, introduces a unique component to the electoral dynamics of the province. As we have seen, the Bloc suffered very few defections to the Greens between the 2006 and 2008 elections, yet Bloc voters seemed to have more favourable perceptions of the Greens than did supporters of the other parties. One reason for this puzzling pattern becomes clearer when the role of basic values and beliefs in motivating a vote for the Greens is taken into account. Sovereignty was by far the most powerful value dimension in explaining vote choice in Québec in 2008 (see Chapter 10), and sovereignist voters were significantly less likely to vote for the Greens.[8] Given the salience of that issue, Bloc voters were the least likely to defect to the Green party in 2008.

By far the single most powerful predictor of a Green vote, though, turns out to have been political disaffection. Other things being equal, the probability of voting for the Green Party in 2008 was 22 points higher if a voter was very disaffected with politics and politicians, as opposed to very satisfied. That finding provides strong support for the hypothesis that a vote for the Green Party in the 2008 federal election was an expression of disaffection with the political status quo. The impact of these particular views on the party's vote share was trivially small, however. Still, the significant interpretive point remains that political disaffection provides a persuasive explanation for why people voted for the Green Party in 2008.[9]

The "new values" hypothesis, on the other hand, receives no support at all. Holding postmaterial values was not significantly related to Green Party voting in 2008.[10] What did matter was moral traditionalism. Socially conservative voters were significantly less likely to vote for the Greens. Given that moral traditionalists were in the minority (see Chapter 3), this worked in the Greens' favour. Had views about matters of traditional morality not mattered, the Green vote would have been at least 1 point lower in 2008. As the evidence presented in Chapter 3 demonstrates, moral traditionalism declined between 2000 and 2008. It may well be that this value shift contributed to the increase in the Green vote in 2008.

Partisanship remains an important barrier to the growth of the Green Party. Many voters have strong attachments to political parties, and while these attachments do not preclude their voting for a different party, they certainly reduce the probability that they will do so. Voters who identified with one of the other four parties were significantly less likely to vote for the Greens in 2008. Had partisanship not been a factor in people's choice of party, the Green vote share might have been over 5 points higher.[11] The problem that this poses for the Greens is compounded by the fact that only about 2 per cent of voters identified with the party. Worse, only 59 per cent of these identifiers actually voted Green.

The Conservatives were very successful in framing the Liberal green shift as just too risky an undertaking in a time of such economic uncertainty (see Chapter 7). It is reasonable to suppose that the Greens might have suffered collateral damage as a result of the Conservative critique of the Liberals' green shift platform. Economic perceptions did matter, but what mattered more were people's evaluations of their personal financial situation, not their evaluations of how the country's economy had been doing. And it was people whose financial situation had improved over the past year who were less likely to vote Green, not those whose finances had deteriorated. In any case, positive evaluations were counterbalanced by an almost equal number of negative evaluations (see Chapter 5),[12] so the net impact on the Green vote share was nil.

Not surprisingly, the Greens attracted some votes from people who approved of the Liberals' proposed green shift. However, views about environmental spending were much more consequential. The balance of opinion clearly favoured increased environmental spending (see Chapter 6), and this helped the Greens, boosting the party's vote share by an estimated 2.5 points, net of other factors. This lends weight to the notion that the Greens were able to capitalize on an issue whose time had come. The Liberals' proposed green shift politicized the issue of the environment in 2008, which worked to the Greens' advantage. When voters were asked which party would be best at protecting the environment, the Greens were the plurality choice (47 per cent), far ahead of the Liberals (18 per cent), the NDP (11 per cent), and the Conservatives (11 per cent).

Protecting the environment is clearly a valence issue (Richardson and Rootes 1995): everyone wants a better environment, and no party is going to campaign on an anti-environment platform. But there are limits to growth when a political party is perceived as a single-issue party. When asked to name the most important issue to them personally in the election, only 10 per cent of voters spontaneously mentioned the environment, and only half of them thought that the Greens were the best party for dealing with the issue. The issues that mattered in 2008, such as health care, day care, and same-sex marriage (see Chapter 6), simply did not factor into the Green vote. Worse for the Greens, the other parties had positioned themselves to compete for the support of "green" voters: only 19 per cent of voters who spontaneously identified the environment as the most important issue ended up voting for the Green Party. Across the country, their votes went to the Liberals (26 per cent), the NDP (22 per cent), and the Conservatives (8 per cent) as well. And in Québec, the Bloc was the clear "green" choice (59 per cent), with only 5 per cent going to the Green Party. Still, there are indications that those supporting the Green Party were not entirely driven by that single issue. In 2008, the Green Party also attracted the support of voters who were opposed to a get-tough approach to youth crime, as well as voters who favoured cuts in welfare spending. In both cases, though, the impact of these issue positions on the party's vote share was minimal.

Did leadership matter? It comes as no surprise to discover that the more people liked Elizabeth May the more likely they were to vote for her party. But, at the end of the day, she was not a big vote getter for the Greens. The problem was twofold. First, despite her participation in the 2008 televised leaders' debates, she lacked visibility. Outside Québec, only 42 per cent of voters could identify her as the leader of the Green Party when they were interviewed in the closing weeks of the campaign. This figure fell to 34 per cent in Québec. This finding reinforces the conclusion that the lack of electoral support for the Green Party in Québec was not attributable to the fact that Québec residents did not care about the environment. They did, but the Green Party lacked profile in the province, and green voters found a ready home with the Bloc in that election. The second problem with respect to leadership was that evaluations of May (among those who were able to rate her) were negative on average. Her mean score on a 0 to 100 scale was 44. Only 35 per cent of voters evaluated her positively, while 45 per cent gave her a negative rating.

Constraints and Opportunities

The question of why people supported the Green Party in the 2008 election might seem to have an obvious answer: "because they cared about the environment." It turns out that the answer is much more complex. The vast majority of Canadians expressed concern about the environment, yet only a small minority voted for the Greens in 2008.

The limited support for the Green Party might well seem to be a classic case of the "wasted vote" phenomenon, the notion that voters are more inclined to support a party that is likely to win rather than "waste" their votes on a party that has no chance of winning (see Chapter 8). It turns out that only a tiny fraction of voters (0.2 per cent) thought that the Green Party had the best chance of winning a seat in their riding, and few voters thought that the party had a chance of coming in second (2.7 per cent). However, when presented with the statement: "There is no point voting for a party that will only win a few seats," a majority of voters strongly or somewhat disagreed with it (56 and 22 per cent, respectively). Moreover, fewer than 3 per cent of voters indicated that they had voted for another party despite preferring the Greens. Thus, even if all of these voters had voted "sincerely" for the party they liked best, the Green Party's share of the vote would have increased by only a small amount.

The Green Party did suffer from strategic defections, but this was not the main reason the party did not do better. A more plausible explanation for why the Greens did not win more votes in 2008—and why their support dropped significantly in 2011—goes to the very nature of single-issue political parties. Single-issue parties, in one sense, seem to represent the electoral face of social movements; they enjoy the luxury of being able to focus on one issue. But that luxury can also become an electoral liability when voters either care more about other issues or care about more than one issue. Both conditions applied in the 2008 election. There were other issues in the mix, and many of those who said that the environment was the most important issue ended up voting for one of the other parties. The Greens' problems were compounded in Québec by the overriding importance of the sovereignty question.

Certainly, people voted for the Green Party in 2008 because they cared about the environment. But this chapter suggests that a more complicated decision calculus helped to shape the Green Party's electoral prospects. This complexity makes for both opportunities and constraints. Political disaffection turned out to be the strongest predictor of a Green vote. The implication is that the Green Party may have an opportunity to grow once again if the public becomes more disappointed with the performance of the traditional mainstream political parties and frustrated with the political status quo. To capitalize on that opportunity, though, the Greens will have to find some way of increasing their visibility, something they were unable to do in 2011.

A second implication of the findings is that the single-issue nature of the Green Party is a constraint. Some Canadians care about the environment. But more care about other things, and those who care about the environment also care about other issues. The challenge, perhaps, is for the Green Party to develop a more expansive issue platform. But such a strategy would move the Green Party closer to the status of being a party *comme les autres*. And that strategy introduces a dilemma with an ironic twist: many people voted for the Green Party because it was not *comme les autres*.

Notes

1 There were too few voters in the three preceding elections to conduct reliable analyses. Even in 2008, the sample size was too small to permit separate analyses for Québec. Note, though, that the Green vote as reported in the 2008 CES was 6.3 per cent, very close to the official figure of 6.8 per cent.

2 Note that the 2008 post-election sample included 117 respondents who reported voting for the Green Party. The relatively small number of Green voters should be borne in mind when evaluating the findings.

3 In effect, the NDP lost 10 per cent of its 2006 vote base to the Greens, compared to 4 per cent each for the Liberals and the Conservatives.

4 Indeed, there was only one respondent in the 2008 CES who reported voting Bloc in 2006 but Green in 2008.

5 The findings reported in this chapter are based on the multistage bloc-recursive model (see Chapter 1). However, there are too few Green voters to permit a multinomial specification. Consequently, we resort to binary logistic regression. This means that we are estimating the effects of various explanatory factors on the propensity to vote Green as opposed to the propensity to vote for any of the other parties. As before, explanatory factors are only retained in the model if their effects are statistically significant at the $p < .10$ level when first entered.

6 Note that the education effect is not masking an age effect. Young Canadians are more likely to have a university education, but, regardless of whether education is included in the model or not, Canadians aged 18 to 34 were no more likely to vote Green in 2008 than middle-aged Canadians. The same holds whether being secular or not is included or left out of the model.

7 This was the case even in the absence of controls.

8 For Québec voters, views about sovereignty were substituted for the question about doing more for Québec, and an interaction term was added to the model to differentiate the impact of these views in Québec.

9 It is reasonable to ask why people who are politically disaffected would bother to vote at all. However, analyses of voter turnout suggest that Green voters are not distinctive in this regard. Political disaffection does not have an independent impact on the propensity to vote or not, once political interest and political knowledge are taken into account (Blais et al. 2002). To be sure, some will register their disaffection by staying home, but others will cast a protest vote or vote for a party that they think might do politics differently.

10 We tested this interpretation by adding postmaterialism to the model. The postmaterialism index was based on the following two questions: (1) "Here's a list of four goals. Which goal is most important to you personally? One, fighting crime; two, giving people more say in important government decisions; three, maintaining economic growth; or four, protecting freedom of speech?" and (2) "And, which is the second most important to you, personally?" Following the original four-item index used by Inglehart (1977), voters who gave "giving people more say in important government decisions" and "protecting freedom of speech" were considered to be postmaterialists. The effect of postmaterialism did not approach conventional levels of statistical significance.

11 To conserve degrees of freedom and minimize the problem of empty cells, we created a dummy variable that was coded 1 for those who identified very

strongly or fairly strongly with the Bloc, Conservatives, Liberals, or NDP and 0 for all other voters. There were too few Green identifiers to include a Green partisanship variable.

12 In the country as a whole, 22 per cent of voters reported that their personal financial situation had improved while 21 per cent said that it had worsened.

CHAPTER TEN

ELECTORAL DYNAMICS IN QUÉBEC

The unique way in which the environmental issue played out in Québec underscores once again the distinctiveness of voting patterns in that province. Since the Bloc Québécois's stunning electoral breakthrough in the 1993 federal election, the single most important factor motivating vote choice in federal elections in Québec—at least until the Bloc's equally stunning defeat in 2011—has been the sovereignty question (Blais et al. 1995; Nevitte et al. 2000). It is because electoral dynamics have been so different in the province that we devote a separate chapter to vote choice in Québec.

Voting in Québec in the four federal elections held between 2000 and 2008 was volatile (see Figure 10.1). No one could have foreseen the electoral upset that was to follow in 2011, but the volatility that was already apparent makes the outcome of that election not quite as surprising as might otherwise have been the case. In 2000, for the first time in three elections, the Bloc Québécois failed to win a plurality of the province's vote.[1] The Liberals edged out their sovereignist rivals. The 2004 election, by contrast, represented a remarkable victory for the Bloc: support for the party jumped by almost 10 percentage points.[2] But the Bloc's share of the vote declined gradually over the next two elections. Meanwhile, the Conservatives achieved a stunning breakthrough in 2006; they took the second largest vote share in the province, although they narrowly lost that position in the following contest. The major loser was the Liberal Party. The Liberal vote share was cut in half between 2000 and 2006. The modest recovery

Figure 10.1 *Party Vote Shares in Québec, 2000–2011*

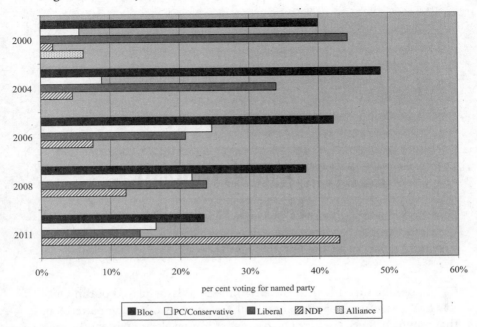

per cent voting for named party

■ Bloc □ PC/Conservative ■ Liberal ▨ NDP ▦ Alliance

in 2008 did little to restore the Liberals to their historic place of electoral strength. The NDP's performance gradually improved, but the party did not win a single seat until 2008.

What explains these dynamics? Given that the Bloc's main mission is to advance the cause of Québec sovereignty, one question to ask is whether the Bloc's changing electoral fortunes during this period reflected the ebb and flow of support for sovereignty. However, there was a crucial novel factor to consider in the 2004 and 2006 elections: the sponsorship scandal may have been responsible for the Bloc's surge and the Liberals' decline. In 2008, Liberal support crept back up a few points, and one possibility is that having a "native son" as party leader helped the Liberals put the sponsorship scandal behind them. The Liberals still lagged far behind the Bloc in the popular vote, though, and barely edged out the Conservatives. This raises the question of the extent to which the Conservatives and the Liberals were splitting the federalist vote. Alternatively, the Conservatives may have owed their new success in Québec not to federalists but to the "soft" centre of lukewarm sovereignists and lukewarm federalists. And a plausible explanation for the NDP's inability to achieve a comparable breakthrough might be that the party was competing with the Bloc for the same left-of-centre constituency, without the benefit of being seen as a credible defender of Québec's interests in Ottawa. But when Bloc support collapsed in 2011, the NDP was well positioned—ideologically, at least—to reap the benefit.

To sort out these possibilities, the Québec data are analyzed with the same multistage model of vote choice that was used in the earlier chapters. As before, the blocs of variables are ordered according to their proximity to the vote decision. Thus, social background characteristics are considered first. That bloc is followed by values, party identification, economic perceptions, issue positions, and leader evaluations.

The Linguistic Divide

Social background characteristics play out very differently in Québec. Language, not religion, has been the dominant social cleavage when it comes to vote choice. The linguistic divide between francophone and non-francophone voters has been evident in provincial elections for decades: francophones typically support the sovereignist party in greater numbers while non-francophones generally back the federalist option (Bélanger and Nadeau 2009; Blais and Nadeau 1984; Lemieux, Gilbert, and Blais 1970; Nadeau and Bélanger 1999). With the emergence of the Bloc Québécois, a similar pattern came to characterize voting in federal elections as well (Blais et al. 2002; Nevitte et al. 2000).

Language was by far the most powerful predictor of vote choice in the four elections held between 2000 and 2008. In three of those elections, the Bloc attracted fully half of the francophone vote (see Figure 10.2).[3] In 2006, its share of the francophone vote hit a high of 61 per cent. Meanwhile, the Liberal share of the francophone vote eroded. In 2000, one francophone in three voted Liberal. In 2004, that figure dropped to one in four. Worse was to follow. The Liberals hit an all-time low in 2006; a sign of things to come, they barely outpolled the NDP among francophone voters. The party did so poorly that francophones only just outnumbered non-francophones in the Liberal ranks (even though francophones comprise by far the largest group in the electorate). No other party experienced such a poor showing in any of the four elections. The Liberals' share of the francophone vote picked up a little in 2008, but the party gained so few additional voters that it is doubtful that any "native son" effect was at work. The main beneficiary of the Liberals' loss of support was the Conservative Party. Between the 2004 and 2006 elections, the Conservatives tripled their share of the francophone vote. The NDP doubled its share, though it still lagged behind the other three parties in 2008.

Figure 10.2 *The Francophone Vote*

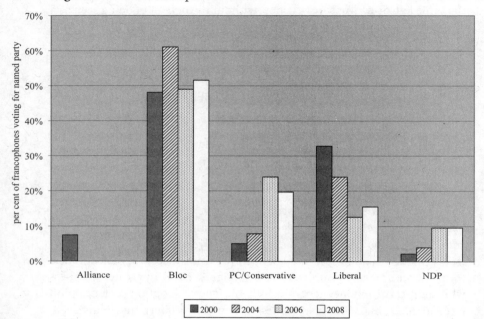

Non-francophones remained significantly more likely to vote Liberal through all four elections. However, even these voters became increasingly unhappy with the party. Between 2000 and 2008, the Liberal share of the non-francophone vote dropped 15 points. The major beneficiary was the Conservative Party in 2004 and 2006, but, in 2008, the NDP managed to outpoll the Conservatives among non-francophones, getting 20 per cent of the popular vote. However, the clearest and most consistent pattern among non-francophones was the Bloc's lack of appeal. The 2008 election was typical: other things being equal, the probability of voting for the Bloc was 44 points lower for voters with a first language other than French.[4]

Language was clearly the most important cleavage in Québec in all four elections, but age, education, gender, and type of community also influenced vote choice, albeit to a lesser extent. When the Bloc ran for the first time in the 1993 election, younger voters were significantly more likely to support the party (Blais et al. 1995, 29). This parallels the pattern of support for its cousin—the Parti Québécois (Bélanger and Nadeau 2009; Blais and Nadeau 1984; Lemieux, Gilbert, and Blais 1970; Nadeau and Bélanger 1999). However, that age effect disappeared in the 1997 and the 2000 elections (Blais et al. 2002; Nevitte et al. 2000). But, in 2004, much of the Bloc gain came from young adults: 64 per cent of those aged 18 to 34 voted for the party compared with 51 per cent of middle-aged voters and 44 per cent of those in the 55-and-over age group. This pattern persisted in the subsequent elections, though it was a good deal weaker in 2008. The Liberals, by contrast, did better among older groups, though their biggest loss of support occurred among those aged 55 and over. In 2006 and 2008, the NDP did best among younger voters while the Conservatives had their best showing among older voters.

Education also structured voting preferences. One group, in particular, behaved differently: voters with the lowest levels of formal education were more likely to reject the Bloc and to embrace the Liberals, though the relationships only reached statistical significance in the 2004 and 2006 elections.[5]

There is evidence of gender effects in all four federal elections held between 2000 and 2008, but they were typically quite modest. Women were less likely than men to vote for the Bloc in three out of four elections; in 2006, the gender gap was a substantial 11 points. And in some elections, women were somewhat more inclined to vote for the Liberals and somewhat less inclined to vote for the Conservatives or the NDP.

Finally, rural residents were somewhat more prone than their urban counterparts to choose the Bloc in 2000. The urban-rural divide in Bloc voting evaporated in the following three elections, but, in each of those elections, rural residents were more likely than city dwellers to prefer the Conservative Party. That pattern was different outside Québec where the Conservatives' gains reflected a narrowing of the urban-rural divide (see Chapter 2). The Liberal Party, meanwhile, did a little better among city dwellers than it did among rural residents, as in the rest of the country. That finding likely reflects the concentration of non-francophones on the Island of Montréal.

So social background characteristics did matter to vote choice in Québec. The impact of language on vote choice, however, was far greater than that of any of the other sociodemographic factors in the four elections held between 2000 and 2008. Apart from language, the political parties did not attract dramatically different voters. Rather, they tended to be a little more or a little less successful among certain groups.

Sovereignists, Federalists, and the "Soft Centre"

Opinion about sovereignty has consistently been the most important value dimension in shaping vote choice among Québec residents in federal and provincial elections alike (Bélanger and Nadeau 2009; Blais et al. 2002). Predictably, sovereignists were much more likely than federalists to vote

Table 10.1 *Basic Values and Beliefs, Québec, 2000–2008 (voters only)*

Year	Market Liberalism	Moral Traditionalism	Religiosity	Continentalism
2000	−0.12	−0.22	0.12	0.13
2004	−0.14	−0.26	0.01	0.02
2006	−0.16	−0.22	0.00	0.08
2008	−0.12	−0.32	−0.13	0.11

for the Bloc in all four elections held between 2000 and 2008. Other things being equal, the probability of a Bloc vote was 31 to 38 percentage points higher when a voter was strongly in favour of a sovereign Québec as compared to when a voter was unsure about sovereignty. The probability of a Liberal vote among that group was 10 to 24 points lower.

The Bloc is the only sovereignist option at the federal level. The Liberal Party, by contrast, has to compete for the votes of those who have federalist inclinations. The signal shift between 2000 and 2008 was that federalists in Québec gradually moved away from the Liberal Party. In 2000, 63 per cent of federalists voted Liberal, and just 10 per cent voted Alliance. By 2006, the Conservatives and the Liberals were neck and neck among federalists with 35 per cent each. And, in 2008, the Liberals were only marginally ahead of the Conservatives (33 per cent to 30 per cent). But focusing only on the sovereignist-federalist divide obscures a troubling trend for the Liberals. In both the 2006 and 2008 elections, the Conservatives easily outpolled the Liberals among "soft" federalists, those voters who were "somewhat opposed" to a sovereign Québec. Only among those who were strongly opposed to a sovereign Québec did the Liberals win the competition for the federalist vote.

Then there is the "soft" sovereignist side of the coin to consider. With the exception of the 2006 election, the Conservatives polled in the single digits among those who were only somewhat favourable to Québec sovereignty, whereas the Bloc's share of the "soft" federalist vote never fell below 28 per cent in any of the four elections. Why would the Bloc attract the support of more than one in four of those who considered themselves "soft" federalists? Part of the answer is to be found in perceptions about which party is the best when it comes to defending the interests of Québec. In 2008, two-thirds of "soft" federalists identified the Bloc as that party, as did almost half (48 per cent) of "hard" federalists.[6]

Sovereignty	Racial Outlook	Political Disaffection	Regional Alienation
−0.20	0.21	0.12	0.29
−0.09	0.38	0.08	0.18
−0.14	0.17	0.02	0.25
−0.05	0.20	0.01	0.16

Note: The column entries are mean values. All of the items run from −1 to +1. See Appendix B for details of question wording.

The Bloc's appeal to "soft" federalists may help to explain why changes in the Bloc's share of the vote between 2000 and 2008 did not necessarily coincide with shifts in support for sovereignty. True, the Bloc's strong showing in the 2004 election did coincide with an upswing in support for sovereignty (see Table 10.1).[7] And the drop in the Bloc's share of the vote coincided with a drop in support for sovereignty in 2006. But support for sovereignty increased in 2008, yet the Bloc's share of the vote fell to its lowest point in the four elections held between 2000 and 2008. The implication is clear: the Bloc's stunning defeat in 2011 should not necessarily be interpreted as sounding the death knell of sovereignty in Québec.

Sovereignty trumped other basic values and beliefs when it came to voting in the four federal elections held between 2000 and 2008, but other value dimensions mattered. Views about the appropriate balance between the state and the market mattered too. They played into the choice between the Bloc and the Conservatives in the 2004 and 2008 elections, as well as in the choice between the Conservatives and the NDP in 2006. Québec voters have been consistently more inclined than their counterparts in the rest of the country to support government intervention in the economy.[8] Predictably, the NDP did best among voters who favoured a strong role for the state, but the party was competing with the Bloc for the votes of these market sceptics, and, in these four elections, the NDP clearly lost this competition. As they did elsewhere, the Conservatives had their best showing among voters who favoured the free market.

Conventional wisdom has it that Québec is more open to alternative lifestyles and "progressive" views about gender roles. The CES data provide some support for that conclusion. In 2000, certainly, Québec voters scored noticeably lower on the moral traditionalism index than their counterparts elsewhere. That said, moral traditionalism was declining outside Québec (see Chapter 3), so the gap between Québec and the rest of the country in these outlooks narrowed significantly between 2000 and 2008. In three of the four elections, the NDP attracted more votes among those who scored low on the moral traditionalism index. And, like the Alliance in 2000, the Conservatives attracted the support of those who endorsed traditional social roles and norms. The impact of moral traditionalism, however, was only statistically significant in 2006, and, in 2008, it was the Liberals who attracted significantly more support from moral traditionalists. This Québec-specific finding stands in striking contrast to the party's appeal to socially liberal voters in the rest of the country (see Chapter 3).

In the 2008 election, the Bloc was clearly the magnet for moral liberals. Other things being equal, the probability of voting for the Bloc was 25 points higher among those who scored very low on the moral traditionalism index than it was among those who scored very high. Social liberals easily outnumbered moral traditionalists, and thus the impact of this value dimension on vote shares was significant. In 2008, the Bloc gained 8.5 points as a result of its appeal to social liberals. But the NDP also appealed to socially liberal voters, netting almost 2 points on average in the three elections held between 2000 and 2006. The parties that appealed to traditionalists lost out: 2 points for the Alliance in 2000 and the Conservatives in 2006, and 5 points for the Liberals in 2008.

Quebecers' orientations toward continentalism have traditionally differed from those in the rest of the country (Inglehart, Nevitte, and Basáñez 1996), but the CES data suggest that this may no longer be the case. The balance of opinion favoured a closer relationship with the United States. And, like their counterparts outside Québec, those who favoured a closer relationship were significantly less likely to vote NDP. That finding is consistent across the four elections, and it worked to reduce the party's share of the vote. On balance, however, continentalism was not an important factor in vote choice. The only exception was in 2006 when it boosted the Conservative and Liberal vote shares by 1 point each at the expense of both the Bloc and the NDP.

It comes as little surprise to discover that Québec voters were fairly dissatisfied with politics and politicians in 2000 and 2004. Disaffected voters were more likely to vote Alliance in 2000 and Conservative in 2004 and 2006. The Liberals bore the brunt of that dissatisfaction in all three elections. It cost the party over 1.5 points in 2000 and just over 1 point in 2004. Voters were less disaffected in 2006, however, so the impact of dissatisfaction on the Liberal vote share was minimal. Dissatisfaction with the government's performance and with politics and politicians generally works to the disadvantage of incumbents. The evidence points to a similar pattern in Québec. The Liberals were the incumbents going into all three of the elections between 2000 and 2006, but, in 2008, it was the Conservatives who were in power, having formed a minority government after the 2006 election. And, on that occasion, political disaffection worked against the Conservatives. The same pattern holds in the rest of Canada, but, in the Québec case, the Bloc not the NDP attracted the protest vote. The scale of these effects, though, was quite modest, and the impact on vote shares was trivial.

Voters in Québec were more likely than their counterparts elsewhere to think that their province was treated worse than others by the federal government. This sense of regional alienation boosted the Bloc's share of the vote by over 2 points in 2000 and by almost 3 points in 2006. These two elections coincided with the periods when levels of regional alienation were highest in the province.

Finally, there are some noteworthy findings regarding values and beliefs that appeared to have no effect or only a limited one on the vote. Two values had no significant impact on vote choice in Québec—personal religiosity and racial outlooks. Between 2000 and 2008, the proportion of voters who said that religion was very or somewhat important in their lives declined. This trajectory reinforces the image that Québec is becoming an increasingly secular society. But the perception that Quebecers are less open to racial diversity receives no support whatsoever. Quite the reverse: in all four elections, Québec voters were much more likely than others to favour doing more for racial minorities. However, neither personal religiosity nor racial outlooks had any appreciable impact on vote choice in Québec.

When it comes to values and beliefs, the overriding importance of views about sovereignty is apparent. No other value or belief came even close to having a comparable effect on individual vote choice or party vote shares in the four elections held between 2000 and 2008. Views about sovereignty had a consistently strong impact in all four elections. In 2000, the Liberals could count on attracting the support of the majority of the federalist votes. After that election, the party's diminishing appeal to federalist voters is clearly a key part of the explanation for the declining electoral fortunes of the Liberal Party.

Partisanship and Vote Choice

In Quebec as elsewhere in Canada, vote choices between 2000 and 2008 do not make sense unless the role of partisan loyalties is taken into account. Substantial numbers of Quebecers thought of themselves as Liberals or Bloquistes, and these loyalties had a powerful impact on the way they voted. The problem for the Liberals was that the number of Liberal partisans declined with every election. The number of Bloc partisans, by

Figure 10.3 *The Distribution of Partisanship in Québec*

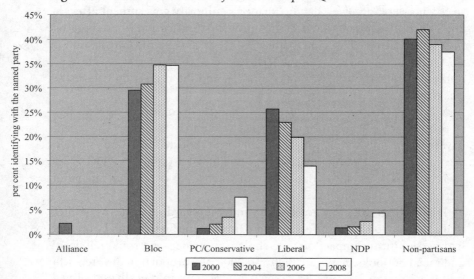

Note: Those who identified very strongly or fairly strongly with a party in the campaign survey are considered partisans.

contrast, grew (see Figure 10.3).[9] The Liberals lost partisans in the rest of the country too, but the losses in Québec were much larger. The evidence is truly striking; the Liberals lost almost half of their partisans in the province. In 2000, one Quebecer in four was a Liberal partisan; the Liberals had almost as many partisans as the Bloc. By 2008, only one Quebecer in seven identified with the party; the Bloc had two and a half times as many partisans as the Liberals.

The Bloc was not the only party to reap rewards from the Liberals' partisan collapse. The Conservatives and the NDP both made some gains over the same period. That the Conservative Party's partisan core experienced much less growth than that party's share of the vote signifies the fragility of Conservative gains in Québec. In contrast to the rest of the country (see Chapter 4), Québec experienced only a small net decline in the number of non-partisans.

Liberal partisans in Québec, as elsewhere, became much less likely to vote for the party between 2000 and 2008 (see Figure 10.4). In 2000, Liberal partisans were as loyal to the party as Bloc partisans were to the Bloc. By 2006, though, barely two Liberals in three were actually voting Liberal. Bloc partisans, by contrast, were much more loyal to their party. Liberal partisans

Figure 10.4 *Vote Choice by Campaign Partisanship in Québec*

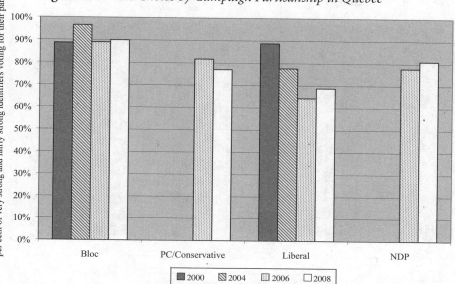

per cent of very strong and fairly strong identifiers voting for their party

■ 2000   ◩ 2004   ▦ 2006   ☐ 2008

Note: There were too few NDP and Conservative partisans in 2000 and 2004 for percentages to be meaningful.

were somewhat more loyal in 2008 than they were in 2006; there were just fewer of them. There were even fewer Conservative and NDP partisans. They showed more loyalty to their party than their Liberal counterparts, but they were still more likely than Bloc partisans to vote for another party.

The Liberals' decline in Québec is also reflected in their diminishing appeal to non-partisans (see Figure 10.5). In 2000, the Bloc and the Liberals finished neck and neck in this key segment of the electorate. Each attracted the votes of more than one non-partisan in three. By 2008, however, only one non-partisan in four was voting Liberal. In 2004, the Bloc won almost half of the non-partisan vote, and the party mobilized almost every Bloquiste to vote BQ (see Figure 10.4). But the party was unable to replicate that measure of success in the following election. In 2006, it was the Conservatives who did by far the best among non-partisans, and they did so at the expense of the Bloc as well as the Liberals. The Conservative share fell in 2008, but the party still managed to do as well among non-partisans as the Liberals.

Partisan identification confers a notable advantage on parties fortunate enough to attract the loyalties of numerous voters. But a large partisan core is not enough. To win, a party must mobilize its partisans to vote for the

Figure 10.5 *The Vote Choices of Non-partisans in Québec*

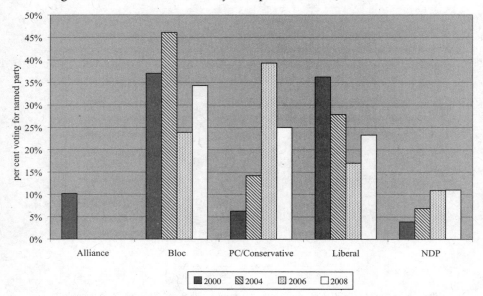

party and also appeal to those who lack a party affiliation. In Québec, as in the rest of the country, the Liberals failed on both counts. They lost partisans, they failed to mobilize those partisans who stayed with the party, and they failed to appeal to many non-partisans. If there was one feature of the Liberal landscape that qualified as good news it was that many of the Liberals who voted against the party still considered themselves Liberal partisans when they were re-interviewed after the 2008 election. Twenty-seven per cent of those who identified with the party in the post-election survey reported that they had voted for a different party yet still thought of themselves as Liberals. That finding reinforces once again an important conclusion (see Chapter 4): party identification does not necessarily travel with the vote.

The Economy

Outside Québec, economic considerations had a minor impact on vote choice in the four elections held between 2000 and 2008 (see Chapter 5). These considerations do not explain why the Liberals were able to dominate in the 2000 election, and they are even less help in accounting for the Liberal decline in the next three elections. The very same findings also apply to Québec. Economic conditions and perceptions have influenced elec-

Figure 10.6 *Economic Perceptions in Québec*

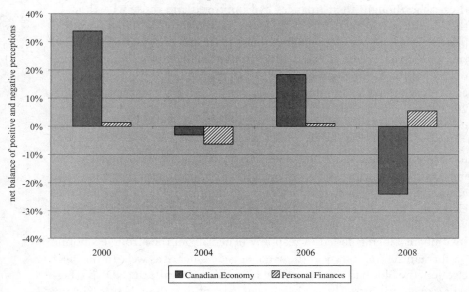

tion results in Québec at both the provincial (Bélanger and Nadeau 2009; Guérin and Nadeau 1995) and federal (Crête and Simard 1984; Nevitte et al. 2000) levels. They also played a role in these four elections, but their impact on the outcomes can be described as only modest.

Quebecers had more positive perceptions of how the country's economy had been doing in 2000 than did other Canadians (see Figure 10.6). Indeed, the net balance of opinion was very positive: close to half of all Québec voters (46 per cent) believed that the economy had improved over the previous 12 months. Quebecers were much less optimistic about the state of the economy four years later. A little more than half saw no change, and the others were more or less equally divided between the positive and the negative camps. They were more positive in 2006, though perceptions were less rosy than they were in the rest of the country. Predictably, the most negative perceptions emerged during the 2008 election at the onset of the financial crisis. In 2008, voters who thought the state of the economy had deteriorated (34 per cent) outnumbered by almost three to one those who deemed it had improved (12 per cent).

Voters' perceptions of their own financial situation, by contrast, fluctuated within a much narrower range. In all four elections, almost two-thirds of voters reported that their personal finances had stayed about the same over the past year. The rest were more or less evenly divided between those who thought their finances had improved and those who thought their finances had deteriorated. Negative perceptions slightly outweighed positive ones in 2004; in 2008, the positive slightly outweighed the negative. Given that so many voters thought that their personal finances were unchanged, it comes as no surprise to find that perceptions of their financial situation had little impact on vote choice. The only exception was in 2004 when voters who thought that they were personally worse off were more likely to support the Conservative Party.

Assessments of the country's economy were more consistently linked to voting preferences. In 2000, the Canadian Alliance and the NDP had more success in attracting voters who were unhappy with the state of the economy. These voters, however, were very much in the minority in that election. The failure of both parties to appeal to voters who had a rosier view of the economy cost them about 1 point each. More important, the incumbent Liberals failed to reap any benefit from the strong economic performance. The story was the same outside Québec as well. In the 2004 election, the Bloc had more success with pessimists while the NDP did better among optimists. The net balance of perceptions, though, was trivially small, so the repercussions for vote shares were minimal.

In the 2006 and 2008 elections, these dynamics changed; the economy had a more decisive impact on vote choice. Significantly, these economic considerations worked to differentiate support for the two main federalist parties. In 2006, Canada's economic performance was judged positively, the Liberals were governing, and they reaped a reward at the Conservatives' expense. If the economy had not mattered, the Conservatives' vote share would have been at least 2 points higher, and the Liberals would have lost 1.5 points. In 2008, the tables were turned. The economy soured, and the Conservatives, who were in power, paid the price. People with negative evaluations rallied more toward the Liberals, whereas the incumbent Conservatives were more successful among the smaller group with positive appraisals. As a result, the Liberals gained almost 1.5 points while the Conservatives dropped just over 1 point.

Economic perceptions affected vote choice in Québec during the last decade, but the effects were small regardless of whether the times were good or bad. Neither the 2000 economic boom nor the 2008 financial collapse had major electoral repercussions. But, in Québec as in the rest of Canada, the Liberals would have suffered worse defeats in both 2006 and 2008 had they not benefited from positive economic perceptions in 2006 and negative perceptions two years later.

Figure 10.7 *Perceptions of the Sponsorship Scandal in Québec*

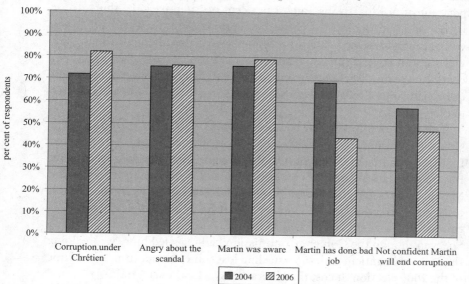

The Issues

The most influential issue in Québec in any of the four elections held between 2000 and 2008 was the sponsorship scandal. In 2004, many voters believed that there had been corruption when Jean Chrétien was prime minister, and they were angry about the sponsorship scandal (see Figure 10.7). Quebecers were more inclined than people in the rest of the country to believe that Paul Martin knew about the scandal before he became prime minister. And the small minority who gave him the benefit of the doubt typically thought that he should have known (76 per cent). Many voters thought that he had done a poor job of handling the scandal and lacked confidence that he could prevent a similar scandal in the future.

The Liberals paid the electoral price for these negative perceptions in Québec as elsewhere. The more negative voters' perceptions of the scandal, the more likely they were to punish the Liberals by voting for other parties. The scandal ended up costing the Liberal Party almost 7 percentage points in 2004. All of the other parties gained at the Liberals' expense, particularly the federalist ones. The Liberals might have paid a higher price were it not for the fact that many voters reacted to the scandal through the prism of their party attachments. Only 28 per cent of Liberal identifiers could be characterized as being very critical of the scandal and its handling (as indicated by a score above +.25 on the scandal index) compared with 57 per cent of non-partisans and 77 per cent of Bloquistes. In short, those voters who had the most negative perceptions were the least likely to be voting Liberal anyway. Voters' perceptions were also filtered through their views about sovereignty: sovereignists were much more critical (70 per cent) than federalists (44 per cent). That said, federalists were nonetheless quite critical too, reflecting perhaps a sense that "their" side had resorted to dirty tricks.

The sponsorship scandal had less impact in 2006. In the wake of the Gomery Commission hearings, an even larger number of voters believed that there had been corruption under the previous Liberal government. But these negative perceptions were tempered by more charitable views of Martin's role (see Figure 10.7). Québec voters were more likely than others to report correctly that the Gomery report had exonerated Martin: two-thirds knew that the report said Martin was not to blame for the scandal. So, even though the Gomery Commission had revealed more wrongdoing than was first anticipated, the issue had lost some momentum by the time of the 2006 election. It cost the Liberals only a little over 1 point.

Other issues mattered in Québec too, though which issues mattered and how much they mattered varied from one election to the next. In 2000, issues were not very salient. In this respect, at least, the election played out quite similarly in Québec as in the rest of the country (see Chapter 6). Indeed, there were only two issues that made more than a trivial difference to the parties' vote shares. The first was defence spending. Québec voters who favoured cuts to defence spending were more likely to vote Bloc and less likely to vote Liberal. The balance of opinion favoured cuts (38 per cent) over increased spending (11 per cent), so the effect was to boost the Bloc vote share by almost 1.5 points, mostly at the Liberals' expense. The other issue that mattered to Quebecers was health care. Indeed, this was the one issue that mattered in all four elections. In 2000, voters who favoured more health spending were much more likely to vote for the Bloc or the Liberals. A massive majority (90 per cent) of voters favoured increased spending, and the issue gave the Bloc a 6-point boost and the Liberals just over 3 points. These votes came mostly at the NDP's expense.

In 2004, the vast majority of voters (88 per cent) once again wanted to see increased government expenditures on health care, and, once again, those voters divided their votes between the Bloc and the Liberals. On this occasion, both parties gained about 5 points each while the Conservatives lost out along with the NDP. In Québec as in the rest of the country, the electoral consequences were clear: the health care issue helped to save the Liberals from defeat by offsetting the impact of the scandal. Clearly, the Conservatives benefited from the scandal. And they might have gained more votes but for the issue of tax cuts. Voters who wanted personal income taxes to be cut were more likely to prefer the Bloc or the Liberals to the Conservatives. That position cost the Conservatives 2 points. The other issue that cost the Conservatives votes was the war in Iraq. The main beneficiary was the NDP, which did particularly well among voters who believed steering clear of engagement in the second Persian Gulf War was a good decision. The vast majority of voters (94 per cent) shared this view, and it ended up costing the Liberals some votes as well (even though the decision had been made by the Chrétien government).

In the 2006 election, health-care spending was again a top priority for voters. In this election, however, it was the Conservatives who attracted the support of those who favoured increased spending and the Liberals who ended up being the net losers. Indeed, that issue goes some distance toward explaining the Conservatives' breakthrough; it garnered the party as many as 6 points, almost entirely at the Liberals' expense. The only other issue that had more than a trivial effect on party vote shares was gun control. Voters who thought that only the military and the police should be allowed to have guns were more inclined to favour the Liberals over the Conservatives. In Québec, 43 per cent of voters strongly agreed and another 26 per cent somewhat agreed with that position, and that distribution of opinion helped the Liberals, boosting the party's vote by over 1.5 points.

Issues were more important determinants of vote choices in the 2008 election, but, on that occasion, the most influential issue was the environment. The Liberals put all their eggs into the environment basket, but the gamble did not pay off. Opinion on the green shift was divided; a sizeable minority (39 per cent) accepted the Conservative argument that it would hurt the economy; only a bare majority (51 per cent) disagreed. Those disagreeing with the Conservative argument were more likely to vote Liberal, but the party only netted about .5 of a point. The winner on the environment was the Bloc. It "out-greened" the Liberals on an even more important issue: spending on the environment. The Bloc did better than any other party among the 74 per cent of Québec voters who wanted to increase environmental expenditures, and, as a result, it increased its share of the vote by over 5.5 points. Unlike in the rest of the country, in Québec, the Liberals were unable to capitalize on this desire for increased spending on the environment, though the Conservatives were the bigger losers on this issue.

Both the Liberals and the Conservatives ended up losing on all three of the issues that mattered most in the 2008 election. Health spending was once again a salient factor in voters' choice of party. The Bloc was typically the party of choice for those who favoured increased spending on health, and this netted the party well over 3 points. The NDP also had some appeal to this constituency. In striking contrast to the previous election, the 2008 election proved the Conservatives to be the biggest losers on the issue of health spending: had views about health spending not mattered, the party's share of the vote would have been over 4 points higher. The Conservatives were also the biggest losers on the issue of defence spending. Voters who wanted cuts in defence spending were more likely to vote Bloc. While the Bloc gained almost 4 points in consequence, the Conservatives lost 2.5 points.

The war in Afghanistan was another issue that helped the Bloc. Fifty-seven per cent of Québec voters were opposed to having Canadian troops in Afghanistan, and they were more likely to opt for the Bloc. The issue, however, carried little weight in voters' choice of party, so the net gains for the Bloc were correspondingly modest—less than 1.5 points.

The Conservatives' promise to cut spending on the arts generated a good deal of controversy in Québec, but the impact on the parties' vote shares was negligible. Voters who opposed the proposed cuts were significantly less likely to vote Conservative, but this did little damage to the party's share of the vote.

Considered together, it is clear that very few issues had consistent leverage across all four elections. Health care was the single exception. It was the only issue that consistently influenced the parties' fortunes, but the issue played differently from one election to the next. In Québec, the repercussions of the sponsorship scandal were essentially confined to a single election. And other issues that did sporadically emerge had a limited impact on the electoral bottom line—the parties' vote shares.

The Leadership Factor

Evaluations of party leaders have been an important determinant of vote choice in Québec both in provincial and federal elections (Bélanger and Nadeau 2009; Lemieux, Gilbert, and Blais 1970; Nevitte et al. 2000). Lucien Bouchard's personal popularity was a critical ingredient in the Bloc's historic electoral breakthrough in 1993. However, his successor, Gilles Duceppe, was burdened by a serious image problem that cost the party a substantial number of votes in 1997 (Nevitte et al. 2000). Jean Charest's personal appeal in that election, by contrast, produced a significant electoral dividend; it boosted the Progressive Conservatives' vote share a substantial 12 points.

The Conservatives' breakthrough in 2006, though, had little to do with their leader's popularity (see Figure 10.8). Indeed, Harper's average ratings were negative, and they were no higher in 2006 (or 2008) than they

Figure 10.8 *Evaluations of Party Leaders in Québec*

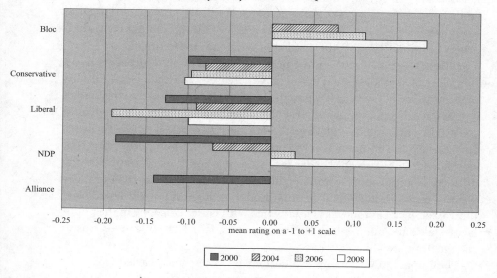

mean rating on a -1 to +1 scale

■ 2000 ▨ 2004 ▦ 2006 ☐ 2008

had been in 2004. Harper rated somewhat higher in Québec than Stockwell Day had in 2000, but his personal popularity was no greater than Joe Clark's had been. The problem for Harper was the lingering perception that he was just too extreme. Fifty-six per cent of voters agreed with that assessment in 2004; little had changed by 2008 (58 per cent). Equally problematical, 63 per cent of voters endorsed the view that Harper had a hidden agenda in 2008.[10]

The Liberal Leader's ratings were hardly any better. Jean Chrétien was not popular in his home province. When asked which leader they would describe as arrogant, almost half (48 per cent) named Chrétien, whose role in the patriation of the Constitution was controversial, to say the least. Paul Martin's ratings were slightly better in 2004 in spite of the sponsorship scandal. But when voters were asked to rate each leader's honesty, Martin was the only leader to score below the neutral point (4.5 on a 0 to 10 scale). He was more unpopular by the time the 2006 election came around, perhaps reflecting the "fallen heroes" syndrome (Clarke et al. 1991; Gidengil and Blais 2007; A. Turcotte 2001). People rated Martin to be the least honest and the least competent of any of the four party leaders. And there was a widespread perception (shared by 77 per cent of respondents) that all he cared about was staying in power. Stéphane Dion fared better in 2008, but his ratings still hovered in negative territory, and he was no more popular than Stephen Harper. That said, perceptions of Dion's leadership were less negative in Québec than they were in the rest of the country (see Chapter 7): "only" one voter in two (47 per cent) agreed with the statement that Dion was a weak leader. But Québec voters were more likely (43 per cent) than others to think that all Dion cared about was the environment.

Gilles Duceppe was the most popular leader among Quebecers in all four elections. His personal popularity increased with each election. This made him one of the very few party leaders in Canada to escape the "fallen heroes" syndrome, though, as the 2011 election was to prove, he would eventually succumb. In 2004 and 2006, voters were asked to rate the leaders' honesty and competence. Duceppe scored highest on both traits. But, significantly, it was NDP Leader Jack Layton whose ratings improved the most. His ratings moved from slightly negative territory in 2004 to fairly positive territory in 2008. A popular leader, though, is not always an electoral asset. Jack Layton was virtually tied with Gilles Duceppe in the popularity stakes in 2008, yet the NDP came in fourth. That, of course, was to change dramatically in 2011.

The impact of leadership evaluations on vote choice varied from one election to the next. Leadership was not much of a factor in the 2000 election. It mattered more in 2004, at least for the two main federalist parties. Harper helped the Conservatives while Martin hurt the Liberals. Had leadership not mattered, the Conservative vote share would have been 4 points lower. This gain came mostly at the Liberals' expense. Duceppe's growing personal popularity did not help the Bloc in 2004, but, in 2006, his increased personal appeal produced a net gain of almost 6 points. Meanwhile, Layton's improved ratings netted his party 3 points, and those came mostly at the expense of the Conservatives. Had leadership not mattered, the Conservative vote share might have been as many as 7.5 points higher in 2006. Even Conservative voters were lukewarm about the party's leader, giving Harper an average rating of only .16 (on a −1 to +1 scale).

Leadership was even more important in 2008. On this occasion, it was the Liberal Party that lost votes. Dion was not very popular even among those who voted for his party. Liberal voters gave him an average rating of only .16. This lack of appeal may have cost the party as many as 11 points. The major beneficiary was the Conservative Party: but for the leadership factor, that party's vote share could have been as many as 8 points lower. The NDP, meanwhile, gained almost 3 points at the Liberals' expense. This time, Duceppe's personal popularity did not net his party many more votes.

Strategic Considerations
Like their counterparts in the rest of the country, Québec voters were apt to overstate their preferred party's chances of winning, and most voted

"sincerely" regardless of "their" party's perceived chances of success in the local riding. But this was not always the case: in 2000, voters who liked the NDP or the Progressive Conservatives best were just as pessimistic about their party's prospects as other voters. Despite their pessimism, though, only half of them opted to vote for one of the other parties. The NDP's chances were not rated much better in 2004, and the party was even more vulnerable to strategic defections. Significantly, though, as the party's vote share increased, voters who liked the party best were less willing to switch. Indeed, the pattern was clear: the more competitive the party, the less vulnerable it was to strategic defections. For example, when the Liberals hit bottom in 2006, they were more vulnerable to strategic defections. The same applied to the Conservatives before their breakthrough. As the NDP suddenly became competitive in 2011, this pattern may well have worked to the party's advantage.

Predictably, the Bloc proved to be the least susceptible to strategic defections. The 2006 election was the single exception to that rule: in 2006, almost a third of voters who liked the Bloc best but thought it had no chance of winning in their riding voted for another party. Half of these vote switchers opted for the Conservatives. Strategic defections, it seems, might well have contributed to the Conservatives' breakthrough in those ridings where voters thought the party had a chance of winning.[11] But, in 2006, the vast majority of voters who liked the Bloc best believed that it had a good chance of winning the local race.

The 2004 and the 2006 elections both had a relatively high level of strategic voting in Québec. Fully 9 per cent of voters may have switched parties because they thought their preferred party had no chance of winning their riding. In both elections, the three federalist parties lost votes as a result of this type of strategic calculation. In 2000 and 2008, the level of strategic voting in Québec was similar to that in the rest of the country: around 6 per cent of voters did not vote for their preferred political party but voted instead for a party with a better chance of winning. In 2000, all of the parties were affected, but, in 2008, most of the strategic voters were voters who liked the NDP the best of any party.

The other strategic consideration potentially in play in the 2004, 2006, and 2008 elections was the prospect of minority government. It is reasonable to suppose that such an outcome might have helped the Bloc; the party's ability to leverage policies that benefit Québec, after all, should be greater when the governing party lacks a majority in parliament. Recall that even federalist voters considered the Bloc to be the best party when it came to defending the interests of Québec. It is somewhat surprising, then, that the distribution of opinion about minority government in 2004

Figure 10.9 *Views about Minority Government in Québec*

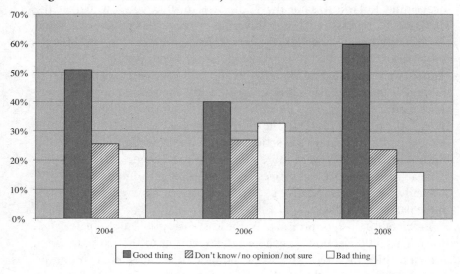

Good thing   Don't know / no opinion / not sure   Bad thing

in Québec was indistinguishable from that in the rest of the country (see Figure 10.9). The view that minority governments are a good thing outweighed the view that they are a bad thing by a margin of two to one. However, Québec voters were more likely than their counterparts elsewhere to re-evaluate the merits of minority governments. In 2004, one in four Québec voters thought of minority governments as a bad thing. By 2006, that figure rose to one in three. In the rest of the country, voters' views just became more ambivalent. Opinion shifted again in 2008. Opinion became much more favourable in Québec, with 60 per cent of the province's voters sharing the view that minority governments are a good thing and only 16 per cent holding a negative opinion.

In all three elections, voters who thought of minority governments as a good thing were much more likely to vote Bloc. This is hardly surprising given that the Bloc stood to gain from a minority outcome. Equally predictably, the Liberals fared best in 2004 among voters who disliked minority governments. In both 2006 and 2008, though, it was the Conservatives who did better with these voters. These patterns highlight the relationship between partisan considerations and views about minority government, but there is little evidence that these views had much *independent* impact on voters' choice of party. When voters confronted the prospect of a minority government for the first time in 2004, their views had no independent effect on their vote.[12] In the next election, voters who thought minority governments were a good thing were more likely to choose the Bloc over the Liberals and the Conservatives alike, but the impact on the parties' vote shares was negligible. There was a similar pattern in 2008, but the effects fell short of statistical significance. Once we take into account other motivations, we find that views about minority government had little traction. Voters who liked minority government were inclined to vote for the Bloc anyway. Conversely, those who disliked minority governments had other reasons not to vote for one of the federalist parties.

Distinct Dynamics

As the 2011 election once again demonstrated, elections play out in distinctive ways in Québec. Language has a much more powerful impact on vote choice in Québec than does any other single social background characteristic elsewhere in the country. And no other part of the country has a value divide that even approaches the impact that the sovereignty question has had in Québec. It is not possible to make sense of vote choice in Québec without taking these two fundamental factors into account. Precisely how these factors play out in any given election, though, is moderated by shorter-term influences.

There were some dramatic changes in the parties' vote shares in both the 2004 and 2006 elections. The sponsorship scandal pummelled the Liberals in 2004. Two years later, the Liberals' share of the vote declined still further but then so did that of the Bloc Québécois. The 2006 election marked a major Conservative breakthrough in the province. The sponsorship scandal played a surprisingly small role in explaining these dynamics. What mattered in Québec was health care. In 2000 and 2004, both the Bloc and the Liberals appealed to voters who wanted more spending on health care. In 2006, there was a complete reversal. This time, the Conservatives attracted the support of voters wanting more spending on health, and the previous winners were now losers. The message is clear: issues *can* matter a good deal. Whether and when they matter and how much they matter, though, depends very much on the electoral context. In 2000, issues were hardly a decisive factor in the election outcome.

Assertions that elections hinge on the popularity of the party leaders may make good copy and help to sell newspapers, but they do not accurately characterize voting behaviour in Québec during this period any more than they do in the rest of Canada. Voters' evaluations of the party leaders certainly influenced their choice of party in all four of the elections held between 2000 and 2008, but these evaluations had what might be characterized as an important impact only on the outcome of the 2008 election. Had leadership not mattered in Québec in 2008, the Conservative Party would have fallen far behind the Liberals.

Between 2000 and 2008, the single most constant and powerful theme reverberating through Quebecers' voting behaviour continued to be the question of sovereignty. In all four elections, the best predictor of vote choice was a voter's opinion about whether Québec should become an independent country or not. In 2000, the Liberals were the only viable federalist option. By 2008, they could only count on the votes of committed federalists; the Conservatives outpolled the Liberals among "soft" federalists. The ability of the Conservatives to capitalize on their 2006 breakthrough, however, was constrained by their lack of appeal to "soft" sovereignists. The Bloc, meanwhile, was able to attract enough "soft" federalists to win a plurality of the Québec vote in three of the four elections. If the distribution of opinion about sovereignty sets the essential parameters of electoral competition in the province, the parties' electoral prospects within those parameters hinge very much on their ability to attract "soft" federalists and "soft" sovereignists—the "soft centre." In 2011, the Bloc may well have been reduced to its "hard" sovereignist core.

Notes

1 The Bloc did manage to improve slightly over its weak performance in the 1997 election. In that election, its share of the vote plummeted from 49.5 per cent to 37.9 per cent, and it lost almost a quarter of the votes that it had received in the 1993 election.

2 The party did as well in 2004 as it had in its very first contest in 1993, under the leadership of the charismatic Lucien Bouchard.

3 A francophone was defined as someone whose first language was French. For the few voters who did not answer the question about first language, the language of the interview was used as a proxy.

4 This estimate is derived from a simulation based on a multistage bloc-recursive model similar to the one used for the other chapters (see Chapter 1). The choice set consisted of Bloc, Conservative, Liberal, and NDP.

5 Educational attainment, however, does not distinguish the clienteles of the two main provincial parties (Bélanger and Nadeau 2009; Blais and Nadeau 1984; Nadeau and Bélanger 1999).

6 The role of perceptions of competence with respect to defending Québec's interests is consistent with the valence model (see Chapter 1), but the fact that many voters did *not* vote for the party that they perceived to be the best on this issue also underlines the limitations of the model.

7 There are at least two possible explanations for this surge in support for sovereignty. One possibility, proposed by Maurice Pinard (2005), is that support for sovereignty increases in Québec when the provincial Liberals are in power, when there is a good deal of dissatisfaction with the government, and when there is no referendum in sight. All three conditions were in place in 2004. A second possibility is that support for sovereignty increased in response to the sponsorship program scandal.

8 Note, though, that the average score on the market liberalism index was not as tilted toward the side of government intervention as we might expect, given the strong role assumed by the Québec state since the Quiet Revolution.

9 As explained in Chapter 4, we only count people as partisans if their party identification is very strong or fairly strong.

10 In 2008, random half samples received one or other of the two statements.

11 The number of respondents in these ridings was too small to allow for any firm conclusion on this point.

12 These conclusions are based on the multistage vote model. Views about minority government were added as a final bloc.

CHAPTER ELEVEN

THE SHIFTING CONTOURS OF CANADIAN ELECTIONS

The four federal elections held between 2000 and 2008 witnessed dramatic changes in the parties' electoral fortunes and set the scene for the even more dramatic shifts in 2011. At the start of the period, the Canadian public had delivered, for the first time in Canadian history, three consecutive Liberal majorities in a row. By the end of the period, Canadian voters had delivered three consecutive minority governments in a row. In 2011, the Conservatives finally succeeded in winning a majority, the Liberals were reduced to third-party status with only 34 seats in the House of Commons, the NDP assumed the role of official opposition for the first time ever, and the Bloc was reduced to a handful of seats. These striking shifts raise obvious questions: Did the four elections held between 2000 and 2008 precipitate a fundamental shifting of the tectonic plates? And, if so, what were the major fault lines, and what forces propelled such a shift?

Explaining Changing Party Fortunes: Outside Québec

The Liberal Decline

The analyses in the preceding chapters suggest that the sponsorship scandal was the critical fault line that destabilized the electoral landscape between 2000 and 2008. It clearly shook voters' attachments to the "natural party of government." Voters fled the Liberal Party in large numbers in 2004. The reverberations of the scandal in the 2006 election kept many of those voters from returning to the party, and other erstwhile Liberals joined them.

Many Catholics left the Liberal fold, and so did members of union households. Those defections inflicted severe electoral damage on the Liberals.

The Liberals did not just lose voters between 2000 and 2008; they also lost partisans. The distinction between voters and partisans is important. Partisanship is not just an affective attachment to a particular party; it also works as a cognitive device that encourages supporters to evaluate the leaders and the issues of the day through a partisan prism. Analyses of voting behaviour in both the 1997 and 2000 federal elections revealed that the Liberals had far more partisans than any of the other federal parties (Blais et al. 2002; Nevitte et al. 2000). The Liberal advantage was certainly not unassailable. The point, rather, was that the Liberals' advantage going into those campaigns was so great that it was as if they started the 100-metre dash with a 20-metre head start. Much of that advantage had disappeared by 2004. The main reason for the loss of the head start was the merger of the Alliance and the Progressive Conservatives, which gave the new Conservative Party almost as many partisans as the Liberals. The absolute size of the Liberal partisan core did not change much between 2004 and 2006. But, by 2008, the impact of the sponsorship scandal on the Liberals' partisan core was clearly evident.

By then, the Liberal Party was under siege on multiple fronts. Not only had the Liberal advantage disappeared as the party's partisan core shrank, but even those Liberals who remained in the partisan ranks were less loyal to the party than were their counterparts eight years earlier. Worse yet, the Liberals had lost their appeal to non-partisans. Thus, by 2008, the Liberals had lost both the long-term and short-term electoral advantages they once had enjoyed. All of these shifts, to a lesser or greater extent, could be put at the door of the scandal.

Meanwhile, there was erosion on other fronts. As a result, the Liberals found themselves increasingly competing with the NDP for the same left-of-centre constituency. By 2008, they were clearly losing out to the NDP in the competition for the votes of those who favoured a stronger role for governments and more distant ties to the United States. They had also lost their traditional advantage on health care to the NDP. The Liberals still enjoyed a competitive edge, though, among voters who rejected traditional definitions of morality.

The Liberals' problems were compounded by the unpopularity of the party's leaders. Paul Martin was not very popular in 2004, and his popularity declined in 2006. The low point in this series of elections came in 2008, when Stéphane Dion recorded the lowest rating of any leader in the four elections held between 2000 and 2008. Clearly, though, the party's problems ran much deeper than simply having an unpopular leader, and the 2008 election proved to be but a foreshadowing of the defeat that was inflicted on the Liberals in 2011.

The Rise of the Conservatives

When voters defect from one major party in droves, as was the case with the Liberals, it is reasonable to expect that the primary beneficiary of these defections would be the other major party, especially in two-party dominant political systems. The Conservative Party was well positioned to reap the benefits of an unravelling Liberal Party on at least two fronts. The merger of the Alliance and the Progressive Conservatives meant that the Conservative Party could speak as a united right with one voice. And Stephen Harper was an uncontested leader around whom the Conservative faithful could rally. In contrast to the Liberals, Conservatives experienced little residual bitterness after the leadership race; infighting did not plague the party or dog the election campaigns.

The shrinking of the Liberals' partisan core did indeed work to the electoral benefit of the Conservatives. In 2004, the Conservative Party had almost as many partisans as the Alliance and Progressive Conservatives combined, and that partisan core continued to expand over the course of the next two elections. By 2008, Conservative identifiers outnumbered Liberal identifiers by a ratio of three to two. The head start once enjoyed by the Liberals had completely evaporated. Now the advantage lay with the Conservatives. Moreover, unlike their Liberal counterparts, Conservative partisans were much more faithful to the party on election day. On top of that, the Conservatives were now more successful than the Liberals at appealing to those more fickle voters who lacked any party attachment.

The expansion of the Conservatives' electoral ranks was mostly due to the sponsorship scandal. Indeed, the party's margin of victory over the Liberals outside Québec in 2006 was almost wholly attributable to the scandal. In the process, the Conservative Party broadened its electoral base beyond the former Reform/Alliance western core. In only four years, the Conservatives managed to narrow the urban-rural divide that had characterized voting for the parties of the right in the previous decade. Equally significant, the Conservatives made important electoral inroads into vote-rich Ontario and outpolled the Liberals among Catholics, once the mainstay of Liberal dominance.

With all of these advantages working to the party's benefit, it is fair to ask why the Conservatives were unable to exploit fully the electoral weaknesses of the Liberals and achieve an electoral majority in 2008.

The answer to that question emerges by piecing together the collective effects of a combination of factors. One factor that limited the party's electoral success concerns its social foundations. In some respects, the Conservative base remained much closer to that of the former Alliance than to the base of its Progressive Conservative counterpart. It appealed more to Christian fundamentalists, married couples, and men. Lack of appeal to women was a key reason that the Alliance failed to achieve its hoped-for breakthrough in Ontario in the 2000 election. A similar lack of appeal hampered the Conservatives. To be sure, women were as likely as men to vote Conservative in 2004. But the gender gap reappeared in both the 2006 and 2008 elections. Arguably, the Conservatives might well have won a majority in 2008 had they had as much appeal to women as to men.

A second factor standing in the way of a Conservative majority lay in the realm of values and beliefs. Once again, there are striking similarities between the Alliance and the Conservatives on this score. Like the Alliance vote, the Conservative vote was more strongly driven by basic values and beliefs than was the case for the former Progressive Conservatives. The growth in the Conservative vote was limited by the perception that the party was the home of social conservatism. Moral traditionalists were much more likely to vote Conservative. The problem was that these voters amounted to only a minority of the electorate. Moreover, that minority was shrinking.

Issues and leadership failed to compensate. One striking finding to emerge concerns how little issues (apart from the sponsorship scandal) mattered to levels of public support for the Conservatives. Indeed, in both 2004 and 2006, the Conservatives were net losers on the issues. The Conservatives eked out a win in 2006 despite the fact that they did not have a single winning issue. And issues had virtually no impact on the Conservative share of the vote in 2008.

Leadership was not much help, either. Stephen Harper was less popular than Paul Martin in 2004, and his leadership ratings were even lower in 2006. Indeed, he proved to be an electoral liability in that election. He was the least popular leader, and he cost his party votes. In 2008, Harper remained less popular than his party, but, on this occasion, he was more popular than the other leaders, and that provided a modest boost to the Conservatives' electoral fortunes. That boost was not enough, though, to push the Conservatives into majority territory. Part of the problem was that the Conservative leader was not able to shed the perception that he was too extreme. That perception was as widespread in 2008 as it was when he contested his first election as party leader in 2004.

It is reasonable to suspect that the onset of the crisis in the US housing and financial markets in 2008 might have been a major reason that the Conservatives failed to win a majority government in the federal election of that year. The evidence clearly shows that voters were pessimistic about the state of the economy during the 2008 federal election campaign. But the evidence also shows that only a small minority of voters blamed the government of the day for the deteriorating economy. Voters punish incumbents when the economy is doing poorly *and* when they hold governments responsible for the state of the economy. In this case, the Conservatives escaped punishment.

The Conservatives finally managed to win a majority in 2011, but that victory was achieved with only a two-point increase in the party's vote share. The implication is that there remain important constraints on the party's ability to grow.

The NDP: Emerging from the Sidelines

In 1993, the NDP appeared to be headed for electoral oblivion. The party won less than 7 per cent of the vote and lost its official party status. The 1997 election signalled the beginning of a period of recovery. Support for the NDP inched back, and it regained official party status. By 2008, almost one in five voters (18 per cent) was supporting the NDP once again.

The NDP owed the improvement in its electoral fortunes between 2000 and 2008 to three groups of voters. First, secular voters remained a mainstay of the NDP vote. Second, the party succeeded in winning back much of the union vote that had been lost between 1993 and 2000. The loss of the union vote in those years had put the party's future in jeopardy. Winning it back was critical to the party's revitalization. Third, the NDP was particularly successful in attracting women back to the party. But important as these groups were to the NDP vote, their attraction to the party remained limited in 2008. In fact, the Conservatives actually fared better than the NDP among women and union households alike. And secular voters divided their support more or less evenly between the NDP, the Conservatives, and the Liberals. Furthermore, in 2008, the NDP found itself facing increasing competition from the Greens for the votes of secular Canadians.

The NDP did see its partisan core expand between 2000 and 2008. The problem was that NDP partisans proved to have even less stable attachments than their Liberal counterparts. Those who did continue to identify with the party, though, proved to be less willing than Liberal identifiers to vote against their party. Still, with only half as many partisans as the Liberals in 2008 and a third as many partisans as the Conservatives, the NDP seemed to be at a significant disadvantage coming out of the 2008 election.

The NDP's support stalled despite the popularity of its leader. Jack Layton was more popular than his predecessor, Alexa McDonough, and his ratings increased with each election. But even in 2008, Layton's growing popularity had little impact on the NDP's share of the vote. People may have liked Jack Layton, but that did not mean they liked his party.

Similarly, the improvement in the NDP's performance between 2000 and 2004 was not attributable to the party's platform. The net impact of issues on the NDP's share of the vote was minimal in both elections. The same was true of the 2006 election. And the NDP failed completely to capitalize on the sponsorship scandal in both 2004 and 2006. But the pattern was very different in 2008: the NDP was clearly the net winner on the issues. Particularly telling is the fact that the party had usurped the Liberals as the champion of increased spending on health care.

Indeed, the NDP was increasingly competing with the Liberals for the same left-of-centre vote, and, until Liberal support collapsed in 2011, that proved to be an important constraint on the party's growth. Notably, in 2008, the NDP lost out to the Liberals in the competition for the support of voters who rejected traditional conceptions of morality and gender roles. The party fared better in appealing to market liberals and to those who favoured looser ties with the United States, but this did not help the NDP's bottom line. The party did succeed, though, in regaining its traditional role as a lightening rod for political disaffection.

As in past elections, the NDP was vulnerable to strategic defections in 2008. If the party was perceived to have little or no chance of winning the local riding, some voters opted to vote instead for their second-choice party. However, the extent of strategic voting was too limited to explain the stalling of the NDP vote.

The Green Party: A One-Shot Wonder?

Although the Green Party became an officially recognized political party in 1983, it remained a marginal electoral force for the first 20 years of its existence. That changed in 2008 when it took nearly 7 per cent of the federal vote. The improvement in the party's fortunes owed something to the fact that it was championing an issue whose time had come.

Environmental concern is a valence issue. Most people want a cleaner environment, and two out of three Canadians reported in 2008 that they wanted the government to spend more on the environment. But it was precisely because environmental concern was a valence issue that the partisan space for pro-environmental policies was a crowded one. Still, the Greens were able to cut into the vote of the Liberals, Conservatives, and NDP alike, though it was the NDP that was hurt the most by defections to the Green Party because its electoral base was smaller. Green Party support came disproportionately from younger, well-educated, secular, socially liberal voters, groups that were the backbone of the NDP's electoral base. The

Green Party also appealed to voters who were dissatisfied with the political status quo. And outside Québec at least, the NDP was the traditional electoral home of the disaffected. When NDP support increased dramatically in 2011, it is not surprising that one casualty was the Greens.

Even in 2008, the Green Party did poorly in Québec. The reasons it failed to make significant inroads in the province are clear. Both the Green Party and the Bloc were appealing to similar constituencies—young, secular, well-educated voters who care about the environment. Bloc voters, in fact, had more positive evaluations of the Greens than did supporters of any of the other political parties. But Bloc voters had other issues that they cared about—most notably sovereignty.

Explaining Changing Party Fortunes: Québec

The political landscape in Québec shifted considerably during the last decade. Support for the Liberals fell by half, and the Conservatives doubled their vote share. The Bloc Québécois grew by almost 10 percentage points in 2004, but the gain proved to be temporary; the Bloc vote shrank in the next two elections. The NDP's showing improved slowly but systematically in all four elections, laying the ground for the party's stunning breakthrough in 2011.

To understand these dynamics, we have to look beyond the ebb and flow of opinion toward the central question of Québec sovereignty. Sovereignists stood firmly behind the Bloc. But there were significant fluctuations in the party allegiances of federalists. The Conservatives stole a sizable portion of the federalist vote from the Liberals, especially federalists who were only *somewhat* opposed to sovereignty. Conservative gains came mostly at the expense of the Liberal Party, not the Bloc.

Partisanship was also part of the story. The Liberals lost not only votes in Québec but also almost half of their partisans between 2000 and 2008. They also became less successful at attracting non-partisans and at mobilizing their remaining partisans. The only silver lining for the Liberals and for their prospects of returning to strength in Québec was the fact that the Conservatives' proportion of partisans did not increase as much as their share of the vote; in terms of partisanship, the Conservatives still trailed the Liberals.

Few issues had a consistent or strong impact on Quebecers' voting behaviour, but two issues were key to the dynamics in party support. The sponsorship scandal was largely responsible for the first stage of the Liberal collapse in the province. It cost the party 7 percentage points in 2004 (when the party's share of the vote fell from 44 per cent to 34 per cent). Even though the next election followed the revelations of the Gomery Commission, the sponsorship scandal exerted little weight in 2006. That year, both the second stage of the Liberal collapse and the stumbling of the Bloc were due to another issue—health spending. In 2000 and 2004, both the Bloc and the Liberal Party won votes among individuals wanting more spending on health care. But, two years later, there was a complete reversal: the Conservative Party now attracted the support of Quebecers who wanted spending on health care to be increased.

Finally, there is little evidence to substantiate the intuitive story that swings in leader popularity were driving shifts in vote shares in these elections. Feelings toward Gilles Duceppe did not explain either the rise in Bloc support in 2004 or its subsequent fall in the next two elections. The Conservatives did not make a breakthrough in 2006 as a result of Harper's sudden appeal. Paul Martin hurt the Liberals' performance in 2004, but he was not the main reason behind the 23-point drop between 2000 and 2006. However, the NDP's small but steady headway in Québec during these elections was partly the product of increasingly positive evaluations of Jack Layton.

Explaining Vote Choice and Electoral Dynamics: What Has Been Learned?

The analyses in the preceding chapters have important implications for understanding voting behaviour and election outcomes. First, the most powerful influences on individual vote choice are not necessarily the most consequential when it comes to explaining vote shares. Leader evaluations are a case in point. Leader evaluations clearly had a powerful influence on individual vote choice, but leader popularity did not necessarily determine a party's electoral fortunes in the four elections held between 2000 and 2008. Jack Layton is a good example: his popularity (and familiarity to voters) increased between the 2004 and 2008 elections, yet his party failed to make gains. Similarly, it would be difficult to argue that leader popularity or unpopularity was the decisive factor in explaining the Conservatives' ascent to power or the Liberals' decline.

Second, it is difficult to make sense of election outcomes unless we take account of factors that are conventionally considered to be distant from the final vote choice. Even in periods of electoral volatility, there is an important element of inertia in voting behaviour that needs to be understood. Electoral volatility does not mean that voters are changing their votes en masse from one election to the next. Even in a time of electoral flux, many will vote as they have in past elections because they approach each election with a standing decision to support a particular party. To understand why, we need to take account of their social background characteristics, their basic values and beliefs, and their partisan attachments. Social background characteristics tend to be downplayed in Michigan-style accounts of voting behaviour, but they shape many of the factors that typically figure more prominently in these interpretations.[1] The fact that party identification is anchored in sociocultural factors such as religion, region, and ethnicity helps to explain why party identification can be relatively stable, even in a period of electoral volatility. Fundamental values and beliefs also help to anchor people to political parties. People are likely to identify with a party that shares their basic value commitments. This grounding in normative beliefs helps explain, for example, why Conservative partisans were so loyal to the party, just as a weaker foundation in fundamental values and beliefs helps us understand why Liberal and NDP partisans were more apt to stray.

Third, the fact that social background characteristics are quite stable does not mean that they cannot contribute to an understanding of electoral dynamics. The characteristics themselves may be stable, but their effects can change. And change they did between 2000 and 2008. Indeed, it would be difficult to make sense of the Liberals' fall from grace without taking account of the changing voting behaviour of Catholics in particular. The same is true of the effects of basic values and beliefs. Similarly, we cannot understand parties' changing electoral fortunes unless we take account of the size of their partisan core and the degree of loyalty of their partisans. The pull of short-term forces may prove strong enough to induce some partisans to vote at odds with their party; they may even be strong enough to shake their attachment to the party.

Fourth, we cannot understand why short-term forces have the effects they do unless we relate them to longer-term factors. Long-term factors affect how the short-term influences play out. Notably, party identification worked to diminish the impact of the sponsorship scandal. Voters' reactions to the scandal were clearly influenced by their partisanship. Liberal partisans were much less critical of the scandal and the way it had been handled. Partisanship also had a predictably strong impact on voters' evaluations of the party leaders: party leaders were much more popular with their party's core supporters. Similarly, partisans tended to like their party's positions, and this tendency worked to constrain the effects of the issues. Party attachments also help to explain why economic voting is not as prevalent as the rational choice approach implies. In 2000, the Canadian economy was doing well. Eight years later, the country was entering a recession. Yet the state of the economy was surprisingly little help in explaining the parties' changing electoral fortunes. What mattered was not necessarily the state of the economy itself but people's perceptions of economic conditions, and those perceptions were influenced by voters' party loyalties: partisans were apt to offer a more charitable assessment when their party was in power. Partisanship even affects strategic calculations. Partisans tend to overstate their party's chances of winning their local riding, which works to constrain the amount of strategic voting that occurs. Similarly, the fact that views about minority government are rooted in partisan considerations helps to explain why their impact was very limited, even with the prospect of the third minority outcome in a row.

Finally, how much any explanatory factor affects the outcome of an election depends on its distribution. A given value or belief can have a powerful effect on individual vote choice, but it does not necessarily affect the parties' vote shares unless the balance of opinion is tipped in one direction or the other. The same is true of issue attitudes. Issues can only affect the election outcome if the balance of opinion is skewed in favour of one side or the other. When opinion is equally divided, with as many voters on one side as on the other, parties will typically lose as many votes among those who are opposed to their stand as they gain from those who are on the same side. The same-sex marriage issue in 2006 is a prime example. That issue had no net effect on the parties' vote shares, even though it was a strong predictor of a vote for the Conservatives. Similarly, leader evaluations will only affect vote shares if one leader is much more popular—or unpopular—than the others.

The Strategic Challenges Facing Canadian Parties

The finding that social background characteristics, values, and partisanship are all important drivers of electoral outcomes presents significant challenges to parties that want to expand their traditional bases of support. Just as these long-term factors help to shape voters' choice of party, they also influence voters' second choices and their perception that a party might be just too extreme for their liking.

One reason breaking out of the cycle of minority governments that characterized elections between 2004 and 2008 proved to be difficult was that ethnocultural and value differences were more important than issue positions or leader evaluations in differentiating one party's supporters from another's. Changing a party's leader or promising a new policy may have some impact on voting behaviour in any given election, but those short-term factors do not necessarily override the underlying influence of the demographic or ideological make-up of the electorate.

From that vantage point, a party's potential for growth depends greatly upon the size of its core constituency. And the demographic make-up and value orientations of its core constituency shape the strategic opportunities and constraints confronting each party. So we need to ask this question: To what extent did each party carve out a distinctive base of support during these years? Was a particular party the sole option for this constituency, or was it competing for the same votes with one or more of its competitors?

In Canada, region, religion, and union membership, along with competing views about government intervention, morality and gender roles, and accommodating Québec, have been the primary factors that distinguish Conservatives from Liberals or New Democrats. Compared to its competitors, the Conservative Party occupies distinct territory in the Canadian political landscape. And, for that reason, the Conservatives were able to solidify the support of their core partisans between 2004 and 2008. But can the Conservatives expand their base of support? Expansion is a real challenge for the Conservatives. There is little evidence that support for free market values is increasing, and there is some evidence that support is declining for both traditional moral values and religiosity. The data concerning voters' second choices are telling. Only 10 per cent of the electorate identified the Conservatives as the second-choice party in 2008. The Liberals and the NDP, by contrast, were the second-choice options for some 25 per cent and 22 per cent of the electorate, respectively. Moreover, 16 per cent of the electorate viewed the Conservatives as just too extreme. Just 4 per cent of the electorate viewed the Liberals that way, and only 8 per cent thought of the NDP as too extreme. Moreover, more than half of the Liberal and NDP voters in the 2008 election indicated that they would never vote for the Conservatives. It is not surprising, then, that the party was only able to increase its vote share by two points in 2011. To broaden the Conservative Party's appeal beyond its current base of support, the Conservatives would have to abandon, or significantly modify, their fundamental ideological values. The dilemma is that those were the very values that fuelled the party's base of support in the first place.

The Conservatives' best chances of forming another majority government may well flow directly from the very different dilemma facing the Liberals and the NDP. Supporters of these two parties occupy a common value space on the centre-left of the political spectrum. They share similar views when it comes to moral outlooks, accommodating Québec, doing more for minorities, and even market liberalism. Once again, the data on second choices are telling: the most common second choice for each party's voters is the other party. Thus, the prospects for the Conservatives ride on the kind of fragmentation and vote splitting on the left that is reminiscent of the vote splitting on the right that limited the electoral opportunities of the Alliance and the Progressive Conservatives in the 1990s. Centre-left vote splitting undoubtedly helped the Conservatives in 2011.

Coming out of the 2008 election, the Liberal Party seemed to hold the edge in the competition for the centre-left vote. The Liberals certainly had a larger base of partisan support. The partisan base of the NDP did expand after the 2000 federal election just as the Liberal base dwindled. But NDP partisans proved to have even less stable party attachments than their Liberal counterparts. So, although the NDP experienced a dramatic increase in its vote share in 2011, there is no guarantee that these voters will evolve into loyal partisans.

A second set of factors that might influence the electoral prospects of the Liberals and the NDP concerns the geographic and partisan shifts in feelings of political disaffection and regional alienation. In the 1980s and 1990s, in particular, the centre of gravity for political disaffection and regional alienation in Canada was located in the West. By the 2008 election, that centre of gravity had shifted to Ontario and the East. Moreover, the relationship between these political orientations and vote choice had changed such that the growing regional alienation in vote-rich Ontario worked to the benefit of the Liberals. That clearly changed in 2011. The increased support for the NDP in Ontario led to vote splits with the Liberals that enabled the Conservatives to win new seats.

The dynamics work somewhat differently in Québec. Language and support for sovereignty have been the two most powerful cleavages framing vote choice in Québec. Prior to 2011, at least, francophones and those supporting sovereignty lined up behind the Bloc, and the Liberals and Conservatives (and more recently the NDP) competed for the votes of non-francophones and federalists. Historically, of course, the Liberals were more successful in capturing those votes. That the Conservatives outpolled the Liberals among "soft" federalist voters was a recent development. The big question coming out of the 2011 election, of course, is whether the NDP's unprecedented surge in support in the province represents a fundamental realignment or a temporary aberration. Based on what we know about voting in Québec, the answer is likely to depend heavily on how successful the party is at defending the interests of the province in Ottawa.

To consolidate their majority status and give substance to the claim of being a national party, the Conservatives may need to find a delicate balance between increasing their share of the vote in Québec and not alienating their support base in the rest of the country. That is a tough challenge, not least because people who believe that less should be done for Québec make up an important part of the Conservative constituency in the rest of Canada. Conservatives may try to appeal to "soft" sovereignists through policies such as recognizing Québec as a nation within a nation. But too many "concessions," too many efforts to accommodate Québec, run the risk of costing the party votes outside the province. At the same time, the constituency for a party that supports morally traditional positions or more market-based views about the role of government is as limited in Québec as it is elsewhere in Canada. To be sure, the Conservatives made significant gains in the province between 2004 and 2008. But the increases in the number of Conservative Party identifiers in the province were far less impressive, and the party lost seats in 2011. The implication is that Quebecers are not yet willing to commit to the Conservatives.

The Liberals have more experience in managing conflicting messages in Québec and in the rest of the country. Both the dramatic loss of partisans between 2000 and 2008 and the growing competition from the Conservatives and especially the NDP for the federalist vote in Québec nonetheless present the Liberals with significant challenges to regaining power at the federal level. The Liberals' traditional distinctiveness as the voice of federalism in Québec enabled the party to build and maintain a stable partisan core. But as the party's demographic and ideological foundations have become less distinct, voters' attachments to the Liberals have weakened. The challenge for the Liberals, then, is to stake out a more clearly identifiable policy terrain that can attract partisans back to the Liberal fold in Québec *and* across the rest of the country.

These challenges for the Liberals in Québec do not necessarily guarantee continued success for the NDP. The NDP's share of the vote gradually increased in the province between 2000 and 2008, before climbing dramatically in 2011. But it remains to be seen whether the party can maintain this support. On the one hand, the NDP is competing with the Liberals and the Conservatives for the "soft" federalist vote. On the other hand, it is also competing with the Bloc for the affections of left-of-centre voters. The problem for the NDP in Québec is that voters who favour a strong state, who are less traditional in their moral outlooks, and who are disaffected with politics and politicians also turn out to be more supportive of sovereignty.

Although the Liberals' fall from grace between 2000 and 2008 was not as dramatic as the Progressive Conservatives' collapse in 1993, it highlights the ever-present potential for electoral volatility. This volatility was made manifest in 2011. Coming out of the 2000 federal election, Liberal dominance had seemed assured. For the Liberals to lose, two things had to happen: the right would have to reunite and short-term factors would have to be strongly against the Liberals. Both conditions were in place by the time of the 2004 election. The Alliance and the Progressive Conservatives had merged to form the Conservative Party, and the sponsorship scandal had angered many Canadians. The sponsorship scandal clearly destabilized voting patterns both inside and outside Québec. Whether it proves to be a short-term shock or the cause of a longer-term shifting of the electoral contours will depend on how the competing parties manage the resulting electoral opportunities and constraints. It remains to be seen whether any party will be able to replicate the "Liberal threepeat" (Clarkson 2001), but, should it do so, the Liberal decline serves as a salutary reminder of just how fragile electoral dominance can prove to be.

Note

1 Social background characteristics can also have a direct effect on vote choice. Even when we controlled for basic values and beliefs, party identification, economic perceptions, issue positions, and leader evaluations, for example, visible minority voters were significantly more likely than other voters to choose the Liberals. Similarly, Christian fundamentalists remained significantly more likely than other voters to choose the Conservatives, and voters from union households were significantly more likely than other voters to choose the NDP.

ESTIMATING THE MULTISTAGE MODELS

The estimations used throughout much of this analysis are based on multinomial logistic regression. The multinomial specification enables us to capture the inter-party dynamics of support (Gidengil et al. 2006; Whitten and Palmer 1996). Rather than simply looking at the impact of a given factor on the decision to vote for a particular party or not, we adopted the approach of assessing the impact of that factor on the choice between that party and each of the other parties. Consider the case of union membership, a factor that might encourage an NDP vote while simultaneously reducing the likelihood of voting Conservative. If the vote was modelled as a choice between the Liberals and these other two parties, these effects might well cancel out one another and point to the conclusion, wrongly, that union membership did not affect people's vote choice. This approach also allows for the possibility that different factors play into different choices. Consider also the case of religion. Being Catholic is very relevant to choosing between the Conservatives and the Liberals, but it is not relevant to the choice between the Conservatives and the NDP. Limiting the focus of the analysis to the choice between Liberals and the other parties would lead us to underestimate the importance of religious affiliation. For the 2000 election, we model the vote outside Québec as a choice among the Alliance, the Liberals, the NDP, and the Progressive Conservatives. For the three subsequent elections, the choice set consists of the Conservatives, the Liberals, and the NDP. The Bloc Québécois is added for the Québec analyses. Unfortunately, the small number of Green voters, even in 2008, makes it difficult to generate reliable estimations if the Green Party is included as well. Variables are retained in the models if they are statistically significant (at $p < .10$) for at least one election when first entered. Any cut-off for statistical significance is necessarily somewhat arbitrary, but, in practice, very few of the non-significant variables even approached the .10 level.

To make the interpretation of the results easier to digest, we specify each variable's independent impact on the probability of voting for each of the parties. For example, we calculate the probability of voting Liberal, assuming, first, that everyone is a member of a visible minority. We then repeat the same calculation using the opposite assumption, namely, that no one is a member of a visible minority. In both cases, all other social background characteristics are held constant statistically. The difference in the mean probabilities indicates the average impact of being a visible minority on voting Liberal, everything else being equal.

An explanatory factor can have a strong impact on the probability of voting for a party and yet have little effect on the party's share of the vote. Feelings about the party leaders, for example, can strongly affect how people vote, but, unless one leader is much more (or much less) popular than the others, the net effect on party vote shares will be small (see Blais et al. 2002; Johnston 2002). The impact on vote shares can be estimated by setting the coefficient for a given explanatory factor to zero (leaving all other coefficients unchanged) and observing how much the average estimated probability of voting for a given party changes. In effect, we are asking this: What if a given variable had simply not mattered? If opinions about the green shift had been irrelevant to people's choice of party in 2008, for example, would the Liberals have won more votes?

VALUES AND BELIEFS

Market Liberalism

The Cronbach's α scores for the market liberalism index are 0.52 (2000), 0.52 (2004), 0.54 (2006), and 0.60 (2008) outside Québec and 0.35 (2000), 0.39 (2004), 0.43 (2006), and 0.49 (2008) in Québec. This scale is based on responses to the following five questions: (1) "When businesses make a lot of money, everyone benefits, including the poor. Do you strongly agree, somewhat agree, somewhat disagree, or strongly disagree?" (2) "The government should leave it entirely to the private sector to create jobs. Do you strongly agree, somewhat agree, somewhat disagree, or strongly disagree?" (3) "If people can't find work in the region where they live, they should move to where the jobs are. Do you strongly agree, somewhat agree, somewhat disagree, or strongly disagree?" (4) "How much do you think should be done to reduce the gap between the rich and the poor in Canada: much more, somewhat more, about the same as now, somewhat less, or much less?" and (5) "People who don't get ahead should blame themselves, not the system. Do you strongly agree, somewhat agree, somewhat disagree, or strongly disagree?" All of the items have been rescaled to run from −1 to +1 with positive values indicating a pro-market stance.

Moral Traditionalism[1]

The Cronbach's α scores for the moral traditionalism index are 0.55 (2000), 0.57 (2004), 0.56 (2006), and 0.54 (2008) outside Québec and 0.31 (2000), 0.52 (2004), 0.56 (2006), and 0.51 (2008) in Québec. This scale is based on responses to the following four questions: (1) "Society would be better off if more women stayed home with their children. Do you strongly agree, somewhat agree, somewhat disagree, or strongly disagree?" (2) "How much do you think should be done for women: much more, somewhat more, about the same as now, somewhat less, or much less?" (3) "Are you very sympathetic towards feminism, quite sympathetic, not very sympathetic, or not sympathetic at all?" (2000), or "How do you feel [. . .] about feminists? Use any number from zero to one hundred. Zero means you really dislike feminists, and one hundred means you really like feminists" (2004/2006/2008). (4) "Gays and lesbians should be allowed to get married. Do you strongly agree, somewhat agree, somewhat disagree, or strongly disagree?" (2000), or "How do you feel [. . .] about gays and lesbians. Use any number from zero to one hundred. Zero means you really dislike gays and lesbians, and one hundred means you really like gays and lesbians" (2004/2006/2008). All of the items have been rescaled to run from −1 to +1 with positive scores indicating a morally traditional stance.

Continentalism

The Cronbach's α scores for the continentalism index are 0.54 (2000), 0.56 (2004), 0.53 (2006), and 0.52 (2008) outside Québec and 0.42 (2000), 0.41 (2004), 0.40 (2006), and 0.49 (2008) in Québec. This scale is based on responses to the following three questions: (1) "Overall, free trade with the U.S. has been good for the Canadian economy. Do you strongly agree, somewhat agree, somewhat disagree, or strongly disagree?" (2) "Do you think Canada's ties with the United States should be much closer, somewhat closer, about the same as now, somewhat more distant, or much more distant?" (3) "How do you feel about the United States? Use any number from zero to one hundred. Zero means you really dislike the United States, and one hundred means you really like the United States." All of the items have been rescaled to run from −1 to +1 with positive scores indicating a continentalist orientation.

Québec

This is a single-item measure constructed from the question: "How much do you think should be done for Québec: much more, somewhat more, about the same as now, somewhat less, or much less?" Responses were rescaled to run from −1 (much less) to +1 (much more). In Québec, a question about sovereignty was substituted: "Are you very favourable, somewhat favourable, somewhat opposed, or very opposed to Québec sovereignty, that is Québec is no longer a part of Canada?" Responses have been rescaled to run from −1 (very unfavourable) to +1 (very favourable).

Political Disaffection

The Cronbach's α scores for the political disaffection index are 0.70 (2000), 0.67 (2004), 0.64 (2006), and 0.69 (2008) outside Québec and 0.63 (2000), 0.57 (2004), 0.62 (2006), and 0.68 (2008) in Québec. This scale is based on responses to the following six questions: (1) "On the whole, are you very satisfied, fairly satisfied, not very satisfied, or not satisfied at all with the way democracy works in Canada?" (2) "Do political parties keep their election promises: most of the time, some of the time, or hardly ever?" (3) "And on the same scale, how do you feel about politicians in general? Use any number from zero to one hundred. Zero means you really dislike them, and one hundred means you really like them." (4) "How do you feel about the federal political parties in general? Use a scale from zero to one hundred. Zero means you really dislike the parties in general, and one hundred means you really like the parties in general." (5) "I don't think the government cares much what people like me think. Do you strongly agree, somewhat agree, somewhat disagree, or strongly disagree?" (6) "All federal parties are basically the same; there isn't a real choice. Do you strongly agree, somewhat agree, somewhat disagree, or strongly disagree?" All of the items have been rescaled to run from −1 to +1 with positive scores indicating political disaffection.

Regional Alienation

This single-item measure is constructed from this question: "In general, does the federal government treat your province: better, worse, or about the same as other provinces?" Responses have been rescaled to run from −1 (better) to +1 (worse).

Religiosity

Religiosity is a single-item measure constructed from this question: "In your life, would you say religion is very important, somewhat important, not very important, or not important at all?" Responses have been rescaled to run from −1 (not important at all) to +1 (very important). Respondents who had no religious affiliation were not asked this question. They have been coded −1.

Racial Minorities

Racial minorities is a single-item measure constructed from this question: "How much do you think should be done for racial minorities: much more, somewhat more, about the same as now, somewhat less, or much less?" Responses have been rescaled to run from −1 (much less) to +1 (much more).

Sponsorship Scandal

The Cronbach's α scores for the sponsorship scandal index are 0.70 (2004) and 0.63 (2006) outside Québec and 0.64 (2004) and 0.60 (2006) in Québec. The scale is based on responses to the following four questions: (1) "When Jean Chrétien was Prime Minister, do you think there was a lot of corruption in government, some, a little, or none?" (2) "Now some questions about the sponsorship scandal. Does it make you very angry, somewhat angry, not very angry, or not angry at all?" (3) "Since becoming Prime Minister, how good a job has Paul Martin done in dealing with the sponsorship scandal? A very good job, quite a good job, not a very good job, or not a good job at all?" (4) "If re-elected, how confident are you that Paul Martin will prevent this type of scandal from happening again? Very confident, somewhat confident, not very confident, or not confident at all?" All of the items have been re-scaled to run from -1 to +1 with positive values indicating negative opinions.

Note

1 The sympathy for feminism and gay marriage items were substituted in 2000 because the 2000 Canadian Election Study did not ask respondents to rate their feelings about feminists or gays and lesbians.

THE DETERMINANTS OF VOTE CHOICE

In the following tables, entries are marginal effects based on multinomial logistic regression estimations. For dummy coded variables, they represent the marginal effect of being in the named category. For variables coded from -1 to +1, they represent the marginal effect of a change in value from -1 to +1. Statistical significance is indicated by these symbols: * < .10; ** < .05.

Table C1.1 *The Determinants of Vote Choice, Outside Québec, 2000*

	Alliance	Liberal	NDP	Progressive Conservative
Sociodemographics (0/1)				
Under 35 years old	10.4**	-3.1	-2.0	-5.3**
Over 54 years old	-2.5	2.5	0.4	-0.4
Female	-12.5**	4.7	5.1**	2.7
Atlantic resident	-21.3**	-6.0*	10.7**	17.1**
Western resident	19.3**	-18.9**	2.2	-2.6
Rural resident	9.3**	-9.1**	-1.5	1.3
Catholic	-9.8**	13.4**	1.0	-4.6*
Fundamentalist Christian[1]	16.3**	-7.3**	-6.5**	-2.5
No religion	-12.4**	1.8	13.9**	-3.3
French first language	-5.2	8.9	4.7	-8.3**
Visible minority	-24.8**	44.1**	-10.9**	-8.4**
Northern European ancestry	8.2*	-5.8	0.8	-3.2
Married/Common law	10.2**	-2.4	-8.3**	0.6
Public sector worker	1.5	-0.4	-0.8	-0.3
Union household	-3.4	1.5	4.3*	-2.4
Less than high school	-1.1	3.3	4.4	-6.7**
University graduate	-4.9	-1.5	3.8	2.6
Values (-1 to +1)				
Market liberalism	25.8**	-18.8**	-26.8**	19.8**
Moral traditionalism	48.0**	-32.0**	-9.2*	-6.8
Continentalism	31.0**	1.2	-25.2**	-7.0
Personal religiosity	10.2*	4.7	-9.4**	-5.6
Racial outlooks	-13.2*	8.4	6.5	-1.8
Accommodating Québec	-4.4	-5.4	6.0	3.8
Political cynicism	39.6**	-63.0**	12.8**	10.6*
Regional alienation	12.2**	-8.6*	-3.0	-0.7
Party identification (0/1)	43.5**	25.6**	40.6**	15.4**
Economic perceptions (-1 to +1)				
National retrospective	-1.6	-5.6	2.1	5.2*
Personal retrospective	-7.6**	7.5**	-4.9**	4.9*
Issues (-1 to +1)				
More defence spending	10.9**	-9.6**	-0.0	-1.3
Personal tax cuts	-1.2	-4.3	3.7**	1.7
More welfare spending	-9.0**	-2.5	2.1	9.3**
Favour gun control	0.8	0.6	2.3	-3.7
Favour death penalty	0.3	1.3	-5.0**	3.3
Oppose private hospitals	-6.2**	2.1	1.4	2.7
Provincial powers	10.2**	-10.3**	2.5	-2.4
Leader evaluations (-1 to +1)	54.8**	31.0**	24.2**	31.2**

1 This question was only asked in the self-administered mail-back survey in 2000. Accordingly, values have been imputed for voters who did not complete the mail-back survey.

Table C1.2 *The Determinants of Vote Choice, Outside Québec, 2004*

	Conservative	Liberal	NDP
Sociodemographics (0/1)			
Under 35 years old	4.5	-7.4**	2.9
Over 54 years old	3.8	4.0	-7.9**
Female	-4.1	-1.0	5.1**
Atlantic resident	-12.0**	7.2	4.8
Western resident	14.0**	-16.7**	2.7
Rural resident	9.8**	-4.7	-5.1*
Catholic	-8.4**	8.1**	0.3
Fundamentalist Christian	17.2**	-9.0**	-8.2**
No religion	-7.8**	-3.4	11.2**
French first language	-5.8	18.1**	-12.2**
Visible minority	-26.5**	24.2**	2.3
Northern European ancestry	-4.0	1.6	2.4
Married/Common law	11.1**	-3.4	-7.7**
Public sector worker	-2.8	-0.3	3.1
Union household	-8.5**	0.9	7.6**
Less than high school	-12.0**	-3.4	15.4**
University graduate	-2.8	4.8	-2.0
Values (-1 to +1)			
Market liberalism	26.2**	-0.1	-26.1**
Moral traditionalism	39.8**	-3.5	-36.3**
Continentalism	62.4**	-28.2**	-34.1**
Personal religiosity	10.0	-9.6	-0.3
Racial outlooks	0.2	-1.1	0.9
Accommodating Québec	-18.6**	16.1**	2.5
Political cynicism	40.0**	-76.1**	36.2**
Regional alienation	14.0**	-6.4	-7.5**
Party identification (0/1)	28.1**	26.6**	26.7**
Economic perceptions (-1 to +1)			
National retrospective	-1.3	2.5	-1.2
Personal retrospective	-0.3	0.1	0.1
Issues (-1 to +1)			
More defence spending	5.4**	0.4	-5.0**
Personal tax cuts	6.6*	-11.5**	4.9
More health spending	-10.0**	11.7**	-1.6
Scrap gun registry	12.1**	-7.3**	-4.8*
Oppose private hospitals	-8.7**	1.6	7.1**
Staying out of Iraq	-7.5**	8.1**	-0.6
Favour same-sex marriage	-5.1*	-9.2**	14.3**
Sponsorship scandal	30.1**	-35.9**	5.8
Leader evaluations (-1 to +1)	46.1**	51.9**	34.5**

Table C1.3 *The Determinants of Vote Choice, Outside Québec, 2006*

	Conservative	Liberal	NDP
Sociodemographics (0/1)			
Under 35 years old	-3.4	1.8	1.6
Over 54 years old	-5.0*	5.2*	-0.2
Female	-6.5**	0.4	6.1**
Atlantic resident	-12.2**	3.9	8.2**
Western resident	14.4**	-17.9**	3.5
Rural resident	6.1**	-7.0**	0.9
Catholic	-4.2	4.8	-0.6
Fundamentalist Christian	23.5**	-10.4**	-13.0**
No religion	-10.2**	0.9	9.4**
French first language	-10.4*	10.5*	-0.1
Visible minority	-28.2**	31.5**	-3.3
Northern European ancestry	-2.1	0.9	1.2
Married/Common law	5.7**	0.1	-5.9**
Public sector worker	-11.5**	9.5**	1.9
Union household	-1.5	-8.2**	9.8**
Less than high school	1.7	-5.4	3.7
University graduate	-3.5	0.7	2.8
Values (-1 to +1)			
Market liberalism	46.3**	-3.6	-42.7**
Moral traditionalism	38.1**	-14.8**	-23.2**
Continentalism	46.7**	-25.8**	-20.8**
Personal religiosity	11.4*	-0.6	-10.8**
Racial outlooks	-15.8**	11.0	4.8
Accommodating Québec	-14.6**	-4.0	18.7**
Political cynicism	7.7	-42.7**	35.1**
Regional alienation	5.8	-8.3**	2.4
Party identification (0/1)	33.8**	25.2**	23.1**
Economic perceptions (-1 to +1)			
National retrospective	-6.5**	14.0**	-7.5**
Personal retrospective	-3.9	4.7	-0.8
Issues (-1 to +1)			
Fund national day care	-7.7**	4.3*	3.4
Increase corporate taxes	-3.1	10.4**	-7.2**
Spend more on environment	-7.5**	2.6	4.9
Pro-life	4.5	-6.2	1.7
Oppose private hospitals	-2.3	-4.6*	7.0**
Oppose allowing people to pay for faster medical care	-4.0	8.1**	-4.1
Favour same-sex marriage	-9.6**	4.0	5.6**
Sponsorship scandal	35.2**	-45.9**	10.7*
Leader evaluations (-1 to +1)	49.9**	47.2**	43.6**

Table C1.4 *The Determinants of Vote Choice, Outside Québec, 2008*

	Conservative	Liberal	NDP
Sociodemographics (0/1)			
Under 35 years old	-0.0	-6.6*	6.6*
Over 54 years old	0.3	0.2	-0.4
Female	-6.0*	-1.4	7.4**
Atlantic resident	-11.5**	4.9	6.6
Western resident	11.8**	-17.9**	6.1**
Rural resident	7.0*	-4.6	-2.3
Catholic	-6.8*	4.6	2.2
Fundamentalist Christian	17.8**	-12.9**	-4.9
No religion	-16.8**	7.8**	9.0**
French first language	-13.0*	15.4**	-2.5
Visible minority	-20.8**	25.9**	-5.1
Northern European ancestry	2.4	-1.7	-0.8
Married/Common law	8.7**	-1.6	-7.1**
Public sector worker	0.2	1.7	-2.0
Union household	-5.1	-8.4**	13.5**
Less than high school	-6.3	-4.9	11.1**
University graduate	-10.0**	11.2**	-1.2
Values (-1 to +1)			
Market liberalism	42.2**	-12.0	-30.2**
Moral traditionalism	38.5**	-23.8**	-14.7*
Continentalism	62.6**	-21.2**	-41.3**
Personal religiosity	4.3	5.7	-10.1*
Racial outlooks	-7.8	-5.2	13.0*
Accommodating Québec	-31.6**	19.8**	11.7*
Political cynicism	-33.1**	3.8	29.4**
Regional alienation	-13.1**	11.3**	1.8
Party identification (0/1)	28.7**	23.3**	21.5**
Economic perceptions (-1 to +1)			
National retrospective	5.0*	-7.8**	2.8
Personal retrospective	5.3	-0.7	-4.6
Issues (-1 to +1)			
Fund national day care	-6.7**	1.5	5.2**
More health spending	4.2	-11.2**	7.0
Spend more on environment	-4.1	8.2**	-4.1
Spend more on arts	-10.2**	7.3**	2.9
Get tough on youth crime	6.5**	-4.3*	-2.2
Oppose private hospitals	0.0	-4.4*	4.4**
Favour 'green shift'	-18.5**	15.5**	3.0
Favour same-sex marriage	-1.6	-8.5**	10.2**
Oppose war in Afghanistan	-8.7**	2.9	5.8**
Leader evaluations (-1 to +1)	43.8**	35.4**	28.4**

Table C2.1 *The Determinants of Vote Choice, Québec, 2000*

	Bloc	Progressive Conservative	Liberal	NDP	Alliance
Sociodemographics (0/1)					
Under 35 years old	-2.0	-4.5**	1.7	3.7*	1.1
Over 54 years old	-9.0*	-0.6	14.9**	0.2	-5.5**
Female	-3.5	-0.3	8.4**	-3.8**	-0.8
Rural resident	10.3**	-3.8**	-6.7	3.1	-3.0
Non-francophone	-34.7**	-5.1**	36.4**	5.3**	-1.9
Less than high school	-5.7	1.2	7.4	-3.6**	0.6
University graduate	2.4	1.5	-9.0*	4.9**	0.2
Values (-1 to +1)					
Continentalism	3.0	0.4	5.0	-12.6**	4.2
Political cynicism	10.2	9.6**	-46.6**	10.0*	16.8**
Market liberalism	0.2	5.4	-0.6	-11.2**	6.0
Moral traditionalism	-11.0	-8.6	9.8	-12.2**	22.0**
Québec sovereignty	60.6**	-1.0	-44.4**	-5.6**	-9.8**
Regional alienation	12.6**	-1.6	-19.6**	-0.4	9.2**
Party identification (0/1)	24.4**	49.8**	18.7**	7.7	46.7**
Economic perceptions (-1 to +1)					
National retrospective	6.0	0.6	2.6	-3.8**	-5.2**
Issues (-1 to +1)					
More defence spending	-7.6*	1.2	9.6**	2.0	-5.0
More health spending	9.0	-4.6	4.0	-9.2**	0.8
More welfare spending	4.4	2.8	-0.8	1.4	-7.8**
Favour gun control	2.0	0.6	3.4	-1.2	-4.8*
Oppose private hospitals	0.6	-3.2*	3.0	0.0	-0.4
Leader evaluations (-1 to +1)	31.8**	3.8	19.2**	5.2**	34.2**

Table C2.2 *The Determinants of Vote Choice, Québec, 2004*

	Bloc	Conservative	Liberal	NDP
Sociodemographics (0/1)				
Under 35 years old	12.0*	-2.1	-8.4	-1.5
Over 54 years old	-6.9	1.6	9.2*	-3.8**
Female	3.1	-4.1	5.3	-4.3*
Rural resident	-3.7	7.5*	-5.8	2.0
Non-francophone	-55.5**	7.5	46.2**	1.7
Less than high school	-12.6*	0.0	16.5**	-3.9**
University graduate	-0.7	-0.4	-1.7	2.7
Values (-1 to +1)				
Continentalism	2.8	13.0*	-3.6	-12.0**
Political cynicism	20.4	26.8**	-36.0**	-11.2*
Market liberalism	-27.6**	22.0**	10.0	-4.4
Moral traditionalism	5.2	3.8	5.8	-15.0*
Québec sovereignty	54.6**	-9.8*	-43.0**	-1.6
Regional alienation	8.0	2.8	-9.0	-1.8
Party identification (0/1)	29.0**	18.2	21.9**	23.2*
Economic perceptions (-1 to +1)				
National retrospective	-11.4**	1.4	4.4	5.6**
Personal retrospective	5.4	-8.4**	7.0	-4.0
Issues (-1 to +1)				
More health spending	9.8	-11.0**	9.4	-8.2**
Get tough on youth crime	-8.4**	7.2**	0.0	1.0
Personal tax cuts	6.2	-9.4**	4.4	-1.0
Favour same-sex marriage	3.2	-7.4**	4.0	0.2
Sponsorship scandal	10.8	14.8**	-51.6**	26.0**
Staying out of Iraq	-11.8	-8.2*	-14.2	34.2**
Leader evaluations (-1 to +1)	31.0**	37.0**	33.4**	18.4**

Table C2.3 *The Determinants of Vote Choice, Québec, 2006*

	Bloc	Conservative	Liberal	NDP
Sociodemographics (0/1)				
Under 35 years old	11.5**	-14.5**	-1.9	4.8
Over 54 years old	-6.2	1.7	6.8	-2.3
Female	9.4**	-7.9**	1.7	-3.3
Rural resident	0.4	5.7	-4.5	-1.5
Non-francophone	-49.3**	3.3	47.3**	-1.4
Less than high school	-15.1**	2.1	17.0**	-4.0
University graduate	-3.2	-5.6	4.6	4.2
Values (-1 to +1)				
Continentalism	-24.6**	28.6**	15.6*	-19.8**
Political cynicism	2.2	34.6**	-24.6**	-12.0
Market liberalism	-9.2	40.4**	-13.8	-17.6**
Moral traditionalism	-15.4	20.0*	10.8	-15.4*
Québec sovereignty	50.0**	-10.0*	-34.0**	-6.0*
Regional alienation	14.6**	1.2	-11.0**	-4.6
Party identification (0/1)	25.0**	63.4**	17.6**	44.5**
Economic perceptions (-1 to +1)				
National retrospective	-1.6	-17.8**	11.6**	7.8
Personal retrospective	5.2	-8.4	5.4	-2.4
Issues (-1 to +1)				
More health spending	-5.0	15.6**	-16.2**	5.6
Fund national day care	2.8	-4.4	5.4**	-3.8
Favour death penalty	-3.8	6.4*	-5.2**	2.6
Favour gun control	6.4	-10.0**	7.6**	-4.0
Oppose allowing people to pay for faster medical care	-10.2**	-4.0	7.6**	6.8*
Sponsorship scandal	1.2	23.0**	-33.4**	9.0
Leader evaluations (-1 to +1)	33.6**	54.0**	23.6**	32.6**

Table C2.4 *The Determinants of Vote Choice, Québec, 2008*

	Bloc	Conservative	Liberal	NDP
Sociodemographics (0/1)				
Under 35 years old	-0.1	-3.3	-4.8	8.2*
Over 54 years old	-2.9	2.6	5.2	-4.9
Female	2.8	-8.7**	2.7	3.3
Rural resident	0.3	5.7	-2.8	-3.2
Non-francophone	-44.3**	-5.8	37.2**	12.9*
Less than high school	-10.7	6.2	5.2	-0.7
University graduate	-1.5	-1.1	5.7	-3.0
Values (-1 to +1)				
Continentalism	0.6	23.0	-1.0	-22.6**
Political cynicism	20.0	-22.0	3.0	-1.0
Market liberalism	-29.6**	43.6**	-17.0	3.0
Moral traditionalism	-48.2**	17.6	28.4**	2.0
Québec sovereignty	53.8**	-16.8**	-30.8**	-6.2
Regional alienation	15.0*	-5.0	2.2	-12.4**
Party identification (0/1)	22.4**	34.4**	25.6**	68.0**
Economic perceptions (-1 to +1)				
National retrospective	-0.6	13.4**	-10.4**	-2.4
Personal retrospective	-3.0	3.6	1.2	-2.0
Issues (-1 to +1)				
Spend more on arts	5.2	-14.4**	8.2	1.0
More defence spending	-16.0**	12.6**	6.0	-2.6
Spend more on environment	15.0*	-9.2	-2.2	-3.4
More health spending	8.4	-10.8*	-6.0	8.4
Favour death penalty	-1.0	7.0**	-3.2	-2.8
Favour 'green shift'	-9.4	-8.4	14.4**	3.6
Oppose private hospitals	-1.8	3.8	7.6**	-9.6**
Oppose war in Afghanistan	5.6	-1.2	4.2	-8.6**
Leader evaluations (-1 to +1)	46.6**	63.8**	37.6**	38.8**

REFERENCES

Aarts, Kees, André Blais, and Hermann Schmitt, eds. 2011. *Political Leaders and Democratic Elections*. Oxford: Oxford University Press.

Abramson, Paul R., and Ronald Inglehart. 1995. *Value Change in Global Perspective*. Ann Arbor: The University of Michigan Press.

Abramson, Paul R., John H. Aldrich, and David W. Rohde. 2010. *Change and Continuity in the 2008 Elections*. Washington, DC: CQ Press.

Alford, Robert R. 1963. *Party and Society: The Anglo-American Democracies*. Chicago: Rand McNally.

Alvarez, Michael R., Jonathan Nagler, and Shaun Bowler. 2000. "Issues, Economics, and the Dynamics of Multiparty Elections." *American Political Science Review* 94: 131–94.

Andersen, Robert, and Tina Fetner. 2008. "Cohort Differences in Tolerance of Homosexuality: Attitudinal Change in Canada and the United States, 1981–2000." *Public Opinion Quarterly* 72 (2): 311–30. doi:10.1093/poq/nfn017.

Anderson, Cameron D. 2006. "Economic Voting and Multilevel Governance: A Comparative Individual-Level Analysis." *American Journal of Political Science* 50 (2): 449–63. doi:10.1111/j.1540-5907.2006.00194.x.

Anderson, Cameron D. 2008. "Economic Voting, Multilevel Governance and Information in Canada." *Canadian Journal of Political Science* 41 (2): 329–54. doi:10.1017/S0008423908080414.

Anderson, Cameron D. 2010. "Economic Voting in Canada." In *Voting Behaviour in Canada*, ed. Cameron D. Anderson and Laura B. Stephenson. Vancouver: University of British Columbia Press, 139–62.

Anderson, Cameron D., and Laura B. Stephenson. 2010a. "The Puzzle of Elections and Voting in Canada." In *Voting Behaviour in Canada*, ed. Cameron D. Anderson and Laura B. Stephenson. Vancouver: University of British Columbia Press, 1–39.

Anderson, Cameron D., and Laura B. Stephenson. 2010b. "Reflecting on Lessons from the Canadian Voter." In *Voting Behaviour in Canada*, ed. Cameron D. Anderson and Laura B. Stephenson. Vancouver: University of British Columbia Press, 279–89.

Anderson, Christopher J. 1995. *Blaming the Government: Citizens and the Economy in Five European Democracies*. Armonk: M.E. Sharpe.

Anderson, Christopher J. 2000. "Economic Voting and Political Context: A Comparative Perspective." *Electoral Studies* 19 (2-3): 151–70. doi:10.1016/S0261-3794(99)00045-1.

Anderson, Christopher J., and Christine A. Guillory. 1997. "Political Institutions and Satisfaction with Democracy: A Cross-National Analysis of Consensus and Majoritarian Systems." *American Political Science Review* 91 (1): 66–81. doi:10.2307/2952259.

Archer, Keith. 1985. "The Failure of the New Democratic Party: Unions, Unionists, and Politics in Canada." *Canadian Journal of Political Science* 18 (2): 353–66. doi:10.1017/S0008423900030298.

Artés, Joaquín, and Antonio Bustos. 2008. "Electoral Promises and Minority Governments: An Empirical Study." *European Journal of Political Research* 47 (3): 307–33. doi:10.1111/j.1475-6765.2007.00722.x.

Ayres, Jeffrey M. 1996. "Political Process and Popular Protest: The Mobilization against Free Trade in Canada." *American Journal of Economics and Sociology* 55 (4): 473–88. doi:10.1111/j.1536-7150.1996.tb02646.x.

Bafumi, Joseph, and Robert Y. Shapiro. 2009. "A New Partisan Voter." *Journal of Politics* 71 (1): 1–24. doi:10.1017/S0022381608090014.

Banducci, Susan A., and Jeffrey A. Karp. 2000. "Gender, Leadership and Choice in Multiparty Systems." *Political Research Quarterly* 53: 815–48.

Banting, Keith, George Hoberg, and Richard Simeon. 1997. *Degrees of Freedom: Canada and the United States in a Changing World*. Montréal: McGill-Queen's University Press.

Barnea, Marina F., and Shalom H. Schwartz. 1998. "Values and Voting." *Political Psychology* 19 (1): 17–40. doi:10.1111/0162-895X.00090.

Bartels, Larry M. 2002. "Beyond the Running Tally: Partisan Bias in Political Perceptions." *Political Behavior* 24 (2): 117–50. doi:10.1023/A:1021226224601.

Baum, Matthew A. 2002. "Sex, Lies, and War: How Soft News Brings Foreign Policy to the Inattentive Public." *American Political Science Review* 96 (1): 91–109. doi:10.1017/S0003055402004252.

Bean, Clive, and Anthony Mughan. 1989. "Leadership Effects in Parliamentary Elections in Australia and Britain." *American Political Science Review* 83 (4): 1165–79. doi:10.2307/1961663.

Bélanger, Éric. 2004. "Antipartyism and Third-Party Vote Choice: A Comparison of Canada, Britain, and Australia." *Comparative Political Studies* 37 (9): 1054–78. doi:10.1177/0010414004268847.

Bélanger, Éric, and Richard Nadeau. 2005. "Political Trust and the Vote in Multiparty Elections: The Canadian Case." *European Journal of Political Research* 44 (1): 121–46. doi:10.1111/j.1475-6765.2005.00221.x.

Bélanger, Éric, and Richard Nadeau. 2009. *Le comportement électoral des Québécois.* Montréal: Les Presses de l'Université de Montréal.

Bélanger, Paul, and Munroe Eagles. 2006. "The Geography of Class and Religion in Canadian Elections Revisited." *Canadian Journal of Political Science* 39 (3): 591–609. doi:10.1017/S0008423906060227.

Bennulf, Martin. 1995. "Sweden: The Rise and Fall of Miljöpartiet de Gröna." In *The Green Challenge: The Development of Green Parties in Europe*, ed. Dick Richardson and Chris Roots. London: Routledge, 94–107.

Bennulf, Martin, and Sören Holmberg. 1990. "The Green Breakthrough in Sweden." *Scandinavian Political Studies* 13 (2): 165–84. doi:10.1111/j.1467-9477. 1990.tb00435.x.

Berelson, Bernard, Paul F. Lazarsfeld, and William N. McPhee. 1954. *Voting.* Chicago: Chicago University Press.

Betz, Hans-Georg. 1990. "Value Change and Postmaterialist Politics." *Comparative Political Studies* 23 (2): 239–56. doi:10.1177/0010414090023002004.

Bibby, Reginald W. 1979. "The State of Collective Religiosity in Canada: An Empirical Analysis." *Canadian Review of Sociology* 16 (1): 105–16. doi:10.1111/ j.1755-618X.1979.tb01013.x.

Bibby, Reginald W. 2008. "The Perils of Pioneering and Prophecy: A Response to Thiessen and Dawson." *Studies in Religion* 37 (3-4): 417–25. doi:10.1177/ 000842980803700302.

Bilodeau, Antoine, and Mebs Kanji. 2010. "The New Immigrant Voter, 1965–2004: The Emergence of a New Liberal Partisan." In *Voting Behaviour in Canada*, ed. Cameron D. Anderson and Laura B. Stephenson. Vancouver: University of British Columbia Press, 65–85.

Birch, Sarah. 2009. "Real Progress: Prospects for Green Party Support in Britain." *Parliamentary Affairs* 62 (1): 53–71. doi:10.1093/pa/gsn037.

Bittner, Amanda. 2010. "Personality Matters: The Evaluation of Party Leaders in Canadian Elections." In *Voting Behaviour in Canada*, ed. Cameron D. Anderson and Laura B. Stephenson. Vancouver: University of British Columbia Press, 183–207.

Blais, André. 2002. "Why is There So Little Strategic Voting in Canadian Plurality Rule Elections?" *Political Studies* 50 (3): 445–54. doi:10.1111/1467-9248.00378.

Blais, André. 2005. "Accounting for the Electoral Success of the Liberal Party in Canada." *Canadian Journal of Political Science* 38: 821–40.

Blais, André, Shaun Bowler, Todd Donovan, and Ola Listhaug. 2005. *Losers' Consent, Elections, and Democratic Legitimacy.* Oxford: Oxford University Press.

Blais, André, and Martin Boyer. 1996. "Assessing the Impact of Televised Debates: The Case of the 1988 Canadian Election." *British Journal of Political Science* 26 (2): 143–64. doi:10.1017/S0007123400000405.

Blais, André, Elisabeth Gidengil, Agnieszka Dobrzynska, Neil Nevitte, and Richard Nadeau. 2003. "Does the Local Candidate Matter?" *Canadian Journal of Political Science* 36: 657–64.

Blais, André, Elisabeth Gidengil, Richard Nadeau, and Neil Nevitte. 2001. "Measuring Party Identification: Canada, Britain, and the United States." *Political Behavior* 23 (1): 5–22. doi:10.1023/A:1017665513905.

Blais, André, Elisabeth Gidengil, Richard Nadeau, and Neil Nevitte. 2002. *Anatomy of a Liberal Victory: Making Sense of the 2000 Canadian Election.* Peterborough: Broadview Press.

Blais, André, Elisabeth Gidengil, Richard Nadeau, and Neil Nevitte. 2003. "Campaign Dynamics in the 2000 Canadian Election: How the Leader Debates Salvaged the Conservative Party." *PS: Political Science and Politics* 26: 45–50.

Blais, André, and Richard Nadeau. 1984. "L'appui au Parti Québécois: Évolution de la clientèle de 1970 à 1981." In *Comportement électoral au Québec*, ed. Jean Crête. Chicoutimi: Gaëtan Morin, 279–318.

Blais, André, and Richard Nadeau. 1996. "Measuring Strategic Voting: A Two-Step Procedure." *Electoral Studies* 15 (1): 39–52. doi:10.1016/0261-3794(94)00014-X.

Blais, André, Richard Nadeau, Elisabeth Gidengil, and Neil Nevitte. 2001a. "The Formation of Party Preferences: Testing the Proximity and Directional Models." *European Journal of Political Research* 40: 81–91.

Blais, André, Richard Nadeau, Elisabeth Gidengil, and Neil Nevitte. 2001b. "Measuring Strategic Voting in Multiparty Plurality Elections." *Electoral Studies* 20 (3): 343–52. doi:10.1016/S0261-3794(00)00017-2.

Blais, André, Neil Nevitte, Elisabeth Gidengil, Henry Brady, and Richard Johnston. 1995. "L'élection fédérale de 1993: Le comportement électoral des Québécois." *Revue québécoise de science politique* 27: 15–49.

Blais, André, Mathieu Turgeon, Elisabeth Gidengil, Neil Nevitte, and Richard Nadeau. 2004. "Which Matters Most? Comparing the Impact of Issues and the Economy in American, British, and Canadian Elections." *British Journal of Political Science* 34 (3): 555–63. doi:10.1017/S0007123404220178.

Blake, Donald E. 1982. "The Consistency of Inconsistency: Party Identification in Federal and Provincial Politics." *Canadian Journal of Political Science* 15 (4): 691–710. doi:10.1017/S000842390005201X.

Blake, Donald E. 2002. "Personal Values and Environmental Attitudes." In *Citizen Politics: Research and Theory in Canadian Political Behaviour*, ed. Joanna Everitt and Brenda O'Neill. Toronto: Oxford University Press, 126–41.

Bowler, Shaun, and David J. Lanoue. 1992. "Strategic and Protest Voting for Third Parties: The Case of the Canadian NDP." *Western Political Quarterly* 45 (2): 485–99. doi:10.2307/448722.

Brettschneider, Frank, and Oscar Gabriel. 2002. "The Nonpersonalization of Voting Behaviour in Germany." In *Leader's Personalities and the Outcomes of Democratic Elections*, ed. Anthony King. Oxford: Oxford University Press, 127–57.

Brodie, M. Janine, and Jane Jenson. 1988. *Crisis, Challenge and Change: Party and Class in Canada*. Ottawa: Carleton University Press.

Campbell, Angus, Philip E. Converse, Warren E. Miller, and Donald E. Stokes. 1960. *The American Voter*. New York: John Wiley.

Canada. Commission of Inquiry into the Sponsorship Program and Advertising Activities. 2005. *Who is Responsible: Phase 1 Report*. Ottawa: Public Works and Government Services Canada. http://epe.lac-bac.gc.ca/100/206/301/pco-bcp/commissions/sponsorship-ef/06-02-10/www.gomery.ca/en/phase1report/summary/es_full_v01.pdf.

Canada. Parliament of Canada. 2011. *Electoral Results by Party*. Ottawa: Library of Parliament. http://www.parl.gc.ca/parlinfo/Compilations/ElectionsAndRidings/ResultsParty.aspx.

Carmines, Edward G., and James A. Stimson. 1980. "The Two Faces of Issue Voting." *American Political Science Review* 74 (1): 78–91. doi:10.2307/1955648.

Carty, R. Kenneth, D. Munroe Eagles, and Anthony Sayers. 2003. "Candidates and Local Campaigns: Are there Just Four Canadian Types?" *Party Politics* 9 (5): 619–39. doi:10.1177/13540688030095006.

Clarke, Harold, and Allan Kornberg. 1992. "Support for the Canadian Federal Progressive Conservative Party since 1988: The Impact of Economic Evaluations and Economic Issues." *Canadian Journal of Political Science* 25 (1): 29–53. doi:10.1017/S0008423900001906.

Clarke, Harold D., Jane Jenson, Lawrence LeDuc, and Jon H. Pammett. 1984. *Absent Mandate: The Politics of Discontent in Canada*. Agincourt: Gage.

Clarke, Harold D., Jane Jenson, Lawrence LeDuc, and Jon H. Pammett. 1991. *Absent Mandate*, 2nd ed. Toronto: Gage.

Clarke, Harold D., Allan Kornberg, and Thomas J. Scotto. 2009. *Making Political Choices: Canada and the United States*. Toronto: University of Toronto Press.

Clarke, Harold D., Lawrence LeDuc, Jane Jenson, and Jon H. Pammett. 1979. *Political Choice in Canada*. Toronto: McGraw-Hill Ryerson.

Clarke, Harold D., David Sanders, Marianne C. Stewart, and Paul Whiteley. 2004. *Political Choice in Britain*. Oxford: Oxford University Press. doi:10.1093/019924488X.001.0001.

Clarke, Harold D., and Marianne C. Stewart. 1987. "Partisan Inconsistency and Partisan Change in Federal States: The Case of Canada." *American Journal of Political Science* 31 (2): 383–407. doi:10.2307/2111081.

Clarkson, Stephen. 2001. "The Liberal Threepeat: The Multi-System Party in the Multi-Party System." In *The Canadian General Election of 2000*, ed. Jon H. Pammett and Christopher Dornan. Toronto: Dundurn, 13–58.

Clarkson, Stephen. 2002. *Uncle Sam and Us: Globalization, Neoconservatism, and the Canadian State.* Toronto: University of Toronto Press.

Cody, Howard. 2008. "Minority Government in Canada: The Stephen Harper Experience." *American Review of Canadian Studies* 38 (1): 27–42. doi:10.1080/02722010809481819.

Converse, Philip. 1964. "The Nature of Belief Systems in Mass Publics." In *Ideology and Discontent*, ed. David Apter. New York: Free Press, 206–61.

Cox, Gary. 1997. *Making Votes Count: Strategic Coordination in the World's Electoral Systems.* Cambridge: Cambridge University Press.

Crête, Jean, and Johanne Simard. 1984. "Conjoncture économique et élections: une étude des élections au Québec." In *Comportement électoral au Québec*, ed. Jean Crête. Chicoutimi: Gaëtan Morin, 165–97.

Crewe, Ivor, and Anthony King. 1994. "Are British Elections Becoming More Presidential?" In *Elections at Home and Abroad: Essays in Honor of Warren E. Miller*, ed. Kent Jennings and Thomas Mann. Ann Arbor: University of Michigan Press, 181–206.

Cutler, Fred. 2002. "The Simplest Shortcut of All: Socio-Demographic Characteristics and Electoral Choice." *Journal of Politics* 64 (2): 466–90. doi:10.1111/1468-2508.00135.

Cutler, Fred, and Richard Jenkins. 2001. "Where One Lives and What One Thinks: Implications of Rural-Urban Opinion Cleavages for Canadian Federalism." In *Canada: The State of the Federation 2001: Canadian Political Culture(s) in Transition*, ed. Hamish Telford and Harvey Lazar. Montréal: McGill-Queen's University Press, 367–92.

Dalton, Russell J. 1988. *Citizen Politics: Public Opinion and Political Parties in Advanced Western Democracies.* Chatham, NJ: Chatham House.

Dalton, Russell J. 1999. "Political Support in Advanced Industrial Democracies." In *Critical Citizens: Global Support for Democratic Governance*, ed. Pippa Norris. Oxford: Oxford University Press, 57–77.

Dalton, Russell J. 2009. "Economics, Environmentalism and Party Alignments: A Note on Partisan Change in Advanced Industrial Democracies." *European Journal of Political Research* 48 (2): 161–75. doi:10.1111/j.1475-6765.2008.00831.x.

Dalton, Russell J., Scott C. Flanagan, and Paul Allen Beck. 1984. *Electoral Change in Advanced Industrial Democracies: Realignment or Dealignment?* Princeton: Princeton University Press.

Dalton, Russell J., and Martin P. Wattenberg. 2001. *Parties without Partisans.* New York: Oxford University Press.

Dalton, Russell J., and Steven Weldon. 2005. "Public Images of Political Parties: A Necessary Evil?" *West European Politics* 28 (5): 931–51. doi:10.1080/01402380500310527.

De Haan, Jakob, Jan-Egbert Sturm, and Geert Beekhuis. 1999. "The Weak Government Thesis: Some New Evidence." *Public Choice* 101: 163–76.

Delli Carpini, Michael X., and Scott Keeter. 1996. *What Americans Know about Politics and Why it Matters.* New Haven: Yale University Press.

Dobrzynska, Agnieszka, André Blais, and Richard Nadeau. 2003. "Do the Media Have a Direct Impact on the Vote? The Case of the 1997 Canadian Election." *International Journal of Public Opinion Research* 15 (1): 27–43. doi:10.1093/ijpor/15.1.27.

Docherty, David. 2008. "Minority Government in Canada." In *No Overall Control?* ed. Alex Brazier and Susanna Kalitowski. London: Hansard Society, 83–94.

Downs, Anthony. 1957. *An Economic Theory of Democracy.* New York: Harper Collins.

Duch, Raymond M., and Randolph T. Stevenson. 2008. *The Economic Vote: How Political and Economic Institutions Condition Election Results.* New York: Cambridge University Press. doi:10.1017/CBO9780511755934.

Duverger, Maurice. 1954. *Political Parties.* New York: Wiley.

Ebeid, Michael, and Jonathan Rodden. 2006. "Economic Geography and Economic Voting: Evidence from the US States." *British Journal of Political Science* 36 (3): 527–47. doi:10.1017/S0007123406000275.

Edin, Per-Anders, and Henry Ohlsson. 1991. "Political Determinants of Budget Deficits: Coalition Effects versus Minority Effects." *European Economic Review* 35 (8): 1597–603. doi:10.1016/0014-2921(91)90021-A.

Erickson, Lynda, and Brenda O'Neill. 2002. "The Gender Gap and the Changing Woman Voter in Canada." *International Political Science Review* 23 (4): 373–92. doi:10.1177/0192512102023004003.

Erikson, Robert S. 1989. "Economic Conditions and the Presidential Vote." *American Political Science Review* 83 (2): 567–73. doi:10.2307/1962406.

Erikson, Robert S. 1990. "Economic Conditions and the Congressional Vote: A Review of the Macrolevel Evidence." *American Journal of Political Science* 34 (2): 373–99. doi:10.2307/2111452.

Erikson, Robert S., Michael B. MacKuen, and James A. Stimson. 2002. *The Macro Polity.* New York: Cambridge University Press.

Esmer, Yilmaz, and Thorlief Pettersson. 2007. "The Effects of Religion and Religiosity on Voting Behaviour." In *The Oxford Handbook of Political Behaviour,* ed. Russell J. Dalton and Hans-Dieter Klingemann. Oxford: Oxford University Press, 481–503. doi:10.1093/oxfordhb/9780199270125.003.0025.

Feldman, Stanley. 1988. "Structure and Consistency in Public Opinion: the Role of Core Beliefs and Values." *American Journal of Political Science* 32 (2): 416–40. doi:10.2307/2111130.

Feldman, Stanley, and John Zaller. 1992. "The Political Culture of Ambivalence: Ideological Responses to the Welfare State." *American Journal of Political Science* 36 (1): 268–307. doi:10.2307/2111433.

Finer, Samuel E. 1975. *Adversary Politics and Electoral Reform*. London: Wigram.

Fiorina, Morris P. 1981. *Retrospective Voting in American National Elections*. New Haven: Yale University Press.

Fiorina, Morris P. 2002. "Parties and Partisanship: A 40-year Retrospective." *Political Behavior* 24 (2): 93–115. doi:10.1023/A:1021274107763.

Forsey, Eugene. 1964. "The Problem of 'Minority' Government in Canada." *Canadian Journal of Economics and Political Science* 30 (1): 1–11. doi:10.2307/139166.

Fournier, Patrick. 2002. "The Uninformed Canadian Voter." In *Citizen Politics: Research and Theory in Canadian Political Behaviour*, ed. Joanna Everitt and Brenda O'Neill. Oxford: Oxford University Press, 92–110.

Franklin, Mark N. 1992. "The Decline of Cleavage Politics." In *Electoral Change: Responses to Evolving Social and Attitudinal Structures in Western Countries*, ed. Mark N. Franklin, Tom Mackie, and Henry Valen. Cambridge: Cambridge University Press, 383–405.

Gabriel, Oscar W. 1995. "Political Efficacy and Trust." In *The Impact of Values*, ed. Jan W. Van Deth and Elinor Scarbrough. Oxford: Oxford University Press, 357–89.

Gélineau, François, and Éric Bélanger. 2005. "Electoral Accountability in a Federal System: National and Provincial Economic Voting in Canada." *Publius: The Journal of Federalism* 35: 407–24.

Gibbins, Roger. 1980. *Prairie Politics and Society: Regionalism in Decline*. Toronto: Butterworths.

Gibbins, Roger. 1982. *Regionalism: Territorial Politics in Canada and the United States*. Toronto: Butterworths.

Gibbins, Roger, and Loleen Berdahl. 2003. *Western Visions, Western Futures: Perspectives on the West in Canada*. Peterborough: Broadview Press.

Gidengil, Elisabeth. 1992. "Canada Votes: A Quarter Century of Canadian National Election Studies." *Canadian Journal of Political Science* 25 (2): 219–48. doi:10.1017/S0008423900003966.

Gidengil, Elisabeth. 1995. "Economic Man—Social Woman? The Case of the Gender Gap in Support for the Canada–US Free Trade Agreement." *Comparative Political Studies* 28 (3): 384–408. doi:10.1177/0010414095028003003.

Gidengil, Elisabeth. 2002. "The Class Voting Conundrum." In *Political Sociology: Canadian Perspectives*, ed. Douglas Baer. Don Mills: Oxford University Press, 274–87.

Gidengil, Elisabeth. 2007. "Beyond the Gender Gap." *Canadian Journal of Political Science* 40: 1–17.

Gidengil, Elisabeth. 2011. "Voter Characteristics and Leader Effects." In *Political Leaders and Democratic Elections*, ed. Kees Aarts, André Blais, and Hermann Schmitt. Oxford: Oxford University Press, 147-64.

Gidengil, Elisabeth, and André Blais. 2007. "Are Party Leaders Becoming More Important to Vote Choice in Canada?" In *Political Leadership and Representation in Canada: Essays in Honour of John Courtney*, ed. Hans Michelmann, Donald Story, and Jeffrey Steeves. Toronto: University of Toronto Press, 39–59.

Gidengil, Elisabeth, André Blais, Joanna Everitt, Patrick Fournier, and Neil Nevitte. 2006. "Back to the Future? Making Sense of the 2004 Canadian Election Outside Quebec." *Canadian Journal of Political Science* 39 (01): 1–25. doi:10.1017/S0008423906060069.

Gidengil, Elisabeth, André Blais, Richard Nadeau, and Neil Nevitte. 1999. "Making Sense of Regional Voting in the 1997 Canadian Federal Election: Liberal and Reform Support Outside Quebec." *Canadian Journal of Political Science* 32 (2): 247–72. doi:10.1017/S0008423900010489.

Gidengil, Elisabeth, André Blais, Richard Nadeau, and Neil Nevitte. 2003. "Women to the Left? Gender Differences in Political Beliefs and Policy Preferences." In *Gender and Electoral Representation in Canada*, ed. Manon Tremblay and Linda Trimble. Oxford: Oxford University Press, 140–59.

Gidengil, Elisabeth, André Blais, Richard Nadeau, and Neil Nevitte. 2004. "Language and Cultural Insecurity." In *Québec: State and Society*, 3rd ed., ed. Alain Gagnon. Peterborough: Broadview Press, 345–67.

Gidengil, Elisabeth, André Blais, Neil Nevitte, and Richard Nadeau. 2001. "The Correlates and Consequences of Anti-Partyism in the 1997 Canadian Election." *Party Politics* 7 (4): 491–513. doi:10.1177/1354068801007004005.

Gidengil, Elisabeth, André Blais, Neil Nevitte, and Richard Nadeau. 2004. *Citizens*. Vancouver: University of British Columbia Press.

Gidengil, Elisabeth, Matthew Hennigar, André Blais, and Neil Nevitte. 2005. "Explaining the Gender Gap in Support for the New Right: The Case of Canada." *Comparative Political Studies* 38 (10): 1171–95. doi:10.1177/0010414005279320.

Goerres, Achim. 2008. "The Grey Vote: Determinants of Older Voters' Party Choice in Britain and West Germany." *Electoral Studies* 20: 1–20.

Graetz, Brian, and Ian McAllister. 1987. "Party Leaders and Election Outcomes in Britain, 1974–1983." *Comparative Political Studies* 19 (4): 484–507. doi:10.1177/0010414087019004002.

Green, Donald P., Bradley Palmquist, and Eric Schickler. 2002. *Partisan Hearts and Minds: Political Parties and the Social Identities of Voters*. New Haven: Yale University Press.

Green, Donald P., and David H. Yoon. 2002. "Reconciling Individual and Aggregate Evidence Concerning Partisan Stability: Applying Time-Series Models to Panel Survey Data." *Political Analysis* 10 (1): 1–24. doi:10.1093/pan/10.1.1.

Grofman, Bernard. 1993. "Is Turnout the Paradox that Ate Rational Choice Theory?" In *Information, Participation and Choice: An Economic Theory of Democracy in Perspective*, ed. Bernard Grofman. Ann Arbor: University of Michigan Press, 93–103.

Guérin, Daniel, and Richard Nadeau. 1995. "Conjoncture économique et comportement électoral au Québec." *Recherches sociographiques* 26: 65–76.

Hall, Elaine J., and Marnie Salupo Rodriguez. 2003. "The Myth of Postfeminism." *Gender & Society* 17 (6): 878–902. doi:10.1177/0891243203257639.

Haranda, Susan. 2004. "The Others: A Quest for Credibility." In *The Canadian Federal Election of 2004*, ed. Jon H. Pammett and Christopher Dornan. Toronto: Dundurn, 170–202.

Hayes, Bernadette C., and Ian McAllister. 1997. "Gender, Party Leaders, and Election Outcomes in Australia, Britain, and the United States." *Comparative Political Studies* 30 (1): 3–26. doi:10.1177/0010414097030001001.

Hellwig, Timothy T. 2001. "Interdependence, Government Constraints, and Economic Voting." *Journal of Politics* 63 (4): 1141–62. doi:10.1111/ 0022-3816. 00104.

Henry, Shawn. 2001. "Revisiting Western Alienation: Towards a Better Understanding of Political Alienation and Political Behaviour in Western Canada." In *Regionalism and Party Politics in Canada*, ed. Keith Archer and Lisa Young. Toronto: Oxford University Press, 77–91.

Holmberg, Sören, and Henrik Oscarsson. 2011. "Party Leader Effects on the Vote." In *Political Leaders and Democratic Elections*, ed. Kees Aarts, André Blais, and Hermann Schmitt. Oxford: Oxford University Press, 35–51.

Inglehart, Ronald. 1977. *The Silent Revolution: Changing Values and Political Styles among Western Publics*. Princeton: Princeton University Press.

Inglehart, Ronald. 1995. "Public Support for Environmental Protection: Objective Problems and Subjective Values in 43 Societies." *PS: Political Science and Politics* 28 (1): 57–72. doi:10.2307/420583.

Inglehart, Ronald. 1997. *Modernization and Postmodernization: Cultural, Economic, and Political Change in 43 Societies*. Princeton, NJ: Princeton University Press.

Inglehart, Ronald, and Wayne E. Baker. 2000. "Modernization, Cultural Change, and the Persistence of Traditional Values." *American Sociological Review* 65 (1): 19–51. doi:10.2307/2657288.

Inglehart, Ronald, and Hans-Dieter Klingemann. 1976. "Party Identification, Ideological Preference, and the Left-Right Dimension among Western Mass Publics." In *Party Identification and Beyond*, ed. Ian Budge, Ivor Crewe, and Dennis Farlie. London: John Wiley, 243–73.

Inglehart, Ronald, Neil Nevitte, and Miguel Basáñez. 1996. *The North American Trajectory: Cultural, Economic, and Political Ties among the United States, Canada, and Mexico.* New York: Aldine.

Inglehart, Ronald, and Pippa Norris. 2003. *Rising Tide: Gender Equality and Cultural Change around the World.* New York: Cambridge University Press. doi:10.1017/CBO9780511550362.

Irvine, William P. 1974. "Explaining the Religious Basis of the Canadian Partisan Identity: Success on the Third Try." *Canadian Journal of Political Science* 7 (3): 560–63. doi:10.1017/S0008423900040786.

Janowitz, Morris, and Warren E. Miller. 1952. "The Index of Political Predisposition in the 1948 Election." *Journal of Politics* 14 (4): 710–27. doi:10.2307/2126448.

Jenkins, Simon. 2008. "Hung Parliaments are a Nightmare." In *No Overall Control?* ed. Alex Brazier and Susanna Kalitowski. London: Hansard Society, 101–3.

Jennings, M. Kent. 1988. "Preface." In *The Politics of the Gender Gap,* ed. Carol M. Mueller. Beverly Hills: Sage, 7–12.

Johnston, Richard. 1985. "The Reproduction of the Religious Cleavage in Canadian Elections." *Canadian Journal of Political Science* 18 (1): 99–113. doi:10.1017/S000842390002922X.

Johnston, Richard. 1991. "The Geography of Class and Religion in Canadian Elections." In *The Ballot and its Message,* ed. Joseph Wearing. Toronto: Copp-Clark Pitman, 108–35.

Johnston, Richard. 1992. "Party Identification Measures in the Anglo-American Democracies: A National Survey Experiment." *American Journal of Political Science* 36 (2): 542–59. doi:10.2307/2111490.

Johnston, Richard. 2002. "Prime Ministerial Contenders in Canada." In *Leaders' Personalities and the Outcomes of Democratic Elections,* ed. Anthony Stephen King. New York: Oxford University Press, 158–84.

Johnston, Richard, André Blais, Henry Brady, and Jean Crête. 1992. *Letting the People Decide: The Dynamics of a Canadian Election.* Montréal: McGill-Queen's University Press.

Johnston, Richard, André Blais, Elisabeth Gidengil, and Neil Nevitte. 1996. *The Challenge of Direct Democracy: The 1992 Canadian Referendum.* Montréal: McGill-Queen's University Press.

Johnston, Richard, Patrick Fournier, and Richard Jenkins. 2000. "Party Location and Party Support: Unpacking Competing Models." *Journal of Politics* 62 (4): 1145–60. doi:10.1111/0022-3816.00050.

Joslyn, Richard. 1984. *Mass Media and Elections.* Reading, MA: Addison-Wesley.

Kaase, Max. 1994. "Is There Personalisation of Politics? Candidates and Voting Behaviour in Germany." *International Political Science Review* 15 (3): 211–30. doi:10.1177/019251219401500301.

Kanji, Mebs, and Keith Archer. 2002. "Theories of Voting and their Applicability in

Canada." In *Citizen Politics: Research and Theory in Canadian Political Behaviour*, ed. Joanna Everitt and Brenda O'Neill. Toronto: Oxford University Press, 160–84.

Kanji, Mebs, and Antoine Bilodeau. 2006. "Value Diversity and Support for Electoral Reform in Canada." *PS: Political Science & Politics* 39 (4): 829–36.

Katzenstein, Peter. 1986. *Small States in World Markets*. Ithaca, NY: Cornell University Press.

Kay, Barry J. 1977. "An Examination of Class and Left-Right Party Images in Canadian Voting." *Canadian Journal of Political Science* 10 (1): 127–43. doi:10.1017/S0008423900039317.

Kinder, Donald. 1983. "Diversity and Complexity in American Public Opinion." In *Political Science: The State of the Discipline*, ed. Ada Finifter. Washington, DC: American Political Science Association, 389–425.

Knutsen, Oddbjørn. 1995a. "Left-Right Materialist Value Orientations." In *The Impact of Values*, ed. J.W. Van Deth and E. Scarborough. Oxford: Oxford University Press, 160–96.

Knutsen, Oddbjørn. 1995b. "Party Choice." In *The Impact of Values*, ed. J.W. Van Deth and E. Scarbrough. Oxford: Oxford University Press, 461–91.

Kymlicka, Will. 1995. *Multicultural Citizenship: A Liberal Theory of Minority Rights*. Oxford: Oxford University Press.

Kymlicka, Will. 1998. *Finding Our Way: Rethinking Ethnocultural Relations in Canada*. Oxford: Oxford University Press.

LaForest, Guy. 1995. *Trudeau and the End of a Canadian Dream*. Montréal: McGill-Queen's University Press.

Lambert, Ronald D., James E. Curtis, Steven D. Brown, and Barry J. Kay. 1986. "In Search of Left/Right Beliefs in the Canadian Electorate." *Canadian Journal of Political Science* 19 (3): 541–63. doi:10.1017/S0008423900054573.

Lasswell, Harold D. 1936. *Politics: Who Gets What, When, How*. New York: McGraw-Hill.

Lazarsfeld, Paul, Bernard Berelson, and Hazel Gaudet. 1944. *The People's Choice: How the Voter Makes Up His Mind in a Presidential Campaign*. New York: Duell, Sloan, and Pearce.

Lazarsfeld, Paul, Bernard Berelson, and Hazel Gaudet. 1968. *The People's Choice: How the Voter Makes Up His Mind in a Presidential Campaign*. New York: Columbia University Press.

LeDuc, Lawrence. 1977. "Political Behaviour and the Issue of Majority Government in Two Federal Elections." *Canadian Journal of Political Science* 10 (2): 311–39. doi:10.1017/S0008423900041482.

LeDuc, Lawrence, Harold D. Clarke, Jane Jenson, and Jon H. Pammett. 1984. "Partisan Instability in Canada: Evidence from a New Panel Study." *American Political Science Review* 78 (2): 470–84. doi:10.2307/1963376.

Lemieux, Vincent, Marcel Gilbert, and André Blais. 1970. *Une élection de réalignement, l'élection générale du 29 avril 1970 au Québec.* Montréal: Éditions du jour.

Lewis-Beck, Michael S. 1988. *Economics and Elections: The Major Western Democracies.* Ann Arbor: Michigan University Press.

Lewis-Beck, Michael S., William G. Jacoby, Helmut Norpoth, and Herbert F. Weisberg. 2008. *The American Voter Revisited.* Ann Arbor: University of Michigan Press.

Lewis-Beck, Michael S., and Glenn E. Mitchell. 1993. "French Electoral Theory: The National Front Test." *Electoral Studies* 12 (2): 112–27. doi:10.1016/ 0261-3794 (93)90013-A.

Lewis-Beck, Michael S., and Mary Stegmaier. 2007. "Economic Models of the Vote." In *The Oxford Handbook of Political Behaviour,* ed. Russell Dalton and Hans-Dieter Klingemann. Oxford: Oxford University Press, 518–37.

Lupia, Arthur, and Mathew D. McCubbins. 1998. *The Democratic Dilemma: Can Citizens Learn What They Need to Know?* Cambridge: Cambridge University Press.

Luskin, Robert C. 1987. "Measuring Political Sophistication." *American Journal of Political Science* 31 (4): 856–99. doi:10.2307/2111227.

Lusztig, Michael, and Matthew Wilson. 2005. "A New Right? Moral Issues and Partisan Change in Canada." *Social Science Quarterly* 86 (1): 109–28. doi:10.1111/ j.0038-4941.2005.00293.x.

Macdonald, Stuart E., Ola Listhaug, and George Rabinowitz. 1991. "Issues and Party Support in Multiparty Systems." *American Political Science Review* 85 (4): 1107–31. doi:10.2307/1963938.

MacKuen, Michael B., Robert S. Erikson, and James A. Stimson. 1992. "Peasants or Bankers? The American Electorate and the U.S. Economy." *American Political Science Review* 86 (3): 597–611. doi:10.2307/1964124.

Mallory, James Russell. 1949. *The Structure of Canadian Politics.* Mount Allison University Publications, No. 4. Sackville, NB: Mount Allison University.

Manning, Haydon. 2003. "Profiles: The Environment, the Australian Greens and the 2001 National Election." *Environmental Politics* 12: 123–49.

McAllister, Ian. 1994. "Dimensions of Environmentalism: Public Opinion, Political Activism, and Party Support in Australia." *Environmental Politics* 3: 22–42.

McAllister, Ian. 1996. "Leaders." In *Comparing Democracies: Elections and Voting in Global Perspective,* ed. Lawrence LeDuc, Richard G. Niemi, and Pippa Norris. Thousand Oaks: Sage Publications, 280–98.

McCandless, Henry E. 2004. "Public Accountability in a Minority Government." *Canadian Parliamentary Review* 27 (3): 31–35.

McRoberts, Kenneth. 1997. *Misconceiving Canada: The Struggle for National Unity.* Toronto: Oxford University Press.

Meisel, John. 1975. *Party Images in Canada: A Report on Work in Progress*. Working Papers on Canadian Politics. Montréal: McGill-Queen's University Press.

Mendelsohn, Matthew. 1993. "Television's Frames in the 1988 Canadian Election." *Canadian Journal of Political Science* 26:149–71.

Mendelsohn, Matthew. 1996. "Television News Frames in the 1993 Canadian Election." In *Seeing Ourselves: Media Power and Policy in Canada*. 2nd ed., ed. Helen Holmes and David Taras. Toronto: Harcourt Brace. (8–22).

Mendelsohn, Matthew, and Richard Nadeau. 1999. "The Rise and Fall of Candidates in Canadian Election Campaigns." *Harvard International Journal of Press/Politics* 4 (2): 63–76. doi:10.1177/1081180X99004002006.

Merolla, Jennifer L., and Laura B. Stephenson. 2007. "Strategic Voting in Canada: A Cross Time Analysis." *Electoral Studies* 26 (2): 235–46. doi:10.1016/j.electstud.2006.02.003.

Miller, Warren E., and J. Merrill Shanks. 1996. *The New American Voter*. Cambridge, MA: Harvard University Press.

Miller, William L. 1983. *The Survey Method in the Social and Political Sciences: Achievements, Failures, Prospects*. London: Frances Pinter.

Mughan, Anthony. 2000. *Media and the Presidentialization of Parliamentary Elections*. Basingstoke: Palgrave. doi:10.1057/9781403920126.

Nadeau, Richard, and Éric Bélanger. 1999. "L'appui aux partis politiques québécois, 1989–1998." In *L'année politique au Québec 1997–1998*, ed. Robert Boily. Montréal: Les Presses de l'Université de Montréal, 203–14.

Nadeau, Richard, and André Blais. 1993. "Explaining Election Outcomes in Canada: Economy and Politics." *Canadian Journal of Political Science* 26 (4): 775–90. doi:10.1017/S0008423900000470.

Nadeau, Richard, and André Blais. 1995. "Economic Conditions, Leader Evaluations, and Election Outcomes in Canada." *Canadian Public Policy* 21 (2): 212–18. doi:10.2307/3551594.

Nadeau, Richard, André Blais, Neil Nevitte, and Elisabeth Gidengil. 2000. "It's Unemployment, Stupid! Why Perceptions about the Job Situation Hurt the Liberals in the 1997 Election." *Canadian Public Policy* 26 (1): 77–94. doi:10.2307/3552257.

Nadeau, Richard, and Michael S. Lewis-Beck. 2001. "National Economic Voting in U.S. Presidential Elections." *Journal of Politics* 63 (1): 159–81. doi:10.1111/0022-3816.00063.

Nadeau, Richard, Richard G. Niemi, and Antoine Yoshinaka. 2002. "A Cross-National Analysis of Economic Voting: Taking Account of the Political Context across Time and Nations." *Electoral Studies* 21 (3): 403–23. doi:10.1016/S0261-3794(01)00002-6.

Nas, Masja. 1995. "Green, Greener, Greenest." In *The Impact of Values*, ed. Jan W. Van Deth and Elinor Scarbrough. Oxford: Oxford University Press, 275–300.

Nevitte, Neil. 1996. *The Decline of Deference: Canadian Value Change in Cross-National Perspective.* Peterborough: Broadview Press.

Nevitte, Neil, André Blais, Elisabeth Gidengil, and Richard Nadeau. 2000. *Unsteady State: The 1997 Canadian Federal Election.* Don Mills: Oxford University Press.

Nevitte, Neil, and Christopher Cochrane. 2007. "Value Change and the Dynamics of the Canadian Partisan Landscape." In *Canadian Parties in Transition,* 3rd ed., ed. Alain-G. Gagnon and A. Brian Tanguay. Peterborough, ON: Broadview Press, 255–75.

Nevitte, Neil, and Mebs Kanji. 1995. "Explaining Environmental Concern and Action in Canada." *Applied Behavioral Science Review* 3 (1): 85–102. doi:10.1016/S1068-8595(95)80014-X.

Nevitte, Neil, and Stephen White. 2008. "Citizens Expectations and Democratic Performance: The Sources and Consequences of Democratic Deficits from the Bottom Up." Paper presented at the conference *Comparing the Democratic Deficit in Canada and the United States: Defining, Measuring, and Fixing,* Weatherhead Center for International Affairs, Harvard University, Cambridge, MA.

Niemi, Richard G., and Herbert F. Weisberg. 1993. *Classics in Voting Behaviour.* Washington, DC: CQ Press.

Norpoth, Helmut. 1996. "The Economy." In *Comparing Democracies: Elections and Voting in Global Perspective,* ed. Lawrence LeDuc, Richard G. Niemi, and Pippa Norris. Thousand Oaks: Sage Publications, 299–318.

Norris, Pippa. 1988. "The Gender Gap: A Cross-National Trend?" In *The Politics of the Gender Gap,* ed. Carol M. Mueller. Newbury Park: Sage, 217–34.

Norton, Philip. 2008. "The Perils of a Hung Parliament." In *No Overall Control?,* ed. Alex Brazier and Susanna Kalitowski. London: Hansard Society, 109–112.

Nye, J. S., P. Zelikow, and D. C. King. 1997. *Why People Don't Trust Government.* Cambridge, MA: Harvard University Press.

O'Neill, Brenda. 1998. "The Relevance of Leader Gender to Voting in the 1993 Canadian National Election." *International Journal of Canadian Studies* 17: 105–30.

Offe, Claus. 1987. "Challenging the Boundaries of Institutional Politics: Social Movements since the 1960s." In *Changing the Boundaries of the Political,* ed. Charles S. Maier. Cambridge: Cambridge University Press, 63–106.

Ogmundson, Rick. 1975. "Party Class Images and the Class Vote in Canada." *American Sociological Review* 40 (4): 506–13. doi:10.2307/2094436.

Pech, Gerald. 2004. "Coalition Governments versus Minority Governments: Bargaining Power, Cohesion, and Budgeting Outcomes." *Public Choice* 121 (1–2): 1–24. doi:10.1007/s11127-004-4326-7.

Pinard, Maurice. 2005. "The Evolution of Support for Constitutional Choices in Quebec." In *Portraits of Canada 2004.* Montréal: Centre for Research and Information on Canada (CRIC), 15–19.

Popkin, Samuel L. 1991. *The Reasoning Voter: Communication and Persuasion in Presidential Campaigns*, 2nd ed. Chicago: University of Chicago Press.

Powell, G. Bingham, and Guy D. Whitten. 1993. "A Cross-National Analysis of Economic Voting: Taking Account of the Political Context." *American Journal of Political Science* 37 (2): 391–414. doi:10.2307/2111378.

Rabinowitz, George, and Stuart E. Macdonald. 1989. "A Directional Theory of Issue Voting." *American Political Science Review* 83 (1): 93–121. doi:10.2307/1956436.

Regenstreif, Peter. 1965. *The Diefenbaker Interlude: Parties and Voting in Canada, an Interpretation*. Toronto: Longmans.

Resnick, Phillip. 1990. *Letters to a Québécois Friend*. Montréal: McGill-Queen's University Press.

Richardson, Bradley M. 1991. "European Party Loyalties Revisited." *American Political Science Review* 85: 751–75.

Richardson, Dick, and Chris Rootes, eds. 1995. *The Green Challenge: The Development of Green Parties in Europe*. London: Routledge.

Roese, Neal. 2002. "Canadians' Shrinking Trust in Government: Causes and Consequences." In *Value Change and Governance in Canada*, ed. Neil Nevitte. Toronto: University of Toronto Press, 149–63.

Rohrschneider, Robert. 1988. "Citizens' Attitudes toward Environmental Issues: Selfish or Selfless?" *Comparative Political Studies* 21 (3): 347–67. doi:10.1177/0010414088021003002.

Roy, Jason. 2009. "Voter Heterogeneity: Informational Differences and Voting." *Canadian Journal of Political Science* 42 (1): 117–37. doi:10.1017/ S0008423 909090052.

Rüdig, Wolfgang, and Mark N. Franklin. 1992. *Green Prospects: The Future of Green Parties in Britain, France and Germany*. Edinburgh: Edinburgh University Press.

Rüdig, Wolfgang, Mark N. Franklin, and Lynn G. Bennie. 1996. "Up and Down with the Greens: Ecology and Party Politics in Britain." *Electoral Studies* 15 (1): 1–20. doi:10.1016/0261-3794(95)00003-8.

Russell, Peter H. 2008. *Two Cheers for Minority Government: The Evolution of Canadian Parliamentary Democracy*. Toronto: Emond Montgomery.

Savoie, Donald J. 1999. *Governing from the Centre: The Concentration of Power in Canadian Politics*. Toronto: University of Toronto Press.

Savoie, Donald J. 2008. *Court Government and the Collapse of Accountability in Canada and the United Kingdom*. Toronto: University of Toronto Press.

Schwartz, Shalom H. 1992. "Universals in the Content and Structure of Values: Theoretical Advances and Empirical Tests in 20 Countries." *Advances in Experimental Social Psychology* 25: 1–65. doi:10.1016/S0065-2601(08)60281-6.

Sharp, Jacqueline, and Anita Krajnc. 2008. "The Canadian Greens: Veering Away from Grass-Roots Democracy So Soon?" In *Green Parties in Transition: The End of Grass-Roots Democracy?*, ed. Gene E. Frankland, Paul Lucardie and Benoit Rihoux. Surrey: Ashgate, 225–44.

Simeon, Richard, and David J. Elkins. 1974. "Regional Political Cultures." *Canadian Journal of Political Science* 7 (3): 397–437. doi:10.1017/S0008423900040713.

Sniderman, Paul M., Richard A. Brody, and Philip Tetlock. 1991. *Reasoning and Choice: Explorations in Political Psychology*. Cambridge: Cambridge University Press. doi:10.1017/CBO9780511720468.

Sniderman, Paul M., H.D. Forbes, and Ian Melzer. 1974. "Party Loyalty and Electoral Volatility: A Study of the Canadian Party System." *Canadian Journal of Political Science* 7 (2): 268–88. doi:10.1017/S0008423900038336.

Stephenson, Laura B. 2010. "The Catholic-Liberal Connection: A Test of Strength." In *Voting Behaviour in Canada*, ed. Cameron D. Anderson and Laura B. Stephenson. Vancouver: University of British Columbia Press, 86–106.

Stokes, Donald. 1963. "Spatial Models of Party Competition." *American Political Science Review* 57 (2): 368–77. doi:10.2307/1952828.

Taylor, Charles. 1993. "Shared and Divergent Values." In *Reconciling the Solitudes: Essays on Canadian Federalism and Nationalism*, ed. Guy Laforest. Montréal: McGill-Queen's University Press, 155–86.

Thomas, Paul E.J. 2007. "Measuring the Effectiveness of Minority Parliament." *Canadian Parliamentary Review* 30 (1): 22–31.

Thompson, Debra. 2008. "Is Race Political?" *Canadian Journal of Political Science* 41 (3): 525–47. doi:10.1017/S0008423908080827.

Turcotte, André. 2001. "Fallen Heroes: Leaders and Voters in the 2000 Canadian Federal Election." In *The Canadian General Election of 2000*, ed. Jon H. Pammett and Christopher Dornan. Toronto: Dundurn, 277–92.

Turcotte, Martin. 2001. "L'opposition rural/urbain a-t-elle fait son temps? Le cas du traditionalisme moral." *Canadian Journal of Sociology* 26 (1): 1–29. doi:10.2307/3341509.

Van der Brug, Wouter, Cees van der Eijk, and Mark Franklin. 2007. *The Economy and the Vote: Economic Conditions and Elections in Fifteen Countries*. Cambridge: Cambridge University Press. doi:10.1017/CBO9780511618857.

Van Deth, Jan W., and Elinor Scarbrough, eds. 1995. *The Impact of Values*. Oxford: Oxford University Press.

Walks, R. Alan. 2004. "Place of Residence, Party Preferences, and Political Attitudes in Canadian Cities and Suburbs." *Journal of Urban Affairs* 26 (3): 269–95. doi:10.1111/j.0735-2166.2004.00200.x.

Wattenberg, Martin. 2011. "U.S. Party Leaders: Exploring the Meaning of Candidate-Centered Politics." In *Political Leaders and Democratic Elections*, ed. Kees Aarts, André Blais, and Hermann Schmitt. Oxford: Oxford University Press, 76–90.

Webb, Paul, David Farrell, and Ian Holliday, eds. 2002. *Political Parties in Advanced Industrial Democracies*. Oxford: Oxford University Press. doi:10.1093/0199240566.001.0001.

Whitaker, Reginald. 1977. *The Government Party: Organising and Financing the Liberal Party of Canada, 1930–58*. Toronto: University of Toronto Press.

White, Stephen, Neil Nevitte, André Blais, Elisabeth Gidengil, and Patrick Fournier. 2008. "The Political Resocialization of Immigrants: Resistance or Lifelong Learning?" *Political Research Quarterly* 61 (2): 268–81. doi:10.1177/1065912908314713.

Whitten, Guy D., and Harvey D. Palmer. 1996. "Heightening Comparativists' Concern for Model Choice: Voting Behaviour in Great Britain and the Netherlands." *American Journal of Political Science* 40 (1): 231–60. doi:10.2307/2111701.

Wilson, J. Matthew, and Michael Lusztig. 2004. "The Spouse in the House: What Explains the Marriage Gap in Canada?" *Canadian Journal of Political Science* 37 (4): 979–95. doi:10.1017/S0008423904990154.

Zaller, John. 1992. *The Nature and Origins of Mass Opinion*. New York: Cambridge University Press.

INDEX